THE
LORDS OF
STRATEGY

THE
LORDS OF
STRATEGY

The Secret Intellectual History of the New Corporate World

Walter Kiechel III

Harvard Business Press

Boston, Massachusetts

14 13 12 11 10   5 4 3 2 1

Library of Congress Cataloging-in-Publication Data

Kiechel, Walter.
    The lords of strategy : the secret intellectual history of the new corporate world /
Walter Kiechel III.
        p. cm.
    ISBN 978-1-59139-782-3 (hardcover : alk. paper)   1. Business planning.   I. Title.
    HD30.28.K496 2009
    658.4'012—dc22

                                                                                2008050381

The paper used in this publication meets the requirements of the American
National Standard for Permanence of Paper for Publications and Documents in
Libraries and Archives Z39.48-1992.

for Genie Dunstan

and we rose up like wheat,
acre after acre of gold

—Anne Sexton

Contents

CONTENTS

Three Common Beliefs
to Be Discarded

Bruce Doolin Henderson achieved executive position at an early age—
he was the second youngest vice president in Westinghouse's history—
but he was fired from that job and every job thereafter, something
he bragged about. Then, in 1963, he founded the Boston Consulting
Group, which changed the world. The *Financial Times* would say of him,
on his death in 1992, "few people have had as much impact on international business in the second half of the twentieth century." Have you
ever heard of Bruce Henderson?

What he and his consulting firm did was to launch the corporate-
strategy revolution. Revolutions seem to occur every day in the world
of business, or so you would believe if you listen to journalists acclaim-
ing the latest technological wonder or to the authors of most new
books on management. But the rise of strategy qualifies as the genuine, consciousness-transforming article. Strategy's coming to dominance as *the* framework by which companies understand what they're
doing and want to do, *the* construct through which and around which
the rest of their efforts are organized, eclipses any other change
worked in the intellectual landscape of business over the past fifty
years.

Understanding the strategy revolution requires getting beyond three common beliefs. The first is that at bottom, ideas don't really matter that much in business. To be sure, skeptics admit, an idea for a great new product can make a huge difference, for a mass-produced automobile, say, or a personal computer. But ideas for how to think about a business, or analyze its dynamics?

Those of little faith in this regard don't usually state their views flat out. What they say instead is, "Business is mostly a matter of common sense." (How eager we are to believe in the democracy of commerce.) Or, "You can have the best idea in the world, but if you can't execute . . ." (Action trumps cerebration every time, supposedly.)

This lack of enthusiasm for the power of ideas extends more widely than one might suspect. Most people familiar with the field would probably agree that the leading journal of management ideas aimed at practitioners is *Harvard Business Review*. But fewer than 4 percent of the sixty-five thousand living alumni of the Harvard Business School subscribe to that venerable publication. On its op-ed pages, the *Wall Street Journal* routinely mounted closely argued exegeses of economic, political, and policy concepts. Comb through the newspaper's archives for the past four decades, though, and try to find comparably detailed coverage of the experience curve, say, or the value chain, or time-based competition. If you want to make a management consultant squirmingly uncomfortable, even one who churns out articles and books, just ask whether he or she thinks of himself or herself as an intellectual.

Bruce Henderson would probably have pleaded guilty, but not because he was besotted with ideas for their own sake. He was, instead, obsessed with figuring out how the world works. For him, this meant identifying both the principles that explain how companies compete and the means of microeconomic analysis with which to arrive at those principles. More particularly, he sought to understand how one company achieves an advantage over others. Henderson represents the first of the breed that will drive this history, the intellectual as corporate warrior, firebrand, entrepreneur, maverick, and impresario.

He wanted to use the concepts he dug from the messy back-and-forth of competition to change the world of business, beginning with his clients' behavior and performance. In this, his aspirations were utterly representative of the strategy revolution as a whole. Its course features a rowdy parade of ideas and analytical techniques jostling each other down the historical road, the ones further back often sneering at those in the van, but all clamoring for the attention and money of corporations.

In other words—and maybe this helps ward off the dread specter of intellectualism—these were almost always ideas sharp with a purpose, namely, to solve a problem bedeviling a company. The secret intellectual history of the new corporate world is as much about the challenges companies faced, from competing with the Japanese in the 1970s to surviving a crisis in the global financial system in the twenty-first century, as it is about the conceptual solutions devised in response. Our story is, in that sense, an account of how the economy and the world we live in today have become what they are. Stock markets rise, fall, rise again, then come crashing down, as they have done recently. Nations wax and wane in their prosperity. Wars break out on distant frontiers. Through it all, strategy has enjoyed a remarkable constancy, the preferred if ever-evolving framework by which companies understand what is happening to them and how they should react.

To say that fifty years ago, before Henderson, there was no such thing as corporate strategy is to invite incredulity. What do you mean, goes up the cry, haven't well-run companies and their leaders always had strategies? What about Rockefeller with Standard Oil, Ford with his motor company, the Watsons and IBM? Which is as much to say, how could strategy possibly have an intellectual history? Another common belief to be overcome.

To be sure, smart enterprises throughout history have had a sense of how they wanted to make money. They typically knew a lot about the products or services they sold, a middling amount about their customers—often considerably less than they do now—and as little or as much about competitors as their closeness to a monopoly position necessitated. (Think of the American auto companies' obliviousness to the growing threat posed by the Japanese through the 1980s. From his elevated perch as CEO, Henry Ford II dismissed the Toyotas and Datsuns arriving in his market as "those little shitboxes.") Year to year, companies made plans, mostly simple extrapolations of what they had been doing. Plans, not strategy—the latter word making only scattered appearances in the corporate vocabulary before 1960.

What companies didn't have before the strategy revolution was a way of systematically putting together all the elements that determined their corporate fate, in particular, the three Cs central to any good strategy: the company's costs, especially costs relative to other companies; the definition of the markets the company served—its customers, in other words—and its position vis à vis competitors. If an enterprise had different lines of business, it might view these in historical terms—"First we got into radio, which led us into television"—or as a capital allocation puzzle. But it wouldn't think of the array as a portfolio of businesses, each of which might be grown or harvested, bought or sold, in service to a larger corporate purpose. Most dangerous of all, the prestrategy worldview lacked a rigorous sense of the dynamics of competition—"If we do this, the other guy is likely to do that." It was like trying to do large-scale engineering without knowing the laws of physics. As a set of ideas, strategy sought to remedy all these deficiencies.

And the effort was spearheaded by, of all people, management consultants—Henderson and his ilk. For many readers, entertaining this fact will entail reconsidering an even more cherished belief: that consultants are at best hangers-on of only occasional, limited usefulness—in the ancient, tired joke, someone who borrows your watch to tell you the time, which, of course, is not always a bad thing to be reminded of—or at worst, rapacious parasites whose slightest presence in the corporate body indicates gullibility, weakness, and insecurity on the part of its leadership.

There are many sorts and conditions of consultants, and even the best can be fairly hermaphroditic creatures, one minute exhibiting a professor's passion for the great clarifying concept, the next displaying sales skills worthy of a street hustler. Among my contentions is that it was this very combination of natures that animated Henderson and his confreres to launch the strategy revolution.

Today, the revolution reaches everywhere business is done in the world. In its origins, though, in the people and institutions that forged it, the movement strikes me as having a distinctively American quality, particularly in its approach to ideas. One inspiration for this work is a wonderful book, *The Metaphysical Club*, Louis Menand's masterly account of American thought after the Civil War as told through the biographies of four of its protagonists. In his preface, Menand identifies what they shared in their attitude toward ideas:

> If we strain out the differences, personal and philosophical, they had with one another, we can say that what these four thinkers [Oliver Wendell Holmes, William James, Charles S. Pierce, and John Dewey] had in common was not a group of ideas, but a single idea—an idea about ideas. They all believed that ideas are not "out there" waiting to be discovered, but are tools—like forks, knives, and microchips—that people devise to cope with the world in which they find themselves. They believed that ideas are produced not by individuals, but by groups of individuals—that ideas are social. They believed that ideas do not develop according to some inner logic of their own, but are entirely dependent, like germs, on their human carriers and environment. And they believed that since ideas are provisional responses to particular and unreproducible circumstances, their survival depends not on their immutability but on their adaptability.

Bruce Henderson was a management consultant, not a jurist or a philosopher, but his idea about the ideas underlying the strategy revolution tallies point for point with those of Menand's thinkers. Does that put him and his fellow lords somehow, ever so slightly, into their intellectual tradition? Most readers will find this too far a reach, but let it at least raise the possibility that we might afford the ideas of the consultants and business thinkers a leaf or two from the wreaths of dignity we hang around the busts of a Holmes or Dewey.

For better or for worse, in their approach to ideas, Henderson and his fellow revolutionaries embody a new strain of intellectual in business, one standing in slap-in-your-face contrast to the stereotype of the double-domed, ineffectual solipsist. This book will argue their case, warts, major moral disfigurements, and all. As far as I know, the volume in your hands represents the first book-length treatment of the strategy revolution. Know what it aims to be and what not. It's an exercise in journalism more than scholarship, albeit what I think of as the journalism of ideas. That's the sort I've been most interested in for thirty years, first at *Fortune* and then at Harvard Business Publishing.

As a work of journalism, the book is based as much or more on over one hundred interviews—none shorter than an hour and some lasting days—as on texts cited and uncited. (For notes on the sources, a selective bibliography, and photographs please go to *thelordsofstrategy.com*.) With the main exception of Bruce Henderson, whom in my various earlier incarnations, I interviewed three times before his death, most of the lords of strategy are all still alive today, able and usually willing to talk.

Finally, this book is an essay as much as a history, by which I mean an account incorporating the personal observations of the author, including a few of his speculations and prejudices. No self-respecting academic would, I suspect, allow himself or herself the kind of generalizations you'll find here, particularly as to the patterns by which ideas developed. In that sense, too, this is an essay, a first approximation that invites disputation, further research, and still more carefully considered books on the topic.

1.

Strategy as a Case to Be Cracked

CCORDING TO THE STORY, Peter Drucker once remarked that he had "invented management." But how can that be, his listener responded, given that people had been running organizations for centuries, millennia? True, the sage replied, but when he first went to study the subject in the 1930s and 1940s, he could find only two or three books describing the functions he came to group under that rubric. By naming them *management*, pulling them together with that term, he gave those practicing the art a new way of understanding what they were doing. And a new way of studying and improving their practice.

The argument of this book is that precisely the same thing went on with the invention of corporate strategy, except that it didn't spring full-blown from a single, godlike forehead but instead was assembled from the spoils of many an intellectual and business battle. This is a story not of paradigm shift, but of the bit-by-bit creation of the first comprehensive paradigm that pulled together all the elements most vital for a company to take into account if it is to compete, win, and survive.

There are three strands to the narrative, woven into a single braid. First is the history of the critical ideas, how they were devised, out of what forerunner materials, and in response to which particular problems. The second and third strands are the stories of people—Bruce Henderson, Michael Porter, Tom Peters, and others—and of organizations, companies that struggled to put the new concepts to work, consulting firms that fostered so many of the ideas, and business schools that turned strategy into an academic discipline. There were and are many lords of strategy, not just the original thinkers, but also a swelling progress of executives rendered more lordly through its use.

Horsemen of the Corporate Apocalypse

Every historical period feels itself beset with forces making for change, but for the corporate world, the past fifty years have been especially rich with menacing surprises, one response to which was the rise of strategy. Consider a few of the most significant jolts, which sometimes seemed like the Four Horsemen of the Corporate Apocalypse. The first, though not necessarily chronologically, was the deregulation of industries in which competition had traditionally been held in check by government rules, as in airlines, banking, and telecommunications. The second consisted of the ever-widening effect of new technologies, including the increase in computer power, its spread to desktops everywhere, and the coming of the Internet. In the third, capital markets freed themselves up, shedding inhibitions against hostile takeovers, establishing a genuine market for the control of companies. The fourth horseman usually goes by the name *globalization*, the fact that companies find themselves buying from, selling to, and competing with enterprises and customers from around the world.

What all four had in common was that they worked to extend the reach of markets, and hence of competition, into places that

Schumpeterian creative destructiveness had never touched before. If there's one form of mindfulness that strategy has installed in the corporate brain above all others it's an ever-edgy awareness that other guys or gals are out there, trying to take your business, probably gaining on you, and that new miscreants are popping up all the time, increasingly from places whose names you can't pronounce. The title that Intel CEO Andy Grove gave his 1996 book on strategy, *Only the Paranoid Survive*, nicely captures the feeling.

These days, competition and competitiveness are so ingrained in our thinking that we forget what a relatively recent discovery they were, particularly for American companies lulled by thirty years of postwar prosperity. Two of the earliest academic books on corporate strategy, from the early 1970s, had, respectively, two and four pages devoted to competition. In part, this merely reflected the business landscape of that time, where the worry was more about the unchecked power of companies than about the forces that might threaten them.

By way of contrast to his contemporaries, consider Bruce Henderson's attitude toward competition: he was fascinated by it and passionately believed in its power to spur higher performance. So much so that in the late 1960s, after reading books about Darwinian anthropology, he divided the Boston Consulting Group into three minifirms within the firm—the red, blue, and green—and set them to competing with one another. The move had the desired effect, but not in the way Henderson envisioned: less than three years later, virtually the entire blue unit, by far the most successful, decamped to set up Bain & Company, BCG's most formidable competitor for the next fifteen years.

Henderson was also a pioneer in that he looked at the challenges facing his clients as mysteries to be solved, usually through massive and creative data gathering, then fitting the data to a framework, or supplying such a framework, to explain it. Big-league strategy consultants like Orit Gadiesh at Bain & Company still describe their greatest intellectual thrill as "cracking the case," a term they may have picked up in business school but an endeavor to which they bring far more firepower—that is, teams of people—than any professor could.

Part of the argument of this book is that corporate strategy as something that needs to be figured out, a case to be cracked, is relatively new in the world. Certainly new are the realizations that the effort will require unprecedented fact gathering (at the beginning of the strategy revolution, most companies didn't know how their costs compared with competitors'; many still don't), platoons of experts from outside, and a multibillion-dollar consulting industry to deliver that expertise. Indeed, we'll see that strategic concepts were often less important than the newly muscular empiricism their use required, the imperative they gave companies to gather unprecedented amounts of data on costs, markets, and competitors.

Toward a Greater Taylorism

Historians of business still argue about the effect of Taylorism on our world, about whether Frederick Winslow Taylor's time-motion studies of work at the end of the nineteenth century and the resultant push for greater stopwatch-monitored efficiency was a good thing. But all concede that Taylorism represented a major force for change across the corporate landscape.

Part of the strategy revolution was the coming of what I'll call *Greater Taylorism*, the corporation's application of sharp-penciled analytics this time not to the performance of an individual worker—how fast a person could load bars of pig iron or reset a machine—but more widely to the totality of its functions and processes. How much does it cost us to make our steel? How can the Japanese do it so much less expensively? How can we redesign our whole chain of activities, from purchasing raw materials to delivering the final product, so that we can compete with them?

Greater Taylorism has chewed its way across the corporate landscape to virtually everywhere large companies practice twenty-first-century capitalism, which means on just about every continent. Its appetite for more numbers, more data, seems only to increase with the computer power available to crunch those numbers. And it has become steadily less patient for results, in part because now you can get the numbers back from the market overnight. Private equity firms, with their short time horizons and relentless pressure for results, are merely the latest shock troops for Greater Taylorism's ineluctable advance.

In many ways, the steady, relentless spread of empiricism represents a simpler, less disjointed story line than the history of the successive concepts that made up the strategy revolution. "The early history of strategy is fairly linear," observes Pankaj Ghemawat, a Harvard Business School professor and the subject's leading academic historian. Then, about in the mid-1980s, "it turns into a bush," the different branches heading off into wild scrawls of hypothesis and assertion. Just about that time, too, the transcendent purpose of strategy became clear, at least to Wall Street: its aim was to enrich shareholders, boost the stock price.

History of an Idea in Three Stages

So that we don't lose track of the overall shape of the bush in watching the tendrils spread under the harsh sun of shareholder capitalism, it helps to have a framework by which to understand the different stages of growth. Barry Jones, a senior partner of long standing in BCG's London office, provides one with three Ps. Of course, it's an oversimplification—any such framework is—but not one that hacks off too many intellectual limbs to fit our subject onto its Procrustean bed.

According to his schema, the first phase of strategy's history, from its beginnings in the early 1960s until approximately the mid-1980s, was about positioning. Where was your business situated on the experience curve, charting your costs compared with competitors'? Where did a particular business sit in the portfolio of businesses your company

5

owned, according to measures like its market share? Should it be built up or sold off?

In strategy's second stage, extending from the late 1980s to today, its intellectual focus turned to processes, the procedures and routines by which companies get things done. BCG plumps for its discovery of *time-based competition* as the first major breakthrough on the process front, the realization that if you concentrated on designing and manufacturing a product more quickly than your competitors do, you could win a competitive advantage over them. Process thinking lay beneath the early 1990s rage for companies to understand and build their *core competencies*. *Business process redesign*, more popularly known (and often loathed) as *reengineering*, shot up like a skyrocket over the corporate firmament in the 1990s and then fell to earth about as fast, eventually becoming the most commonly cited example of business idea as mindless fad.

The third phase of Jones's schema, strategy as centering on people, remains more nebulous, partly because we've only recently embarked on it and partly because no one can agree on what a focus on people means. Private equity firms, those most rational of investors, seem to view managers as interchangeable parts, to be plugged in to run businesses as necessary and then unplugged as quickly. On more distant, speculative shores others like Philip Evans of BCG assert that the single irreducible unit for the strategist must no longer be the company but rather the individual, that only by figuring out how to get the best from him can a company made up of such atoms hope to compete. Occupying the broader middle ground between these two is a school that maintains that people are the key to innovation, and innovation the modern requisite for competitive success.

What makes the increasing concentration on people a particularly fraught passage in our story is the dawning acknowledgement it represents on strategy's part of the element heretofore most neglected in its calculations. What we might call its Jungian shadow, or its intellectual-history equivalent.

The shadow, as postulated by the Swiss psychotherapist, consists of that part of oneself—energies, desires, ambitions—that we repress as we become the individuals we are, "rejected aspects of ourselves and undeveloped potential," as one expert defines it. What got repressed—sometimes viciously repressed—by the strategy-concept makers, consultants, and data gatherers was a consciousness of people and their importance in the creation and execution of any strategy. Not that there weren't voices in the corporate wilderness crying up the centrality of the human. Indeed, sometimes they were spitting and shouting voices, like that of Tom Peters. The problem was that these couldn't get much of a hearing at the strategy consulting firms—indeed, Peters and his *In Search of Excellence* coauthor Bob Waterman were effectively expelled from McKinsey. In Waterman's case, after twenty-one years there.

The tamer, more conventional way of framing this tension is to see the history of strategy as a struggle between two definitions, strategy as positioning and strategy as organizational learning. The positioning school, led by Harvard's Porter, sees strategy making as the choice of where you want to compete, in what industry and from what spot within that industry, and how—on price, with distinctive products, or by finding a niche.

The organizational-learning school, by contrast, maintains that no company that's already up and running can choose its strategy as if it had a blank slate. Almost gleeful in its derision of the positionists—at least its leading spokesman, McGill's Henry Mintzberg is—the learning school also argues that virtually no strategy ever works as originally planned. The point, they say, is for the company to set off in one direction, learn from the response it gets from markets and competitors, and then adjust accordingly.

Each side liberally besmirches the other. "Where are the people in a Michael Porter strategy?" asks one Harvard Business School professor acidly. "Why doesn't Mintzberg ever say anything new?" asks another, going on to decry the organizational-learning school's lack of rigor, paucity of explanatory models, and all-around neglect of microeconomics.

Framing the history of strategy in terms of this debate has all the limitations of an academic exercise, a struggle to be fought out in the pages of the *Journal of Strategic Management*. Meanwhile, *In Search of Excellence*, a paean to the essentialness of people to a company's success, has gone on to sell more than six million copies, far more than any tome on strategic concepts, pioneering a popular market for business books and ideas—a market that is a part of our story. The narrow framing also runs the risk of dodging the question "Where are the people in the history of corporate strategy?" It's a question this book hopes to begin answering.

The Fiercening of Capitalism

Besides the progress of strategy from one P to another and the struggle to come to terms with its human shadow, two other overarching themes shape our narrative. The first is the sharpening of capitalism over our period, or to revive an old word, its fiercening. While hardly the only force making for a fiercer breed of capitalism in the twenty-first century, strategy has contributed most of the key concepts and analytical techniques by which it has become so.

It is, admittedly, a strange kind of *fierce*, one whose seemingly contradictory elements make it hard to compare with earlier periods in capitalism's history, which in many ways were tougher on people. Overall levels of affluence have risen during the last fifty years, and rates of poverty fallen, not just in the United States but even more dramatically in countries such as China and India, which have newly embraced capitalism's gospel. The crisis in the global financial system of the last two years may have slowed that trend temporarily, but is unlikely to stop it.

Despite this, some in the middle or toward the bottom worry that an undue share of the wealth created is sloshing to a privileged class of entrepreneurs and investors like Bill Gates or Warren Buffet or, even more disturbingly, in their eyes, to a new elite of chief executives and financiers. While the pay of investment bankers, mortgage brokers, and the merchants of derivatives have drawn the most fire of late, CEO compensation represents the issue with larger import for the fabric of corporate life. Heads of companies have always done well, but not this well, not this much better than the rest of their employees.

Blame strategy in part, its influence direct and indirect. Somewhat incongruously for such a distinctively American character, Bruce Henderson was also an elitist. He provoked outrage among students at the Harvard Business School when he placed an ad in the student newspaper saying that BCG was looking to hire not just the run-of-that-mill but, instead, scholars—Rhodes Scholars, Marshall Scholars, Baker Scholars (the top 5 percent of the class). He wanted the smartest of the smart, and to attract them he was prepared to overlook what might have seemed obvious liabilities. Of the first seven professionals at BCG, only one besides Henderson had any consulting experience.

This kind of elitism infused the strategy revolution and helped foment a stratification within companies and society—we are *not* all in this together; some pigs are smarter than other pigs and deserve more money—that contributed to the fiercer feel of today's capitalism. For starters, it fostered an entirely new model of consulting firm, one whose credibility derived not from silver-haired industry experience but rather from the brilliance of its ideas and the obvious candlepower of the people explaining them, even if those people were twenty-eight years old. Make way for the new-style business intellectual. Henderson created competition for the highest-rated talent from the "best" business schools—a competition that continues today.

Companies that adopted strategy as their chief mode of self-definition—and nowadays that's almost every company—have found themselves subtly infected by Hendersonian elitism. While the distinction between the people who make up "management" and everyone else in the organization has been clear ever since Drucker identified the management function in the 1940s, if you're trying to identify who in the top ranks really counts, you need only ask, "Who makes strategy here?"

First among the duties of the modern CEO, whatever else this exalted figure does, is the framing and enunciating of the enterprise's strategy. It helps, of course, if he or she is a former strategy consultant, as has been the case at American Express (a Bain & Company alumnus), eBay (Bain), United Technologies (BCG), Xerox (McKinsey) and a growing number of other big-name companies. (These people end up in the damnedest places: The current dean of the Harvard Business School, Jay Light, worked at BCG early in his career—and Bill Bain tried to hire him away—as did Benjamin Netanyahu, who went on to become prime minister of Israel.)

The elitism that Henderson-style strategy making brought with it represents one of the big reasons so many otherwise well-informed businesspeople hate consultants. This, despite the fact that over three-quarters of the largest American companies, and comparable percentages in countries like France, currently use the services of BCG, McKinsey, Bain & Company, or some combination of them.[1] Most are repeat customers.

As CEOs' compensation reaches ever higher multiples of the average employee's, criticism of them begins to sound more like some of the opprobrium traditionally heaped on consultants: What do they do to be paid that much? Are they really that much smarter than everyone else?

In their own defense, those taking home the multimillion-dollar pay packets point to the depredations of fiercening capitalism that they must contend with: competition and market mechanisms seeping into every corner of the corporate landscape, from whom you sell against to whom you outsource to; Draconian punishments from the stock markets for companies and executives who fail to meet financial targets (even when there wasn't a general market collapse like that at the end of 2008); CEOs fired more quickly and more frequently; companies or businesses bought up, broken up, repurposed at an unprecedented pace—this ever since strategy helped the world discover that the only real purpose of a company is to rack up gains for shareholders.

At the company level, where strategy is supposed to do its magic, a similarly confusing picture of fiercening emerges. Strategic advantages are competed away more quickly in anything but the most innovative businesses. Business models have a shorter life span than ever. At the same time, in some industries more of the assets and the market power accumulates in fewer, giant companies—in banking, telecommunications, retailing, and pharmaceuticals, for example. (These behemoths make ideal clients for the strategy consulting firms and are in fact their principal clients these days. In recent years, right up until the global financial crisis, around 40 percent of BCG's revenues have come from serving companies in financial services or health care. Wal-Mart, which never used consultants in its early years, is now a McKinsey client.)

Not that their king-sized perch is any more secure. "Over the past few years Microsoft has spent billions on research and new product development," observes a professor at Harvard. "What do they have to show for it? Nothing. Zero." The innovations that create wealth come instead from interlopers, start-ups, smaller enterprises more capable of seeing and seizing the opportunities thrown up by change. Or from once smaller enterprises, suddenly grown huge—Google, for instance, though even it may have begun to lose its edge. So, in the latest turn of its wheel, strategy becomes about how to make existing institutions as innovative as start-ups.

The Intellectualization of Business

The last overarching theme running through the book is that strategy has helped bring on the intellectualization of business. Many practitioners will seethe at that notion, as will many consultants. Business is supposed to be practical, not airy-fairy with highfalutin concepts, twenty-minute fads, or the latest buwash jargon. The mysteries and opportunities of commerce are equally open to all, aren't they? (The fact that consultants' very existence gives the lie to this belief is another reason they are widely despised.)

But take the trouble to look for it through unsentimental eyes, and you can find evidence everywhere over the past five decades that increasing numbers of people have come to understand business not just by doing it—as it was done in the past, as company lore said it was to be done—but rather as framed and mediated by ideas. Consider just three pieces of that evidence: The market for business books blasted off in 1982 with the publication of *In Search of Excellence* and now marshals eight thousand new titles a year. The number of MBA degrees pursued and granted increased from less than 4,000 a year in the United States in 1948 to over 140,000 today. And finally, of course, there is the rise of the strategy consulting industry, which currently takes in over $5 billion a year worldwide for nothing more than its ideas, analysis, and general smarts.

Strategy has become the linchpin for how we think about doing business and the central conceit around which a new strain of intellectual has shaped the modern corporate world. So much so that it is difficult to recall a time when this was not so. To find that time, we need go back only about fifty years.

2.

Bruce Henderson
Defines the Subject

T HE BOSTON CONSULTING GROUP opened its doors for
business on July 1, 1963, with "one room, a desk, no telephone, and no secretary," according to the firm's official
history of its early years. Bruce Henderson, founder of what was then
known as the Management Consulting Division of the Boston Safe
Deposit and Trust Company, was its sole employee. If you read his
résumé up until then, you wouldn't have taken Henderson for an entrepreneur. For starters, the forty-eight-year-old had worked his entire
life for established companies.

Early Wonderings

Bruce Henderson was born in Nashville on April 30, 1915, the son of a
man who published and sold Bibles. Southwestern Publishing, which
his father owned, dated back to the 1850s and still claims to be the first
"direct selling"—that is, door-to-door—operation in the United States.
Later in life, the younger Henderson told friends that his father gave

customers the impression that he read scripture every day, something he did not in fact do. The son didn't get along well with the father, indeed had trouble with figures of authority all his life. Through much of his corporate career, he would work as a purchasing agent, someone with the power to lord it over salesmen.

While Henderson did episodically sell Bibles for his father's company, he launched himself in a resolutely different direction by studying initially at the University of Virginia—he thought he might want to be a lawyer—and then at Vanderbilt, where in 1937 he earned an undergraduate degree in mechanical engineering. Engineering degrees were to become the standard credential for the lords of strategy.

Henderson's first serious job, with the Frigidaire division of General Motors, also gave him his first taste of major corporate disruption. He was laid off after nine months, part of a cutback that Henderson later recalled as eliminating 6,300 of the business's 13,500 employees. Seemingly unfazed, he "knocked on a few doors," got an offer from the forerunner to IBM, turned it down, and then went to work for the Leland Electric Co. of Dayton, Ohio.

Leland was a comparatively small enterprise, but as the nation's leading manufacturer of explosion-proof motors used in gasoline pumps, it dominated its niche, more than holding its own against larger competitors such as Westinghouse. How could it do that? Henderson wondered. His duties at headquarters included pulling together all the correspondence from the company's sales force. Their reports produced a steady, generous stream of data—prices offered and taken, order sizes, special customer requirements. To this grist Henderson brought two habits of mind acquired in college. The first, from what he described as the most important course he ever took—calculus, at Vanderbilt—had him constantly looking at phenomena in terms of simultaneous rates of change. As one element varied, what happened with others? The second habit, from an economics course at Virginia—surprising, given his lifelong disdain for conventional economics—was to plumb a business or a market for systems that made it go.

The restless curiosity that fed both habits led Henderson to seek further education, and one incident in particular shaped his choice of where to find it. According to the story, one cold night a friend asked Henderson if he'd like to go with him to an event at the local Harvard Club. The speaker was one Marvin Bower, who was in the process of reconstituting the McKinsey & Company consulting firm. What Bower said about the Harvard Business School—he had graduated from both Harvard Law and Harvard Business Schools—apparently so intrigued Henderson that the younger man decided to apply for admission.

Henderson enrolled as a member of the Harvard Business School class of 1941, took the usual curriculum, and then, about ninety days short of graduation, dropped out. In later years, he never talked much about his reasons for quitting, but acquaintances suggest a couple of possible incentives: Westinghouse had offered him a good job, one that might not wait, and this against a background made all the more anxious by the prospect of war. His premature departure didn't, however, keep Henderson from valuing his ties with the business school. He liked to talk about being historian for his class. He would go on to befriend faculty members, lecture in an occasional class, and, of course, with his firm's hiring practices, propel the starting salaries of the school's MBA graduates to unprecedented heights.

Henderson spent the next eighteen years at Westinghouse, working in purchasing much of the time, being promoted to corporate vice president in 1953. But for all his long tenure and seeming success, neither the man himself, the written record, nor the recollections of his BCG colleagues have much to say about what he did or learned there. For our purposes, one episode may be telling enough.

Early in his career, Henderson found himself having dinner with the president of the company, with whom he discussed his background. Three days later, he was assigned to the small-motors division. The unit fielded a broad line of products, including some that competed with those of Leland Electric. Henderson remembered enough from his Leland days about its products' costs, prices, and margins to begin comparing them with Westinghouse's. What he found astonished him.

Westinghouse was selling its motors for gasoline pumps at the same prices as those charged by Leland, the market leader. But while Leland made a profit on each motor sold, Westinghouse lost money on each. As early as 1776, in *The Wealth of Nations*, Adam Smith had pointed up the virtues of specialization. By the 1890s, the great British economist Alfred Marshall was outlining the concept of economies of scale. And in the 1920s, Henry Ford had demonstrated for all to see the power of mass production to bring down prices. But economists hadn't pushed their analysis far enough to overcome a countervailing assumption then current that if two companies—or "firms," as the economists called them—were in the same business, making the same or similar products, they must have just about the same costs. A manufacturing executive from that era summed up the prevailing view: "Your costs were your costs. If you were buying the same raw materials as the other guy, and you paid your labor what he did, then your overall costs must be just about the same as his." The unstated assumption: there probably wasn't much you could do about your costs, anyway.

Why would Westinghouse persist with a money-losing product? The company believed that it needed to market a full line of products, Henderson later explained, adding a bit dismissively, "for cultural reasons." His own calculations suggested another, related irony. Westinghouse and Leland each had product lines in which each company was not as big as the other one, nor as profitable. If the two firms simply switched ownership of their loser businesses, without any increase in sales volume or changes in cost, each would see its overall profit margin on sales increase by 10 percent, a "hell of a lot," in his words. The insight presaged a more general conclusion that would figure large in the strategy revolution: "Nearly all companies I have known," he would say in 1985, "have a number of businesses they should not be in."

Henderson put his observations to work in overseeing purchasing at Westinghouse, pushing suppliers to cut their prices in line with what he figured their costs must be based on their volume. He also put together an informal network of advisers—consultants, engineers, scientists, and fellow executives—with whom he could discuss his thinking on costs, prices, competition, and perhaps most intriguing, underlying systems that might explain their behavior. It all wasn't enough to win him further promotion, though, and his ambition, restless curiosity, and occasional crankiness apparently came to rub his corporate superiors the wrong way. (As the first speaker at the 1992 memorial service for Henderson would say of him, "He was not always easy to deal with.") In 1959, in another of those departures Henderson would later describe as "firings," he left Westinghouse to join the Arthur D. Little consulting firm, based in Cambridge, Massachusetts. There he became senior vice president for management services.

Named for the MIT professor who founded it, Arthur D. Little (ADL) dated back to 1886 and usually gets credit for being the first management consulting firm. Through most of its history, it focused on technology research for companies or government agencies. In the lobby of its headquarters, for example, it long displayed a sort of silk purse woven of filaments that ADL scientists had spun from a sow's ear, or, more precisely, from gelatin derived from many pounds of pigs' ears, in an early publicity stunt. (When ADL went bankrupt in 2002, this early example of a miracle worked by consultants was among the assets put up for auction to satisfy the firm's creditors, the *Boston Globe* reported.)

Even though he "knew nothing about consulting at the time," as he subsequently admitted, Henderson was given serious responsibilities at ADL, including projects for Shell Oil and United Fruit. Arthur D. Little was "a great company," Henderson would later say, but the work didn't provide the platform he was seeking to try out many of the ideas he had been kicking around.

As he headed into his midforties, his independence of mind and, just possibly, his cantankerousness may have been on the rise. He fell into a power struggle with the leadership of ADL. General James M. Gavin, who won fame as a paratroop commander in World War II, had on his retirement from the army in 1957 joined the consulting firm as its head. In 1961, Gavin went on leave to serve as U.S. ambassador to France. When he returned after two years, Henderson pushed for more authority, Gavin pushed back, and shortly after that, Henderson left ADL.

The Mysteries of Market Segmentation

While at Arthur D. Little Henderson had come to know the Boston Safe Deposit and Trust Company, and its chief executive, William W. Wolbach. Boston Safe Deposit had a long history mostly centered around managing the Lowell family's money, but Wolbach was hoping to grow the sleepy institution by taking it into new lines of business. He and Henderson agreed to start up a management consulting division that Henderson would lead. It was an odd choice of a parent for a consulting operation; Boston Safe wasn't a bank with corporate customers that could become clients. But then, as a later head of BCG noted when asked what Henderson was seeking when he founded his firm, "You have to remember, Bruce didn't have a job."

Henderson brought with him no book of business, no list of clients waiting to be served. As a result, in its first year, his operation accepted a hodgepodge of assignments: a reference check for a Midwestern company, a survey of research firms in the Boston area, a study of factors affecting the purchase of paper for offices. Still, monthly billings—five hundred dollars the first month—doubled every month thereafter.

What Henderson did have, besides a fascination with concepts that might explain the dynamics of competition, was an exquisite eye for talent. He began hiring—a professor here to work part-time, a semi-veteran consultant there. The attraction for them, typically, was Bruce's excitement about ideas.

Being hired by Henderson was no conventional experience. Alan Zakon, then an associate professor of finance at Boston University—and later to displace Henderson as head of BCG—describes his first conversation with the man, a phone call in 1966:

"This is Bruce Henderson. I'd like you to do some consulting for me."

"Wonderful."

"What do you charge?"

Zakon would have worked for a pittance, but since Henderson had made the firm sound so prepossessing, the professor decided to go for what he thought a huge fee:

"I charge $125 a day."

"Wrong, too much!" Henderson shouted back. "Take your annual income, and divide it by 365, multiply by 4, and add 22."

Zakon demurred, allowing that if he knew how to do that, he wouldn't need to go consulting. After a long silence, Henderson relented: "I'll pay you a hundred bucks. Come down tomorrow." Zakon did, and the following year left academe to work for BCG full-time.

In early 1964, the start-up landed its first large client, the Norton Company, a ninety-year-old multinational whose factories dominated the landscape of its home city of Worcester, Massachusetts. Norton's main product, not exactly sexy, was grinding wheels. The family-owned company proudly turned out a dizzying variety of the wheels, some sold in huge volumes to customers like carmakers, others in small lots to manufacturers more specialized.

As with Westinghouse and its line of motors, this variety turned out to be the problem. Smaller competitors that concentrated on making just the high-volume products were coming in and picking off Norton's biggest customers by charging less. Norton found itself in the dismal situation of seeing its costs, averaged across all lines, going up even as the average price it could command for products headed down.

Norton thus posed for the consultants the first example of a kind of case they would encounter repeatedly, soon to be classified under the heading *market segmentation*. Looking at the universe of markets you serve, all the customers to whom you sell different products or services, how do you carve up the totality to figure out where you make money and where not? By customer? Product? Geography? Some combination of the three? (Anyone who asserts "You just take the cost of the product and subtract it from the price" has never worked in a large organization.)

Today, with forty years of Greater Taylorism behind us and massive computerized data-crunching power at our fingertips, this might not seem an insuperable question—though it's still tough enough. For thirty years, strategy consultants were to find that among their best sales pitches to the CEO of a prospective client were the questions "Do you actually know how much business you do across all your divisions with your company's largest customer? And how profitable that business is?" With surprising frequency, the answer would come back, slightly shamefacedly, "Well, now that you mention it . . . "

The solution that Henderson and his consultants devised was called the Norton Plan, and it combined elements of production economics, finance, and thinking about the cost of capital for both Norton and its customers. In the 1960s, companies still worried about running afoul of the Robinson-Patman Act of 1936, which in essence made it illegal to sell the same product to different customers for different prices. Partly as a result, the plan outlined a series of elaborate contractual agreements with the company's major customers: they would pay Norton slightly more for its grinding wheels than the customers would pay for competitors' wheels, but would also receive technical services the smaller sellers didn't offer, along with help financing their inventory. To the extent that those present at the time can recall, the plan was a success: Norton adopted it, and the new arrangements arrested the erosion of its market share, at least for a while.

How to Retail Business Ideas

By the end of 1964, the Management Consulting Division of Boston Safe Deposit had six employees and virtually no reputation. To draw attention to itself, it launched two innovations in the course of that year. Or, as one early BCG partner puts it, "We invented the retail marketing of business ideas." The initiatives also marked the beginning of a shift in how consultants were to compete: BCG was going to build its practice around the drawing power of its ideas, not on its storied history or the time-honed expertise of its senior partners.

The first tool was what became known as BCG *Perspectives*, short, punchy essays—eight hundred words, typically—on a new idea or a nagging business question, published in a brochure format just the right size for tucking into a coat pocket. Up until then, consultants had turned out the occasional article in *Harvard Business Review* and a couple of firms were experimenting with publishing their own journals—ADL had one titled *Prism*, and McKinsey started its *Quarterly* in 1964—suitable for leaving behind with clients. But no one else was sending out substantive, pithy broadsides with titles like "Brinksmanship in Business" and "More Debt or None?"

The original notion for *Perspectives* was that the essays were to be *Reader's Digest*–type condensations of articles published elsewhere. Indeed, the first essay was a pared-down version of a 1963 *Harvard Business Review* article "How to Evaluate Corporate Strategy," by Seymour "Sy" Tilles, a former Harvard Business School lecturer soon to join BCG as a senior presence. Rather quickly, though, Henderson realized that the published work of others wasn't about to capture the concepts he and his consultants were exploring. So he began writing them himself, occasionally enlisting a colleague to compose one.

In the decades that followed, BCG published over four hundred *Perspectives*—at the height of popularity, up to fifteen a year—with some partners calculating that the essays eventually reached an audience as large as that of *BusinessWeek*. To go back and read the early ones is a revelation, particularly today, when so much contemporary business literature babbles and shouts. Henderson's sentences are simple, declarative, unadorned, almost deadpan in their calm. "A businessman can predict his normal costs far into the future if he understands their basic relationship to experience." "Market share has a value directly reflected in relative cost." The authorial certainty conveyed is resolute.

Even colleagues whom he drove crazy in other ways describe Henderson as a good writer, and he worked at it, revising each *Perspectives* article ten or fifteen times, polishing his own efforts with professional help. Of the six people on staff at the end of 1964, one was a full-time editor. His written style stood in bizarre contrast to his way of speaking, which occasionally bordered on the incoherent.

Henderson hated to lose an argument, one aspect of an apparent insecurity that seemed to intensify over time as he surrounded himself with brilliant people. When threatened, he would retreat behind squid-ink bursts of only semicomprehensible verbiage laced with big ideas. "He had to give you a sense that he understood things, particularly large patterns, in ways that you didn't," says one admirer, "even when his grasp of what he was talking about wasn't that great." Other colleagues identified what they termed the Henderson uncertainty principle, apologies to Heisenberg: you might understand the point Bruce was making, or you could have a sense of where he was heading with his argument, but you could never do both at the same time.

In *Perspectives*, though, he was lucid. There his aggressive energy took other forms, namely, opposition to the authority of established ideas and conventional thinking. In the introduction to a 1984 collection of the pieces, he summed up their intent as follows, albeit with a bit more of the passive voice than was typical for him: "Statements that senior business managers would find believable are not supported. Only provocative material is argued. The subject matter is chosen to be deliberately provocative, significant in implication, and relevant to the policy decisions of corporate competition."

Bruce Henderson was disruptive. And strategy was going to be all about disruption—or in the words of one of its wise men, "strategy *is* change"—not something you embark on if you want to go on quietly doing what you've been doing.

The other notable marketing innovation introduced in 1964 was the by-invitation-only business conference. Corporate conferences and "expos" and "thought-leader summits" have become so common today—to mangle a line from Mencken, throw an egg out a window, and you're likely to hit somebody heading to one—that we forget what a relatively recent development they are. But talk to someone at the speakers bureaus that furnish talent for these events and they'll testify to a history of not much more than thirty years. The World Economic Forum, aka Davos, dates from only 1971, for example; its original purpose was to spread the light of the latest American business ideas to the companies of Europe, which knew them not.

BCG held its first business conference in June 1964, a so-called seminar discussion at MIT's Endicott House in Dedham, Massachusetts. The subject was long-range planning, a topic the consultants judged to be drawing increased amounts of interest, some of it sparked by the supposed wonders Robert McNamara and his "whiz kids" had worked at Ford and were now taking to the Defense Department. The seminar attracted a total of eight guests, four of them executive vice presidents of sizable companies. The discussion was lively, moderated by Sy Tilles, with the consultants concluding they learned more than the practitioners. Within the year, BCG was doing work for six of the companies that had attended.

Still, there were problems with the event, one with the subject matter, the other with its design. As he would later attest quite openly, Henderson actually wasn't much interested in planning, didn't think it worked, and preferred not to spend time with corporate functionaries whose titles included the words *planning* or *planner*. While he and his colleagues hadn't yet defined precisely what they meant by *strategy*, he already sensed that what he considered urgent for companies to figure out—where they stood relative to their competitors, and how to respond—wasn't encompassed in most planning.

This distinction between strategy and planning, even so-called strategic planning, is one that most of the lords of strategy would come to embrace. To the consultant or academic who might contest the distinction, pose the following question: Whom would you rather have as your client or research subject, the CEO of a company or its corporate planner, if it still has one? BCG, Bain & Company, and McKinsey are utterly clear in their preference here. For the killer account of the shortcomings of planning, readers should consult one of the magisterial works of modern management literature, *The Rise and Fall of Strategic Planning*, by Canadian scholar Henry Mintzberg.

The design problem with the first conference, as the guests were all too willing to tell Henderson, was that they weren't there to hear each other talk. They wanted to be presented with exciting new ideas they could take back to their companies. Serendipitously, that was exactly what Henderson and his consultants were beginning to focus on.

The Foundation Story

By 1965, it was apparent that the Management Consulting Division needed to change its name. As the firm's history notes, its consultants were always greeted with the same three questions: "Do you work for anyone except the bank's customers? Do you do anything besides financial consulting? Do you charge for your services?" Thus the Boston Consulting Group was born, though still under the same corporate ownership. The name change was all the more propitious in that the new firm was beginning to figure out what it wanted to specialize in: strategy.

Ah, *strategy*. The word goes back to the Greek *stategos*, for "the office or command of a general," according to the *Oxford English Dictionary*. The inner eye pictures a grizzled, helmeted Homeric figure arraying his forces before the enemy hoplites come over the hill. (Once they're in sight it's all tactics, according to the standard military usage.) The faint whiff of battlefield command that still hangs about the word is one reason for the term's popularity among corporate chiefs.

By the early nineteenth century, the word was in use by military theorists, notably Carl von Clausewitz, but it wasn't until the mid-twentieth century that it began to creep into the corporate vocabulary with any regularity. Harvard's Pankaj Ghemawat notes that the New Jersey Bell executive Chester Barnard in his 1938 classic, *The Functions of the Executive*, had recommended paying attention to "strategic factors." In 1950, *Fortune*'s John McDonald, a writerly lion whose assignment to do an article on poker led to a deep immersion in game theory, published *Strategy in Poker, Business, and War.*

Increasingly through the mid-1960s, the word *strategy* was in the corporate air, mostly wafted about by people who were thinking about planning and the organization of companies. In 1962, historian Alfred D. Chandler Jr. published *Strategy and Structure*—another classic—which described how the form of giant American companies such as General Motors and DuPont followed the unfolding of what he called their strategies, as they evolved from monoliths organized around functions (production, marketing) into separate divisions, each resembling a stand-alone business.

But Chandler's definition of strategy did not offer much guidance to practitioners who might want to emulate his corporate examples: "*Strategy* can be defined as the determination of the basic long-term goals and objectives of an enterprise, and the adoption of courses of action and the allocation of resources necessary for carrying out these goals." He had become familiar with the word, and the subject matter, from many sources. In one of those twists of intellectual history that may delight only the obsessed, in 1956 McDonald had hired Chandler, then a young scholar in American industrial history at MIT, to be a research associate on the General Motors book he was writing with Alfred P. Sloan. The book would become the classic *My Years with General Motors*.

If Chandler's definition was baggy and capacious, the notions introduced by Igor Ansoff in his 1965 book, *Corporate Strategy*, were filigreed to an overwrought fault. Ansoff, a PhD in mathematics, had worked at the Rand think tank and served as a senior corporate planner for Lockheed Aircraft before moving on to Carnegie Mellon University. The thrust of Ansoff's ideas in some ways paralleled ruminations already under way at Harvard Business School, namely, that the purpose of strategy was to match a company's capabilities to the opportunities in its environment. But by his book's end, he had plunged the reader into planning processes that mapped out, on a one-page diagram, fifty-seven boxes of objectives and factors to be considered, each to be taken up in the proper order, as indicated by an Alice in Wonderland slalom of arrows.

Thus, for all the gradually mounting interest in it, the concept of corporate strategy was still up for grabs as Henderson and his colleagues discussed their young firm's potential focus. This state of affairs is captured in what might be termed the foundation story of BCG, though like many foundation stories, it may be laced with elements of foundation myth. The tale goes that Henderson and his confreres were debating different possibilities when Henderson finally suggested they take strategy as their specialty; this had, after all, been the subject of the first *Perspectives*. But nobody will know what we're talking about, another objected. "That's the beauty of it." Henderson responded, "We'll define it."

The Primordial Ooze from Which Strategy Emerged

In the process, Henderson and his colleagues would get a big push from the shifting winds of the *zeitgeist*. Writing twenty years after the fact, Peter Drucker said that the original title of his 1964 book, *Managing for Results*, had been *Business Strategies*, but that he and his publisher had been persuaded to change it because everyone they asked told them that strategy "belongs to military or perhaps political campaigns but not to business." While Drucker would go on to claim, with characteristic intellectual modesty, that his had been "the first book on business strategy," he also declared he was glad they had gone with the revised title, because *Managing for Results* more accurately reflected his book's message: that "businesses exist to produce results on the outside, in the market and the economy."

Today, when almost every executive's résumé proclaims the bearer to be "results-oriented"—translation: you can rely on the subject to make his or her numbers—it takes a long swim of the imagination to get one's mind back to an era when the notion that "businesses exist to produce results" was something that had to be called to readers' attention. The same holds true for the concept that a business could be actively, consciously managed to that end, an insight that Drucker would maintain—not inaccurately—had been first fully annunciated in his 1954 book, *The Practice of Management.* Blowing past such hidebound-ness and timidity to install a new, aggressive consciousness in business executives was precisely what the strategy revolution was about.

Can it really be that executives before then felt so unempowered? John D. Rockefeller? J. P. Morgan? The heads of giant companies? The too-easy answer would be that we're not talking about the mind-set of a Rockefeller or a Morgan here—they were exceptional individuals for any age—but rather the outlook of the typical mid-twentieth-century businessperson. Nor does it suffice to observe that by the mid-century, American capitalism had become more decorous, corseted by laws and regulations—some enacted to keep another J.P. Morgan from happening—and plumped up by the postwar recovery and the obliteration of competitors' European and Japanese factories.

In his textbook *Strategy and the Business Landscape*, Ghemawat sketches a history of business's interest in planning that I'd argue can be taken as a rough proxy for the evolution of strategic consciousness in companies. In what he describes as the first industrial revolution, from the mid-1700s to the mid-1800s, markets were wild, competition often desperate, and most companies small. Companies had little confidence they could shape their economic environment or chart their future. The "invisible hand" of market forces ruled, *pace* Adam Smith.

This began to change with the second industrial revolution, whose huge wheels started turning in the United States in the second half of the nineteenth century. The coming of the railroads in the 1850s "made it possible to build mass markets for the first time," Ghemawat notes, and mass markets made for big companies capable of exploiting "economies of scale in production and economies of scope in distribution." These ever-larger enterprises *did* have it in their power to re-grade large tracts of the economic landscape, as Rockefeller amply demonstrated in oil and Carnegie and Morgan in steel. Such companies also required legions of functionaries, usually arrayed in hierarchies, to run and coordinate their far-flung activities. On the controls, increasingly, was what Chandler would wittily call the "visible hand" of the professional manager.

That hand in turn required a guiding intelligence, one equipped to think through new issues of scale and the kinds of competition that came with markets that extended nationwide. Henry Ford might, for example, seize the lead in the auto business by pioneering a modern form of mass production in the 1920s, but Alfred Sloan's General Motors would take that lead away from him in the 1930s in part by realizing that the market had grown big enough to be segmented into customers for Chevrolets, Pontiacs, and the rest.

As Ghemawat observes, World War II provided both an impetus to planning and new tools to use in it. Whole industries had to be redirected into war production. The discipline of "operations research" developed. By the 1950s, at least some of the precursor ideas and analytical techniques that would later be used in the strategy revolution had begun to emerge.

But where was the desire to use them, or the burning sense that your company's destiny could be yours to forge, and you better hop to it? Peter Drucker was raising the cry, but his was still a lonely voice.

As Ghemawat says, Drucker "noted that economic theory had long treated markets as impersonal forces, beyond the control of individual entrepreneurs and organizations." Not right and not good enough, the sage began to assert, arguing—and here it's Drucker's words—that managing "implies responsibility for attempting to shape the economic environment, for planning, initiating and carrying through changes in that economic environment, for constantly pushing back the limitations of economic circumstances on the enterprise's freedom of action."

Stern, inspiring stuff and mostly to fall on ears waxed up with the comforts of postwar prosperity and blocked to dissident, disturbing calls to action. In 1956, another *Fortune* writer, William H. Whyte Jr., published *The Organization Man*, also to become a business classic. Reporting articles that became the basis of the book, Whyte had discovered a new phenomenon, middle-class suburbia. He'd also looked into the training programs companies ran for their next generation of managers.

The experience left him profoundly disquieted, a disquiet he passed along to his readers. The Protestant ethic was pretty much dying among this crop of businessmen, he concluded, along with its hardy work ethic. The new men were technicians, bureaucrats, well trained in their specialties, but principally concerned with fitting in. They "are becoming the interchangeables of our society," Whyte observed, "and they accept the role with understanding. They are all, as they say, in the same boat."

"But where is the boat going?" he went on, in a passage worth quoting at length, it so beautifully captures the torpid corporate mind-set that the strategy revolution would wrench into alertness. "No one seems to have the faintest idea; nor, for that matter, do they see much point in raising the question. Once people liked to think, at least, that they were in control of their destinies, but few of the organization people cherish such notions. Most see themselves as objects more acted upon than acting—and their future, therefore, determined as much by the system as by themselves." Your costs were your costs. Old man corporate river, he just keeps rolling along.

But storm clouds were beginning to gather over the lotus-eaters' company picnic. As attendees awoke to the new threats menacing them, BCG would be there to help. For starters, the firm would show them the ineluctable power of the experience curve.

3.

The Experience Curve Delivers a Shock

L ARGER ECONOMIC FORCES were conspiring to make businesspeople ache and fret for a new way of understanding
the world. As the 1960s unfolded, fattish, complacent
American companies found themselves confronted with competition
from unexpected quarters—foreign manufacturers, smaller upstart
enterprises in their own backyard. What was going on? What to do
about it? The Boston Consulting Group had the answer to both questions in the form of the experience curve.

The experience curve was, simply, the single most important concept in launching the strategy revolution. Despite the reality that its
empirical foundations were in places shaky, that academics gleefully
point out its limitations, and that BCG itself would by the mid-1970s
largely move on to more novel tools, no other idea was to set in motion
such an alteration in corporate consciousness.

What the experience-curve concept did was to instigate a sea change
in the way companies think about their costs. While its basic truths are

so ingrained today that we take them as eternal and unchanging laws of nature—"everyone knows that"—when first proclaimed, they were electrifying: businesses should expect their costs to decline systematically, at a rate that can be accurately predicted. (*You can always do it for less.*) Different companies making the same product may have very different costs—heresy to many economists at the time—and your cost position should reflect your share of the market. (*Somebody out there may be able to do it even more cheaply than you can.*) A bigger market share typically means you have more experience—you've made more of the product—which should mean your costs are lower than theirs. (*Get big or get trounced.*)

These were to be the premises from which Greater Taylorism took off. Anyone today who suffers the depredations of a corporate cost-cutting campaign or who sweats at the prospect of meeting "the China price" is running up against the imperatives of the experience curve.

How Your Costs Should Decline

BCG devised the curve in 1966. A client, General Instruments, was having trouble matching competitors' prices in its television-components business. Bruce Henderson dispatched John Clarkeson, a recently minted Harvard MBA—and twenty years later the elected head of BCG—to study what might be wrong. He also suggested that the younger man gather as much literature as he could find on the learning curve, a subject that had long intrigued Henderson.

Literature there was, including a 1964 *Harvard Business Review* article, "Profit from the Learning Curve," by a professor of chemical engineering, Winfred Hirschmann. As Hirschmann noted, as early as 1925, manufacturers of aircraft had begun to observe that the amount of labor that went into making an aircraft declined predictably as the number of planes manufactured increased. Typically, the fourth plane took only 80 percent of the labor required to make the second, the eighth only 80 percent of what had gone into the fourth.

If you took man-hours of labor per plane as the measure to be charted on the vertical axis of a graph—or, later, costs—and the cumulative number of planes produced on the horizontal, the resultant plot of actual production resulted in a graceful downward curve (graph A in figure 3-1). If, even better, you used logarithmic scales on each dimension, whereby each doubling or halving covers the same distance on the scale, you get an even niftier straight line, whose angle could be readily calculated (graph B)—a downward slope of 20 percent in the case of aircraft manufacture. By the mid-1950s, industry experts realized that the effect obtained even for different types of aircraft—fighters, bombers, transport planes—leading these observers to speculate that something generalizable was going on.

But what? The phenomenon had been noticed in the aggregate, not by identifying specific factors leading to the overall result. Hirschmann and others concluded that the explanation lay in learning—hence the name *learning curve*—but learning not just by individuals (the kind of progress that Frederick Taylor would clock on a stopwatch), but rather by the organization as a whole (which was going to put the *Greater* in *Greater Taylorism*). In his article, he cited other names in use for the

FIGURE 3-1

The experience curve

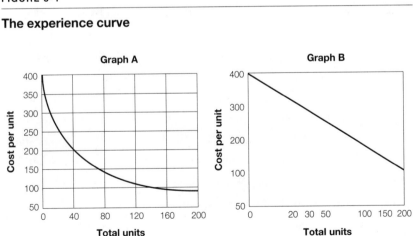

phenomenon—"manufacturing progress function," "cost curve," "efficiency curve," and, yes, "experience curve"—but argued that "learning curve" best captured what was going on. Hirschmann also marshaled evidence to show the learning curve at work in other industries—petroleum refining, heavy-equipment manufacture, steel, even the generation of electric power.

Sure enough, Clarkeson found, in the market for copper-wiring assemblies for televisions, the particular General Instruments product he was studying, the learning curve appeared to working its magic. While a consultant couldn't always get data on competitors' costs, usually available were the prices they were charging. In looking at industry trends, BCG took prices as a proxy for costs and found that prices were declining as the number of units produced increased, in precisely the pattern the learning curve predicted.

The two intellectual steps Clarkeson and his colleagues took next were what transformed the humble learning curve into BCG's distinctive and arresting *experience curve*. First, it broadened the ambit of costs taken into account in calculating the curve, beyond just the costs of labor baked into a product, to include "*all* costs," the firm's literature proclaimed, "including capital, administrative, research, and marketing." These were to be costs based on actual cash flows, not accounting numbers. Instead of the number of units produced, BCG would speak of a company's or industries' accumulated "experience." With each doubling of experience, costs and prices should decline by a predictable amount, typically between 15 and 25 percent.

Second, and vastly more important, BCG posited a direct relationship between a company's position on the experience curve—and hence its costs—and its market share. The competitor with the largest share, the one that sold more of the product than anyone else did, should be the one with the most "experience." Greater experience enabled a company to get the most from all the elements that BCG suggested made the curve work: scale effects, rationalization of costs, redesign, and technology improvements from research and development.

The essential insight here was heartening or terrifying, depending on how your company was situated: the market-share leader should be the low-cost producer in any industry. Provided that it continued to churn out more units than any other competitor and thus drive down the experience curve faster, that company should remain the low-cost producer forever and ever, amen brother. It could charge less for its products, continue to outsell the opposition, and maintain a cost and price advantage over them interminably. "We'd put up the slides explaining the experience curve," says a BCG partner who made presentations at the early conferences, and as the idea sank in, "one or two in the audience would begin nodding and smiling quietly while others started looking like they wanted to throw up."

The call-to-action message, shocking to many at the time, was that you couldn't truly understand how you were doing in a business or likely to do unless you understood exactly how you stood vis à vis your competitors. How did your share of the market compare to theirs? Were your costs lower or higher? If you didn't have any cost advantage, how else might you differentiate your product? With the experience curve, the strategy revolution began to insinuate an acute awareness of competition into the corporate consciousness.

Today, when a jumpy awareness of current or potential competitive threats is the norm for most businesses, it's difficult to recapture the mind-set of an era when that wasn't the case. But the 1950s and 1960s were such an era. The evidence for this particular blind spot in the corporate eye is partly archival, partly testimonial.

Look up "competition" in the indexes to the early books on strategy. In Peter Drucker's *Managing for Results* from 1964, there's a citation to one page, with a quick "*see also* Monopoly," compared with the twenty pages the reader is referred to under "decision-making." His *Practice of Management* has no index entry for "competition" at all. Neither does Alfred Chandler's *Strategy and Structure*, in contrast to the eighty-some pages it offers under "diversification." Igor Ansoff's *Corporate Strategy* from 1965 has precisely three page citations.

Consultants at work during the pre-strategy period report a comparable lack of interest in the subject among their clients. "We just didn't talk about it," recalls one, shaking his head slightly in retrospective amazement. "Nobody did."

How could companies be so unmindful of competitive threats? As Nitin Nohria, Davis Dyer, and Frederick Dalzell point out in their book *Changing Fortunes*, an intriguing study of the growth and—mostly—decline of the large industrial corporation after World War II, in the "golden era" of U.S. capitalism from 1948 to 1973, the economy grew at an average rate of 3.7 percent a year, with the big industrial companies leading the charge. While the shift that would gradually tilt the U.S. economy from a manufacturing base to services was already under way, almost no one saw it at the time. (Nohria and his coauthors observe that manufacturing's share of the gross domestic product peaked between 1953 and 1957. My own preference for demonstrating the trend is employment figures: the proportion of U.S. workers who labored in manufacturing peaked in the early 1940s, at 32 percent; today, it's less than 10 percent, a seeming historical inevitability that ought to be borne in mind by those shocked to discover the migration of "good American jobs" overseas.)

In 1954, *Fortune* magazine began publishing its annual list of the five hundred largest industrial corporations, reflecting the primacy of those sprawling enterprises in the economic order. The worry at the time was not about how these giants might be buffeted by the forces of competition, but rather that their power was too largely unchecked. As Nohria and his colleagues point out, much of the received wisdom at the time came from books like Harvard economist Edward Mason's *Corporation in Modern Society* (1959) or John Kenneth Galbraith's *New Industrial State* (1967). The latter book raised the specter of the modern corporation as "a mighty and largely uninhibited force capable of dictating terms to owners, employees, and unions, while paying little heed to government."

Government responded to the threat, or the snub. In 1950, Congress passes the Cellar-Kefauver Act outlawing mergers that reduced or lessened competition "in any line of commerce." The move would prompt the still-growing industrials to diversify into businesses unrelated to what they knew best, usually resulting in a mess that it would take the strategy revolution to help them sort out. Up through the early 1960s, Washington threatened behemoths such as AT&T and IBM with antitrust action aimed at curbing their market power.

Critics of corporate mightiness need not have worried so much; the horsemen of the apocalypse were on their way, bringing with them competitive forces that would do far more to rein in the power of the big industrial companies than any government policy could. Nohria, Dyer, and Dalzell calculate that the one hundred largest industrials were to reach the summit of their puissance in 1974, when they accounted for more than a third of U.S. economic output. By 1998, their share was half that.

Up until the 1980s at least, most of the clients of BCG and the other strategy consulting firms were industrial companies. The story of the strategy revolution is thus, in some considerable measure, about how these enterprises sought ideas from the consultants and others to help them stem what turned out to be an inexorable decline. The experience curve was to be both a wake-up call for the somnambulist giants and the first strategic concept they would seize on for help.

Black & Decker Uses the Tool

"The fascination of the new toy," recalls John Clarkeson, was what followed BCG's discovery of the experience curve. "For the next five years, maybe more, we applied experience curves to anything that moved, and a lot of things that didn't." Gathering data on prices in one industry after another, and cost information wherever they could, they detected experience-curve effects at work beneath much of the corporate landscape: in chemicals, transistors, appliances, crude oil, facial tissue, and Japanese beer.

The consultants also began to tease out the implications of the curve for company strategy, in the process coming to appreciate the quality that sets it apart from most of the other conceptual tools that we'll encounter in the revolution: the experience curve is dynamic, in the sense that it both tracks change and can be used to predict it, and not just change in costs. Follow the logic of the experience curve, and you'll see how competition between businesses is likely to play out.

Early *Perspectives* explicated this logic with daunting clarity: a company will probably need to sell a new product for less than cost until volume builds. If there's any competition in a market, prices will eventually go down as fast as costs. The competitor with the largest cumulative market share should always be able to remain the lowest-cost producer, but any company that takes on the leader will also have to keep driving down the curve if it hopes to stay competitive. If the market for a product is growing rapidly, then a share of that market can be quite valuable; moreover, that value to a company can be calculated with some precision. The shares that different competitors have in a market will fluctuate until one player establishes dominance, becoming the market-share leader with costs and prices so low that others can no longer grow their share, or until the market stops growing.

Two companies in particular took the logic of the experience curve to heart, and each became a vital early client to the consulting firm (as they also would go on to be, in 1973, for the newly formed Bain & Company). Francis Lucier, a rising executive at Black & Decker, the power-tool manufacturer, had received a mailing from BCG; had attended one, two, then three of its conferences; and had come away intrigued. He invited Henderson to make a presentation to company executives at its headquarters in Towson, Maryland.

"We sat there and listened to Bruce talking about the experience curve," Lucier recalls, "and how it became a strong marketing tool, because you could predict, based on your accumulation of volume, what your costs could be. And if you knew your costs, you could price the product accordingly, instead of doing it the old-fashioned way, where when you brought out a new product, you priced it high to get your money back, and by that time, you had all your competitors in there with you." The Black & Decker crew was impressed and told Lucier to "get" Henderson. "Henderson said, 'You can't get me,'" Lucier remembers, "so I asked him, 'Who is your alter ego?' He said 'Bill Bain.'" Bain had joined BCG in 1967 and was duly dispatched to handle the assignment.

In many respects, Black & Decker was an ideal candidate to take up BCG's ideas. It had been around since 1910 making power tools. After it skated close to bankruptcy in the Depression and then committed itself to war production, its postwar leadership had concluded that greater safety and growth lay in diversification, including into consumer products. Still, by the late 1950s, Black & Decker seemed stuck with about 20 percent of the overall market for power tools. Lucier was brought in to gear up the push into consumer markets, a comparative sideline to the company's main business in tools for manufacturers and the construction industry.

Even before they ran into BCG, Lucier and his team had done enough research to reach two key insights. Most of the outlets Black & Decker sold through, typically hardware stores or small chains of such stores, had no idea which retailers they were competing against in selling power tools to consumers. It was, in fact, Sears, with its Craftsman line and its national distribution. Second, Lucier and the team discovered that if Black & Decker cut product prices, which it could do mostly by squeezing its own margins and those of its distributors, sales volume increased markedly, as the company had proved to itself first with power drills and then with circular saws. When the retail price of the latter was $30.00 to $35.00, the company sold around 50,000 a year. By the time Black & Decker worked the price down to $19.95, it was selling 600,000 circular saws annually. But it took a concerted educational effort to convince distributors, whose eyes were fixed on their margins, that higher turnover at lower margins could mean greater total profit for distributor and manufacturer alike.

The experience curve gave Lucier and his colleagues both an understanding of the logic behind what they were doing and the confidence to apply the same logic to one new product after another, building their market share and scaring off investment from potential competitors. Lucier recounts, for example, what friends of his at Stanley Tools told him of that company's reaction to Black & Decker's introduction of the Workmate workbench: "Their CEO saw our television ads for it and yelled, 'Jeez, that's *our* business, *our* business. What are they doing in *our* business?' But every time they'd cost the thing, they'd come back and say, 'They're not making any money on this.' What we were doing was pricing it for what it was going to be. And you know what, Stanley never got into the business; it proved the point." And the point was what the experience curve could do for you.

The curve wasn't the only learning Black & Decker gained from the consultants. "They showed us on really finding out about your competition," Lucier says. "We started getting market intelligence from them on where we stood relative to competition by product, by this, by that. It was invaluable." The intelligence was particularly helpful to Black & Decker in calculating its next move. By "reading the competitor's numbers," as Lucier puts it, if that competitor were looking for investment dollars, "when they didn't get their money, we knew we had them, they were strapped, and we turned the screws a little harder." Lucier, who had, he says, "no staff," also realized what many consulting clients would in years to follow: "They had the troops to go out and get the information."

With the price of items such as its quarter-inch drill steadily reduced from $15.98 in 1963 to $7.99 in 1970, company sales built steadily, from over $100 million in 1964, to past $200 million in 1969, to more than $500 million in 1974. Black & Decker became a favorite of Wall Street, one of the so-called Nifty Fifty stocks that the go-go market of the late 1960s and early 1970s branded "one-decision" investments: just buy and hold them, so steady was their earnings growth. In 1975, Lucier, who had become president of the company in 1970, was named chief executive, the first in the company's history not to come from either the Black or the Decker families.

TI's Ride Down the Curve Ends Badly

Texas Instruments took a wilder ride down the experience curve with its personal calculator business. Originally in oil-exploration technology, TI was by the 1950s a fast-growing manufacturer of electronics, selling much of its output to the Department of Defense. It was also pioneering new technologies. After licensing the basic invention from Western Electric, TI had developed a new transistor. In 1958, TI engineer Jack Kilby had put together an integrated circuit—essentially transistors and other components such as resistors "printed" on a chip of semiconductor material—based on germanium, this at about the same time that Robert Noyce of Fairchild Semiconductor assembled one based on silicon. Until they finally struck a cross-licensing deal in 1966, the two companies battled over their patents on the technology.

Today it may be difficult to remember that integrated circuits were hardly an instant success. Computers, which the circuits would eventually transform, were only beginning to lumber onto the scene. And like most newly invented wonders, integrated circuits looked expensive compared with the technology they would eventually displace, the transistors being churned out in mass-produced lots.

To spread its customer base, Texas Instruments went looking for new products that incorporated integrated circuits and that could be sold in consumer markets. The company found its answer in the personal calculator, which Kilby and colleagues invented and filed a patent for in 1967. The challenge it faced was as much economic as technological.

When asked in 2005 whether, at the time of the integrated circuit's invention, he had foreseen where it would lead, Kilby observed that "the real story has been in the cost reduction." In 1958, he noted, a single transistor that was not very good sold for about $10. Nowadays, he went on, $10 will buy the equivalent of something over twenty million. "The first calculators tended to sell for $400 or $500," he recalled. "Today, you can get a pretty good one for $4 or $5."

By the mid-1960s, inklings of the potential power of systematic cost reduction in semiconductors were already in the air. In a 1965 *Electronics Magazine* piece titled "Cramming More Components onto Integrated Circuits," Gordon Moore, later to cofound Intel, presented the first version of what came to be known as Moore's law, the idea that the number of transistors on an integrated circuit could be expected to double every eighteen months—Moore originally said two years— or, turning the coin over, that the cost of a given amount of computing power would fall by half in the same period.

Such ideas may have been floating around, but they weren't solidified enough for Texas Instruments to be comfortable building a calculator business around them. For that, it took the Boston Consulting Group and its experience curve. An ambitious TI executive, J. Fred Bucy, knew Henderson and brought in the consulting firm to study the industry emerging around integrated circuits and his company's opportunities with calculators.

Texas Instruments was already producing chip sets for Canon, which in 1970 had brought to market one of the first handheld commercial calculators, selling them for about $400 apiece, and for Bowmar Instrument Corporation, whose Bowmar Brain brought the price down to around $250. TI's prospects in the market were made more complicated, and potentially more exciting, by another technological leap forward: by 1971, its engineers had developed one of the first single-chip microprocessors. Today, the garden-variety definition of *microprocessor* is "a computer on a chip." But in contrast to Intel, which devised its own single-chip microprocessor at about the same time, Texas Instruments conceived of the technology as a calculator on a chip, suspecting that TI could use its new microprocessor to bring down the cost of handheld calculators significantly.

But how fast and by how much? No one had brought out a consumer product based on a microprocessor before. (The first personal computers wouldn't reach the market until 1978.) To calculate answers, BCG assembled a prepossessing team—members would in their later lives go on to found three strategy consulting firms, lead Citigroup's investment banking operations, and in, the person of Jay Light, serve as dean of the Harvard Business School—headed, again, by Bill Bain. For case manager, Bain tapped George Bennett. A native of West Virginia, with an undergraduate degree in engineering—of course—and a PhD from Carnegie Mellon, Bennett had written his dissertation on using artificial intelligence, that is, computer power, to balance assembly lines.

The key to the problem was figuring out that if you were making a component used in a number of different products—in calculators, say, and in missile systems—you needed to take into account the experience-curve effects calculated across all your product lines. "We built an enormous shared-cost system," Bennett recalls. "We had experience curves for each of the fifty major activities in semiconductor production, and got all the data plotted, then built very elaborate models and were able to show that if you would bring out a ten-dollar calculator, and sell two or three million a year, then the reduced costs [of semiconductors] for missiles would be profound."

"Which is what Fred did," Bennett says. The steep slide down to $10 began in July 1972, with the launch of the TI-2500 Datamath calculator. As reported in *Electronics* magazine at the time, retailers were enthusiastic, one observing that TI "seemed more organized than most outfits in the business." Another retailer added: "At that price—$149.99—it should sell up a really big storm." Approximately the size of the Galveston hurricane.

Calculator sales took off—their increase, measured in units, occasionally hitting 40 percent *a month*, according to the recollection of some BCG consultants. TI sold about 3 million of the devices in 1971, 17 million in 1973, 28 million in 1974, and 45 million in 1975, with sales revenue eventually reaching around $100 million a year, about a tenth of TI's total revenue. Costs and prices fell as predicted, with the BCG analysis providing company management the assurance to invest in new semiconductor fabrication facilities well before TI had the actual demand in hand for the output of the "fabs." Also as predicted, Texas Instruments achieved dominant share in the calculator business.

The story doesn't have a happy ending, though, reflecting the bitter competitive dynamics that strategies based on the experience curve and market share can unleash. It was as if competitors hadn't read the same book that TI was operating from. Seeing the rapid growth of the calculator market, new players such as National Semiconductor and Rockwell piled into the business. Even worse, Bowmar, more an assembler than an integrated manufacturer—it didn't build semiconductor plants of its own until too late—refused to cede the market to TI. When recession struck in 1974 and the growth of the business began to slow, the smaller company matched TI's prices, in the process launching a desperate price war. By 1975, prices collapsed, TI's inventories became overvalued, and the Texas company registered a $16 million loss in its second quarter. For its trouble, Bowmar was driven into bankruptcy.

For Texas Instruments, however, the explosion of demand for microprocessors of all sorts was sufficient to mask the sins of particular product lines—company sales would triple from 1973 to 1979. Bucy was promoted to company president in 1976, going on to become CEO in 1984, only to retire, a bit early, the following year. Over the course of his career, he would retain the services of George Bennett in three more of the consultant's incarnations.

More than one BCG consultant from these early days tells a version of the following tale: At a conference, perhaps after giving a presentation, he or she is approached by the CEO of a company, not one that Henderson's firm ever worked for. Angry, vituperative, and, in some recountings, with tears in his eyes, the executive points his finger at the consultant and says, "You guys ruined my company." The aggrieved man's enterprise had adopted a version of an experience-curve strategy, cut prices to gain share, and found itself trapped in an interminable, bloody price war. Inexpert application of the underlying concept, the consultant hastens to explain—probably a failure to define the market segment correctly or to identify where in the overall cost system the curve's dynamics did or didn't apply.

Perhaps, but by the early 1980s, academics and journalists were happy to proclaim the curve's many limitations. A 1985 *Harvard Business Review* article by Harvard's Pankaj Ghemawat ticks them off handily: Slopes varied dramatically from industry to industry, frequently deviating from the 15 percent to 25 percent most companies expected. The curve worked best when demand for a product was growing fast, as with semiconductors, but was a poor basis for strategy in mature industries—beer, cement—where accumulated experience doubled at a glacial pace and many of the inefficiencies had already been wrung out of the business.

And getting locked into an experience-curve strategy, with its relentless drive for ever-lower costs, could leave you open to being blindsided by changes in taste or technology. Everyone's favorite example of the last point is Henry Ford and the Model T: by pursuing an experience-curve strategy *avant la lettre*, he had missed the growing consumer demand for a greater variety and for close-bodied, more aerodynamic automobiles, in the process losing market-share dominance to General Motors for the rest of the twentieth century.

Note, though, that none of these criticisms dispute the curve's existence or call into question its power to discipline a company's thinking around the imperative to cut costs incessantly. Its forcefulness and menace endure into the twenty-first century, as a senior partner of a strategy firm observes: "The experience curve is like what Newton discovered with the law of gravity. It's a fundamental law of nature. People disobey it at their peril."

Loading the Matrix

4.

ALMOST EVERYONE AT BCG in the late 1960s and early 1970s recalls the 8 a.m. Monday staff meetings as formative, heady, and, for some, bordering on intoxicating. Whoever was in Boston—usually a good-sized crew; by 1970, the professional staff there numbered nearly eighty-five—would get together to listen to colleagues presenting their latest casework. Hypotheses would be floated, tested, prodded, and poked. Ideas would emerge and be batted around the room. Around 8:30, Henderson would arrive—that's when his train got in from the suburbs—and "rip everything up," as one participant recalls, asking still more questions, contentiously probing for better explanations.

The excitement that people who were there still register about what they were discovering—even after thirty years, as they talk about it their energy levels rise, their words pour out faster—comports not at all with the standard image of a consultant, an eye fixed unrelentingly on how he or she can wring the most money from clients. But a few factors make somewhat plausible the chorus of claims that at this juncture in consulting's history, this time and place, the wild intellectual adventure was often as intriguing as the prospect of grabbing the brass ring of financial or career success.

Henderson focused on hiring the smartest people, even to the exclusion of other concerns. (Rather in keeping with the spirit of the times. In other circles, this was, famously, the era of what David Halberstam labeled "the best and the brightest.") Prior consulting experience wasn't required. Indeed, looking at the backgrounds of those recruited, such grounding almost appears a disqualification. Henderson was seeking pure conceptual candlepower, preferably the kind demonstrated in competition with other bright lights at some prestigious, hard-to-get-into academic institution. BCG's official account of the year 1970 crows that the firm "discovered we had taken more than one-quarter of the high distinction graduates from HBS . . . no other private company had hired more than one or perhaps two." Plus, the number-one graduates from "at least two of the other major business schools."

The attractions of working there were threefold: First was money—Henderson deliberately sought to pay more than the other companies competing for the same talent. He offered George Bennett a $1,000 monthly retainer while Bennett was still completing his graduate work, before he could actually join the firm; Bennett's rent at the time was $85 a month. The second draw was prestige, at least in the eyes of one's classmates—never underestimate the lemming-express effect that obtains among students at "top" business schools and colleges. You compete to get into the most prestigious college. Then you compete to get into the top-ranked business school. After you've learned and displayed so much independence of mind, what's left but to compete to be hired by the employer all your peers were clamoring to join?

All true, but BCG recruits had plenty of other job offers. What tipped the balance for many was the third attraction, Henderson's excitement about a figuring out how things worked, his quest to explode conventional wisdom to get at the principles that truly governed business competition. *Applied microeconomics*, a few called it, but not the sort that academic economists, with their aggregated, slightly dusty data, could make out. Rather, the hot crucible for a new type of intellectual, and a major step toward the intellectualization of business.

Henderson's passion would come through in the extended, frequently torturous interviews he conducted with potential hires. Sandra Moose, a Harvard PhD in economics, tells of being referred to the firm in 1967, sitting down with its founder and quickly finding herself in "a raging three-hour argument with Bruce," something about long-run average cost curves. When it was over, he told her, "I never heard of a woman at a consulting firm, but I guess I could add one more flake to the mix." She'd go on to become one of BCG's first woman vice presidents and an eminence there.

Another hire from approximately the same time sums up the experience many had working at BCG: "I was an idea junkie. I was surrounded by all these other incredibly smart people who were just as interested in ideas. It was close to heaven."

The last factor lending credence to the notion that the real action at BCG then was intellectual was the paucity of business action. Says Alan Zakon of the period around 1970, with a touch of his characteristically mordant humor, "You were embarrassed to tell people we were doing no business." An overstatement, of course—the enterprise had grown every year through the 1960s, adding staff, becoming incorporated on its own in 1968—but one that nicely captures the insouciance prevailing at the firm. In BCG's own contemporaneous account of its first ten years, the entry for 1969 notes that "we devoted more time and expense to recruiting every year than we did to developing new clients."

Put simply, Henderson cared more about his intellectual explorations and surrounding himself with exciting companions on the voyage than he did about putting the enterprise on a sustainable footing. Put less charitably, this man whose firm aimed to advise companies on their central strategic dilemmas wasn't a particularly good businessman himself.

"He couldn't sell," one early colleague recalls, voicing a sentiment roundly shared by those who knew him. Henderson's willingness, sometimes bordering on eagerness, to get into a fight over ideas or the correct interpretation of data extended to potential clients. Also his unwillingness to lose those fights. Layer in a dislike of authority, suffuse with free-floating insecurity, and you had all the makings for a serious chip carried about unrelievedly on the founder-entrepreneur's shoulder.

Another BCG veteran tells of Henderson slamming down the phone after a brief conversation punctuated with "*Who* are you? What did you say you want? What is your name again?" The caller was Reg Jones, the chief executive of General Electric. "Bruce knew who he was. He was just taking out on Jones all his years of frustration being at Westinghouse competing with GE."

This, together with a few other crotchets, quickly persuaded Henderson's colleagues to try to avoid taking him on sales calls if possible. A colleague recalls journeying down from Boston in a snowstorm with Henderson and Zakon for an appointment with the number-two man at Chase Manhattan Bank, a potential client. "We sat there waiting in this elegant anteroom with snow and slush melting off us. After removing his galoshes while everybody watched, slightly aghast, Bruce patiently and rather proudly unpacked three suits from one of those bags you carry bowling balls in." They didn't get the assignment.

Henderson's independent streak and lack of business acumen showed themselves in other ways as well. In 1965, partly as an effort to give his nascent consulting unit an identity apart from its corporate parent, Henderson had agreed to take over the people and obligations of a consulting firm in Milan, one several times the size of the U.S. operation. The attempt to merge the two firms' cultures quickly failed, with virtually the entire staff in Milan leaving.

A similar attempt 1968 to start up a consultancy in London through a joint venture met a similar result, and about as fast. It was to be BCG's last attempt to set up an outpost along with someone else; thereafter, the firm would only colonize, establishing new offices with people who had been steeped in the true gospel of ideas and analytics back at the mother church.

For all their lack of success, the ventures abroad did signal another way that Henderson's thinking was far ahead of most contemporaries' realizations in the 1960s: he was already alive to the opportunities and dangers posed by globalization. This perspicacity bore the most fruit in the one early foreign adventure that did work for BCG, though the intellectual achievement far outweighed the financial. In 1965, Henderson hired James C. Abegglen, installed him as the second-most-senior member of the staff, and charged him with opening up an office in Japan.

Abegglen had begun to learn Japanese as a marine, been wounded on Guam and Guadalcanal, then first visited the defeated country as part of the postwar Strategic Bombing Survey. While he soon went back to the United States to eventually earn a PhD in anthropology and clinical psychology from the University of Chicago, he remained fascinated with Japan, returning in 1955 as a Ford Foundation fellow, his visit culminating in a book titled *The Japanese Factory*. He would go on to work as an executive in the Far East for ITT, then, disdaining life in a big company, join Arthur D. Little, where he met Henderson. In 1962, Abegglen left ADL for McKinsey, but when that firm proved lukewarm about starting up a branch in Japan, he accepted the offer from Henderson, who had become a friend. They were to remain so, apparently one of the few warm friendships that Henderson maintained with a colleague. (Though even Abegglen, who died in 2007, would admit that Henderson was almost impossible to get to know in any depth, so unyielding were his psychological defenses.)

Abegglen and the Tokyo office he soon opened were to provide BCG and its clients a window on Japan at a time when most American companies had only faint inklings of the competitive threat that its industries were coming to represent. The menace was a perfect fit with what was emerging as BCG's central concern—the dynamics of competition based largely on steadily declining costs. By 1968, the firm would be holding conferences on Japan for clients in the United States and Europe and publishing a *Perspectives* piece titled "What Makes Japan Grow." (The answer was not low labor costs; "Nothing could be further from the truth.")

Recession finally overtook the U.S. economy at the end of 1969, the first such contraction in over eight years. Its arrival would throw into painful relief much of the strangeness and contradiction that had attended BCG's growth since its founding.

Some twenty-six people joined the firm in 1969, and the total staff increased by 60 percent the following year. The retail marketing of the firm's ideas seemed to be going great guns. Even though BCG was charging $1,500 per person or more to attend its conferences, invitations were in heavy and growing demand, so much so that by 1972, it would begin to restrict who could come: only the designated invitee, not some substitute, and only, in the firm's words, "selected officers of a restricted list of companies." By that year, it was conducting biannual conferences on strategy in five countries. BCG was also turning out *Perspectives* at a brisk pace—ten in 1970, fifteen in 1971—which were reaching an audience far beyond the firm's clients.

The problem was that such intellectual engagement didn't necessarily lead to a consulting engagement. In BCG's official early history, the first sentence of the entry for 1971 reads, "This was a depression year," which the firm translated to mean only 10 percent revenue growth. But such growth concealed a lack of underlying, sustaining profitability—all those new people hired—and rumors began to circulate among its denizens that BCG might have to close down.

Two factors were to rescue the firm. First, back-to-back recessions— one in 1970 and then, triggered by oil shocks, another from 1973 to 1975—woke up companies to the need for what BCG was selling in a way that the buoyant 1960s never did. Second, starting in 1968, the firm had begun to capture in one framework all the elements that needed to be integrated into an effective corporate strategy.

Debt and Cash as Imperatives

Tracking the firm's route of discovery entails an excursion over the contested ground of financial theory. On their journey, Henderson and his compadres picked up two conclusions central to the revolution:

First, that in thinking about strategy, one should focus on cash—how much did a business generate, how much consume—rather than on earnings reported for accounting purposes. Second, that for most companies, leverage was a good thing. Or as Henderson put it in a 1972 *Perspectives* essay, "Use more debt than your competition or get out of the business."

In working for a client thinking of buying a small oil company, the consultants concluded that the target's "past and present reported profits were meaningless" to their calculations. The only measure to take seriously was how much cash the company's operations would throw off in the future. Henderson would build on this thinking and tie it in with the experience curve in a 1972 *Perspectives* piece, "Cash Traps." A majority of most companies' products are such snares, he concluded, in that "they will absorb more money forever than they will generate." If they were not market-share leaders, they were likely to be *"not only worthless but a perpetual drain on corporate resources,"* he added with italicized zest.

What converted Henderson into a vociferous advocate of leverage was mostly the work of Alan Zakon, a former associate professor of finance at Boston University. In 1967, Zakon found himself wrestling with one of BCG's largest client engagements to date, helping Weyerhaeuser calculate whether it should diversify out of timber products or acquire still more woodlands. The company viewed the latter as a thoroughly unexciting asset, but some of its competitors—Louisiana-Pacific, Boise Cascade, Georgia-Pacific—seemed to be on a land-acquisition tear and, mysteriously, making lots of money from their investment. Zakon spent nearly a year on the case, trying to devise a framework for understanding Weyerhaeuser's dilemma. Eventually, aided by the intellectual chemistry of the firm's conferences, he came up with a tool with wide applicability, what he calls the "sustainable-growth equation," more often cited in BCG literature as the "sustainable-growth formula."

Zakon figured out that the success of Weyerhaeuser's competitors came from the fact that timber was what would come to be called a *renewable resource*. The cash thrown off by the sale of successive crops of trees, together with any appreciation in the value of the underlying land, exceeded the costs of acquiring and servicing the debt needed to buy that land. Weyerhaeuser's management, older than leadership teams at the competing companies, were reluctant to borrow, trapped as they were in a Depression-era mentality. "What I finally did," Zakon explains, "was an analysis of the value of woodlands based on the proper usage of debt."

The philosophical underpinning of his recommendation "was balancing operating risk and financial risk." If you had a low level of operating risk, as timber companies did, "beef up the financial risk by the use of debt, to get to the appropriate level of debt for the business." Soon thereafter, Weyerhaeuser embarked on a program of acquiring more woodlands.

Henderson was fascinated, in part because Zakon's argument ran against the standard view then coming to prevail. "At that time the pervasive financial theory was Modigliani and Miller, which essentially said that the use of debt was irrelevant," Zakon maintains, oversimplifying slightly. What Franco Modigliani and Merton Miller had argued in an epochal 1958 paper was that the value of a company to investors wasn't affected by changes in its capital structure, its mix of debt and equity. The leading finance textbook of the time translated this into the assertion, "The decision to invest is independent of the decision about finances." Zakon disagreed, and with considerable gusto.

His pitch to Henderson was that it would be valuable to potential clients to work through BCG's formula and apply it to their own companies. "It's obvious in retrospect," argues Zakon, "but the notion of putting together in one expression interest rates, debt usage, dividend policy, and the inherent return on the business into [a determination that] this is the rate at which the company can grow—people hadn't made that linkage." The action-oriented presentation that Zakon crafted began to change the nature of BCG's conferences, away from a quasi-academic discussion of various possibilities toward a fire-bell-in-the-night, look-at-this-breathtaking-insight-and-apply-it directiveness.

Henderson's awakening to the power of leverage led him to probe the debt ratios of every company on which he could get data, including those in Japan, where companies carried much more debt than did their American counterparts. He also became bewitched by the magic of compound interest, an engrossment that some colleagues found baffling, or at least goofy. "At one of the conferences around then," Sandy Moose recalls, "he stood up and said, 'Do you want to know how many years it takes to double if you're growing at fifteen percent? Five years!' He's standing there, reading compound-interest tables out loud for a good fifteen or twenty minutes. The rest of us are sitting there thinking, 'Oh my God.'" Strange, but also telling: in the power of interest compounding, Henderson found another logic that led inevitably to a foreordained future state.

Only Connect

What followed was a dazzling act of intellectual integration, the critical first step enunciating strategy as an inclusive whole. Or as Zakon describes it, "the single biggest intuitive jump that began to put everything together."

He recites how the elements cohered:

We've got example number one of the Japanese using financial policies, combined with a low return. You can have a low return, and lots of debt, and still grow. Now, let's bring in the experience curve. It says the guy that grows fastest reduces his costs relative to his competition. Ah, so if I price down, and I have a low return, I make it back up with debt. I don't pay dividends. I have the wherewithal therefore to continue to reinvest at a rapid pace, enabling me to drive down the experience curve faster than my competition. My costs go down faster than theirs, which allows me now to price down again.

Hey, you know what? Now I have a corporate strategy. I have now integrated my pricing, my look at the competition, my debt policy, a consistency of financial policy, and return on the business, with the growth I want to do. I've got you.

Moose adds, "From there, Bruce and others had the insight that you can kind of equate cumulative experience with market share. Therefore the goal ought to be not maximizing short-term earnings but gaining market share."

In the years that followed, other lords would make the case that being the low-cost producer was hardly the only strategy available to competitors. And academics in particular would chip away at the notion that market share should necessarily be a company's primary goal. What the critics couldn't undermine, though, was the way in which BCG's rudimentary paradigm for corporate strategy linked a forceful if-this, then-that logic to the critical elements a company needed to consider in determining its future—customers, competitors, costs, financial policy.

Still, the paradigm wasn't yet a "product." The experience curve and the sustainable-growth equation provided insight bracing enough to build a strategy around if the company were in a single business, tracking down just one curve. But most of BCG's clients, actual and potential, weren't. For companies in this era, the pressures to diversify continued, in some cases pushing over into conglomeration. Antitrust law ruled out acquisitions in your own industry. You could pay out the money thrown off by your postwar growth as dividends to shareholders, but tax rates on those dividends were confiscatory. So to plow the proceeds back into your company, and to keep getting bigger, you often seemed to have only one choice: buy something in an area unrelated to those you were already in.

The results were frequently disastrous, with executives who had grown up in one business struggling to get their minds around the issues and dynamics of another. In the late 1960s, in an attempt to help clients solve their problems with diversification, BCG conceived the growth-share matrix, whose power and reach over the next ten years would be unparalleled by any other device available to a diversified company's management.

One of the "Duller Things" Gives Rise to the Matrix

As Zakon describes it, the matrix had its origins in musings sparked (probably at a Monday morning meeting) by a colleague, Kent Aldershof, who asserted that there were only three types of investments: the savings account "where you put money in the bank, it compounded, you get nothing back along the way, but at the end you took more money out than you put in"; the bond ("you buy it, it gives you cash flow annually, and at the end of the maturity period you get your money back"); and the third, the mortgage, where, for the holder, "you're getting a return on your investment, plus you're getting your money back, but at the end of the period it's worth nothing." At first, Zakon thought the taxonomy one of the "duller things" he'd encountered.

Then, in 1966 and 1967, he and Sandy Moose found themselves doing a diversification study for Mead Corporation, an Ohio-based enterprise then still mainly grounded in the paper business. After gathering reams of information on the company's different units, their prospects, and their cash requirements, the consultants concluded essentially that if Mead were to stay in paper, the required investment would take all the money the company was generating, and more. If it wanted to get out of paper, it should diversify into businesses that were high-growth, with the money to do so coming from the paper business even if it meant the former centerpiece would be allowed to gradually dwindle in the absence of further financial nourishment. After looking at the results of the study, William Wommack, the Mead executive in charge of strategy, told Zakon, "That's terrific—dress it up."

At first, Zakon didn't know how. Then Aldershof's idea came back to him. "It occurred to me that the savings account is the growth business; it automatically compounds, but you get no cash out of it. The bond is your stable market-share business that's throwing off cash and an equal amount of earnings and maintains its value over time. The mortgage is the business that's declining, and the way you should manage it is to pull cash out." Those were the three pieces of the corporate portfolio, he concluded, "but since I couldn't imagine how to deal with three"—perhaps sensing, too, that he was one element short of some sort of elegant balance—"I added the fourth, the wildcat, meaning wildcat well, a pure speculation, either it pays off or it doesn't." The consultants then arrayed the four into a four-box matrix, savings account on the upper left, bond lower left, mortgage lower right, and wildcat upper right (figure 4-1).

As Zakon and his colleagues recount this bit of intellectual history, it's apparent that the relationship between the boxes or cells—the dynamic that governs which kind of business would be put in which corner—was less than clear in this first cut at what was to become the

FIGURE 4-1

The growth-share matrix: early version

Source: Adapted from BCG working papers.

growth-share matrix. To put it graphically, what were the vertical and horizontal axes? Tight logical relationships between the cells are what give a matrix its power. As HBS professor Clayton Christensen has observed, a four-box matrix is simply another way of conveying the relationship captured in a quadratic equation. And which would you rather look at, displayed on a large screen in a conference room—a four-box structure, perhaps festooned with witty symbols for the content of each cell, or a formula with variables you can't quite remember balanced with an equal sign?

Perhaps because of its visual punch, and despite its logical weaknesses, when Mead saw the framework, its executives "went insane" with enthusiasm, the consultants recall. Working with BCG, the company developed guidelines for how its different businesses were to be managed—for cash or for growth, and what the returns should be. For the first time in its history, Zakon says, BCG had made "an actual product, as to how you ran the business with the corporate portfolio."

Zakon and his team took their new construct back to Boston and showed it to Henderson and the rest of the firm. People saw possibilities, but also limitations. The matrix mostly addressed dilemmas around cash—which businesses in the portfolio threw it off, which ones consumed it. This offered valuable insights to clients struggling with diversification; consultants from that era still shake their heads over how many companies had bought growth businesses without realizing that these used up cash in their early days and would have to be funded from somewhere else.

But the framework didn't seem to speak squarely to the competitiveness of the businesses charted. And the investment-vehicle labels—savings accounts, mortgages—were confusing and, per Zakon's original impression of Aldershof's classification, slightly dull. It would take the suggestion of a newly hired junior consultant to turn the construct into the most famous, influential, and controversial matrix ever devised by the advice-giving industry.

Adding the Stars

Californian Richard K. "Dick" Lochridge, a graduate of Dartmouth and the Stanford Business School, has been described by more than one of his BCG colleagues as "the best natural consultant" they ever encountered, this for the fecundity of his ideas, his ease with clients and coworkers, and his ability to finish work by 6 p.m. Lochridge joined BCG in June 1969.

His transformative insight came out of work BCG was doing for Union Carbide, only the second client assignment he received. The consultants had done small jobs for Carbide when Bill Bain sold the company the largest project the firm had ever undertaken, a six-month study of its entire portfolio. "I'll never forget it," says Lochridge, who was twenty-six at the time, slated to lead the study, and slightly overawed by what Bain had promised. "He told them, 'We're going to put all your businesses along one axis, all your competitors along another; we're going to put all that together and tell you the structure of the industry and what's going to happen.'" BCG had never done anything like it before.

BCG assembled a team of ten consultants, all junior to Lochridge, to try to figure out how to collect and marshal the data. "Talk about kids groping in the dark," recalls Lochridge. "We gradually got a picture, sort of an intuitive, holistic, gestalt of the chemical business by just eating enough data. You got a feeling that Dow was winning a lot of battles, that Union Carbide was not doing very well across the board, that DuPont was kind of losing a lot." Finally, Lorne Weil, a member of the team, proposed a new display to capture what was going on.

It would array a business according to where it fell on two axes, the vertical indicating the recent growth rate of the overall market that the business served—essentially a measure of how fast total sales of all competitors were growing—and the horizontal axis showing the growth rate of just that single business, whether it was the company's own or a competitor's. A forty-five-degree diagonal line bisected the chart starting at the lower left corner. A position to the left of the diagonal would

FIGURE 4-2

The share-momentum graph

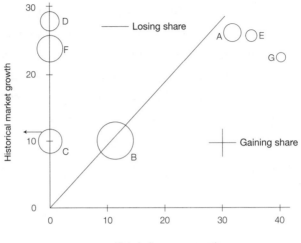

Source: Adapted from BCG working papers.

indicate a business losing market share; one to the right a business gaining share. Hence the name *share-momentum graph* (figure 4-2).

"That got us through about three meetings" with the client, says Lochridge. He and Bain had by this time accumulated a thick loose-leaf notebook of their findings, but were still struggling over how to convey the overall picture, which was baroquely complicated, to Warren Anderson, the Union Carbide executive who was their principal contact. "We rehearsed how we'd present what we learned, kind of telling a story by flipping back and forth between the pages," Lochridge remembers. On the morning they were set to meet with Anderson, he suddenly had a conflict and asked that their session be put off until 3 p.m.

As they waited in Union Carbide's offices, Lochridge wandered over to one of the engineering departments, obtained some semilog graph paper—a straight scale on one axis, a logarithmic scale on the other—and with the rudimentary earlier concepts of the matrix in mind and Bill Bain helping to draw, proceeded to construct the first fully evolved growth-share matrix. At three, they walked into the meeting. "Bill said,

'Warren, we have a lot of things to tell you,'"—and here he laid down a single sheet of paper—"'but here's your portfolio.'" Anderson thought "it was the greatest stuff ever," Lochridge recalls.

Lochridge's great innovation—see the accompanying illustration in figure 4-3—was to quantify the two dimensions along which businesses were arrayed in the matrix. The vertical dimension was to display expected real growth of the market in which the business competed, with zero growth the bottom line of the matrix and a figure such as 25 percent as the top boundary. Thus, slow-growth markets, increasing by less than 12 percent a year, would fall in the bottom half of the matrix, faster-growing markets in the top.

The horizontal dimension would indicate relative market share, indicating how the sales of a company's business compared with those of other companies in the same market. Share was plotted on a logarithmic scale, with high share (e.g., twenty times the size of the next competitor) as the leftmost extreme, and low share (e.g., one-tenth as big) on

FIGURE 4-3

Evolved version of the growth-share matrix

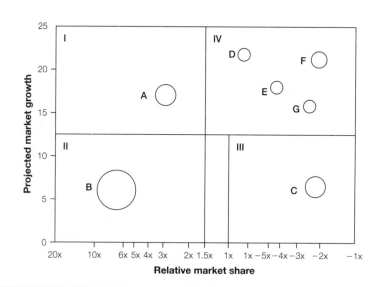

the right. Along this dimension, the middle of the chart would typically fall where a business was 1½ times larger than its nearest competitor, high-share businesses to the left, low-share ones to the right.

In plotting a corporate portfolio, the consultants decided that each
business should be represented by a circle whose size was proportional
to its sales. A company's largest businesses would be displayed as large
circles, its smallest as almost dots.

Powered by Anderson's excitement about the work, Lochridge and
his team worked eighteen-hour days over the next two weeks to chart
similar displays for each of Union Carbide's three main competitors.
Each company's portfolio was portrayed in a different color—red, green,
purple, and blue. "Then Bill had the genius of, instead of telling them
[the client] who the different displays were, we'll show them the different color companies and have them analyze it, and tell us what's going
on," says Lochridge. "And then at the end, the punch line was, 'And
this is you, and that's Dow Chemical, and that's DuPont, and that's
Monsanto.'" BCG had delivered on its promise to profile its client's
strategic situation and those of its competition on a single schematic.

Only one tweak remained to raise the matrix to perfection, and it
fell to others in the firm: the quadrants needed to be renamed. In subsequent deliberations, after considering alternatives—a candle for the
sector Zakon had labeled "mortgages," for example—BCG settled on
the classic formulation. Businesses in the upper left-hand quadrant,
with high market share of a fast-growing market, were labeled *stars*
(figure 4-4). Businesses in the lower left, with high share but of a slow-
growing market, were tagged *cash cows*, almost inevitably leading to the
thought that they should be milked to feed units with better prospects.
The lower right quadrant, with a low share of a low-growth market,
was the home of *dogs*, sometimes pictured as a long-eared, sad-eyed
beagle looking about as forlorn as its corporate future. And in the
upper right, where Zakon had the wildcat oil well, were *question marks*.
These businesses were in high-growth markets, but had only small
shares relative to competitors: should you try to grow them, or not?

FIGURE 4-4

The growth-share matrix: ultimate version

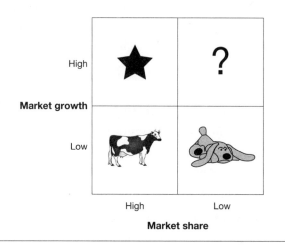

Admire, for a moment, the beauty of the thing. In a single graphic and conceptual device, the Boston Consulting Group had managed to pull together all the elements it thought essential to strategy, including the three Cs. Implicit in your business's market share, itself the most critical indicator of how you were doing relative to competition, was your place on the experience curve and what your costs should be. Taking market share as a surrogate for accumulated experience, if you had the largest share, it meant you should have the lowest costs. Market growth told a great deal about customers. To calculate how their ranks were growing, you'd initially have to figure out how many of them there were now and what was likely to increase their numbers and consumption.

BCG consultants still waffle a bit on the question of whether the growth-share matrix was indicative, suggesting what you ought to do, or merely illustrative. It's clear, though, that most practitioners took it the first way. Star businesses should be defended, the thinking went, funded sufficiently that their growth kept up with overall market growth, so that when market growth slowed, they maintained their high share. Cash cows, with their high share of low-growth markets, needed to be disciplined, their milk mostly channeled off to fund better opportunities—stars or question marks—and the calls of their managers for extra investment resisted. (A bit of prudent reinvestment in the businesses might be okay, though, particularly if it led to continued cost reductions.) Question marks might represent bright prospects for the company, but to gain share, they'd probably have to be funded aggressively. The mistake too many companies made was to put money into all their question-mark businesses, meaning that none got sufficient investment. Pick the best of the lot, give their managers the cash to grow, but do not expect profits in the short haul.

As to dogs, alas. With their low shares of low-growth markets, they represented perfect examples of Hendersonian cash traps. You might squeeze them for whatever meager cash they threw off, or use them to try to block the moves of a competitor. But they also constituted promising candidates for divestiture. Sell them off, and invest the proceeds in your better businesses.

When a client's actual business units were plotted on the matrix (see figure 4-5) the result was often what certain consultants—most of them at Bain & Company—later came to call "the million-dollar slide": a single image that captured and conveyed so much information about a company's strategic situation that by itself, it was worth a million dollars in consulting fees. BCG finally had its first bona fide "product."

The consulting firm quickly began showing off the matrix in its conferences. About the only participant in the concept's genesis unhappy with its public proclamation was the original client. "Mead got totally pissed," says Zakon. "They felt it was proprietary to them, that Wommack had contributed to the naming of some of the elements. It took them about nine months before they talked to me again. But they got over it."

Think of the exchange as an opening contretemps in a debate that was to percolate down through the history of the strategy revolution, feeding and enraging critics of the consulting industry. If the revolution was to be fueled by ideas and those ideas were developed by consultants working with their corporate clients, who ended up owning the idea?

FIGURE 4-5

The growth-share matrix in practice (for General Foods Corporation, 1980–1982)

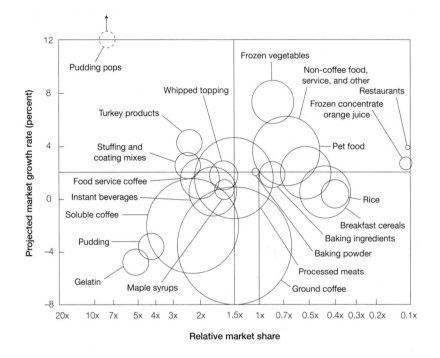

For their part, the veterans of BCG's early years pride themselves that the firm never attempted to copyright, trademark, or patent any of the concepts it developed.

Pushing Back on the Division Heads

With the invention of the growth-share matrix, the process had begun whereby strategy strengthened top management, or what's sometimes called the corporate center, at the expense of the unit heads. "For any of these companies, like ITT or American Standard, that had become conglomerates, there was no way they could keep the whole business in their head" before the matrix, argues Sandy Moose. Since most big corporations in the United States had diversified, BCG's product found a ready market. "Top management knew that the plans that were coming up from each unit seemed unrealistic, but they didn't know how to push back," says Moose. "This was a framework that said, 'Aha, you're showing me a business plan where your earnings are going to grow and you're going to get all this cash out, but this is where you are today. Are you really going to change that? What are you going to do differently?'"

The new framework made for tough discussions, particularly with managers whose businesses had been identified as dogs. "That was a real mistake we made," admits Zakon, "that we didn't see that: the dog manager did not appreciate being labeled a dog." So much for the interpersonal sensitivity of BCG's hotshot conceptualists. Moose tells of making a presentation to the head of a Midwestern manufacturing client and his direct reports. The company's growth-share matrix revealed a plethora of businesses in the lower right-hand quadrant. The troubled silence that followed the slide was finally broken by the CEO's plaintive remark, "Uhhh . . . I always liked dogs." Another lesson for the consultants: "We learned to preview our presentations with the CEO before we gave it to everyone on site."

Smart clients grasped the implications with only a little help. At American Standard, for example, the consultants' analysis indicated that, yes, the company's small air-conditioning business was indeed in a fast-growing market, but its share was perhaps a twentieth of Carrier's—a classic question-mark business. The company was pouring virtually all its available investment capital into the small unit, "to lose market share every year," the consultants concluded. "Their CEO, Bill Marquard, said, 'You know, that's the best business we have in the company in terms of its future,'" recalls Zakon, "'and you're right, we can't afford it. I'm going to sell it, and what's more, I'll get a great price because it's in a growth industry.'" Which they did. BCG took the

American Standard experience, disguised the company's identity, and made it a case study ballyhooed at the firm's conferences.

Given that all the elements on the matrix were readily quantifiable—the major reason for its irrefutability—couldn't clients, once privy to the device, have plotted their portfolios for themselves? To which the consultants predictably answer, "It's not as easy as it might look." Besides the skills required to gather data on market shares and growth, the process required a clear-eyed objectivity about one's own situation—an intellectual honesty that doesn't come easily to corporations. Moose cites as an example a client, a maker of lawn mowers, whose executives complained to the firm, "Your logic can't be right. We dominate our segment, but we're not making any money at it."

The consultants began asking questions. "Do you sell through Sears and other retailers with private-label brands, and how much of the market do they represent?" "Oh no," came the answer, "even though they're maybe 45 percent of the market." Well, what about mass merchandisers like JC Penney, Montgomery Ward, Kmart? "No, we don't sell there. They're another 45 percent." Chain hardware stores? "Ah yes, that's our market, but only in certain markets, and not in California, because it has a kind of grass our mowers don't cut." All in all, the segment of the market the client supposedly dominated represented perhaps 5 percent of the whole, not much room to be profitable.

In the years to come, professors in particular would attack the growth-share matrix and the logic that lay beneath it as simplistic, even dangerous. Market share, they would point out, doesn't always correlate with low costs, profitability, or competitive superiority. What god ordained that you have to balance cash flows among the businesses in a company portfolio? Surely you can find additional funding for a star from outside the company (a lot easier to do now than when the matrix was devised). Critics especially delighted in examples of low-share, low-growth businesses that, when taken under new management, ended up being gratifyingly profitable. Indeed one academic proposed titling his article on the subject "No Bad Dogs."

Looking back, the BCG pioneers of the matrix are prepared to admit they got the dog part slightly wrong, and not just in the nomenclature. "Being inexperienced businesspeople, we didn't walk in there and tell [them] how to run their businesses," says Zakon, without irony. "It didn't dawn on us that the way to manage a dog was not to starve it, but to LBO it," that is, sell it off in a leveraged buyout to its management or to an outfit like Kohlberg Kravis Roberts, which would emerge in the 1980s to pioneer the LBO form. "We focused on the sexy part. There was more money to be made on the dog part, which we didn't do."

Through the rest of the 1970s, BCG would continue to push the growth-share matrix, adding refinements along the way. With time, other consulting firms would devise their own versions of BCG's matrices and toss them onto the bandwagon. In 1979, Phillipe Haspeslagh, an associate professor at the INSEAD business school in France, conducted a survey backed by the *Harvard Business Review*. The goal was to determine how widespread the use of portfolio schema like the growth-share matrix had become in the strategic planning of major companies. Based on the 345 corporate responses he received, he estimated that 45 percent of the *Fortune* 500 were using some form of matrix, and 36 percent of the *Fortune* 1000. The ranks of those employing it were increasing by 25 to 35 companies a year, with diversified industrial corporations leading the charge.

The list of benefits the respondents reported from using the portfolio frameworks vastly outweighed the difficulties some had in putting them to work, and might give a moment's pause to anyone arguing that consultants never contribute much to the corporate weal. To quote Haspeslagh in a 1982 *Harvard Business Review* article summarizing his findings, companies said they had gained "a better understanding of their businesses," enabling them to make "appropriate strategic decisions" in part because they could "decipher industry logic" and better assess their competitive position. And lest anyone think that all the good accrued just at the level of corporate decision making, "Managers even credit the approach with improved operations since it encourages focus, objectivity, and commitment."

The growth-share matrix proved to be the successful "product" that set BCG on its feet and on to the course whereby its business would catch up with its intellectual reputation. "There isn't a lot of money in drawing experience curves for clients," says Zakon. "There is *a whole lot of money* in doing the corporate portfolio. Product number one, you do the portfolio: Here are all your businesses. Are they strong or weak, based on their market share and share momentum? This lets the CEO go to his board and say, 'Okay, I'm going to divest. We're totally changing strategy. My predecessor screwed up. And I'm going to fix it. But to fix it, I'm going to have to clean house.' That was huge, incredible."

"Product number two: Every one of the remaining businesses is now studyable."

Which is precisely what Sandy Moose did over a period of years at American Standard, helping the different business units forge their individual strategies. "I think it took about five years to get through the entire portfolio," recalls Zakon. "Then you can start again." ("And we did," Moose points out.) "This was painting the George Washington Bridge," Zakon gushes, an assignment seemingly without end.

A grand case of consultantly parasitism? Not, of course, to hear the consultants tell it, particularly the story's slightly ironic denouement. Zakon again: "Bill Marquard, American Standard's CEO, did his side, which was to sell barrels of stuff. The company went from losing its ass, on the verge of bankruptcy. Marquard fixes the company. Six or seven years later, he's now got this immense cash cow, because he got rid of all the money-losing stuff. He's got cash up the gazoo, and he's won an award as one of five best-managed companies in America. But he's dead in the water"—the company having sold off its hottest growth prospect, the air-conditioning business.

"So he wants us to do a diversification study," Zakon continues. "One of the things we studied was Trane, the big air-conditioning company which was very successful and completely uninterested in being acquired. A year goes by, someone tenders for Trane, at which point they call up American Standard. We'd done the work, the analysis—Trane helped us update it quickly—but, more importantly, we'd already sold Marquard on the deal. Here was his chance to get back into air-conditioning, with a huge-market share company. Which he did," with the acquisition of Trane in 1984. "If you look at American Standard today, the single biggest business, and the most profitable, is Trane."

Bill Marquard died October 22, 2006, at the age of eighty-six. Obituaries appropriately celebrated his distinguished career, the *Wall Street Journal* crediting him with having "helped save a household name with one of the great corporate turnarounds of the 1970s." Besides praising his work ethic—as CEO, he apparently never missed a day in the office—the newspaper recounted how over the course of the 1970s, he had sold off a raft of businesses purchased the decade before, in the process drastically reducing American Standard's debt. It described how he "required managers to boost market share and become the low-cost producers in their businesses," eliminating a layer of management between them and the CEO to monitor their efforts more carefully. Of the Trane acquisition, the *Journal* quoted him as saying, "It really stretched us . . . But it was the opportunity of a lifetime." In none of the obituaries I've been able to locate has there been any mention of the role of consultants in American Standard's turnaround.

The Rule of Three and Four

In the 1980s, as we will see, the complaint went up that while consultants like BCG might be good at helping you devise a strategy, they were largely useless in helping you put it to work—at "implementation" or "execution." BCG in particular would come to realize that the charge had a lot of merit.

In their defense, though, the pioneers argue that in the early stages of the strategy revolution, through the late 1970s, much of implementation actually consisted of investment and disinvestment decisions, as in the American Standard example. Putting strategy into practice was easier then, in the sense that it often entailed just helping the CEO or division head realize that the company must sell off some businesses and perhaps buy others. Getting the company's "positioning" right, in other words, was the first focus of the revolution.

In 1976, Bruce Henderson would write and publish a *Perspectives* essay titled "The Rule of Three and Four." In it, he argued, "A stable competitive market never has more than three significant competitors, the largest of which has no more than four times the market share of the smallest." The rule was a hypothesis, he admitted, "not subject to rigorous proof," but did seem to fit the facts of industries as diverse as airplanes, automobiles, baby food, soft drinks, and steam turbines.

The essay summed up and reiterated BCG's thinking about the experience curve, cost competition, and the centrality of market share. Its publication can also be seen as the intellectual high-water mark for the concepts that underlay BCG's early success. Increasingly, thereafter, academic critics would point out that market share didn't necessarily equate with competitive success, that costs didn't decline as predictably or automatically as the experience curve would have you believe, and that in some industries, a host of niche competitors thrived.

Among smart practitioners, however, the concepts continued to have currency and power. In his first meeting with security analysts after becoming CEO of General Electric in 1981, Jack Welch told them that henceforth his company would focus on growth markets and—famously—that GE's businesses would be number one or two in their respective markets or leave those battlegrounds to others. (And in 1983, Welch would hire Michael Carpenter, a nine-year veteran at BCG and a consultant to GE to head up the industrial giant's strategic planning efforts.)

Henderson's meditations in 1976 may also have been prompted by the fact that at about that point, for the first time in its history, BCG had begun to face serious competition. McKinsey & Company had begun to take notice of the upstart's success and had begun an intellectual revival of its own. And, in some ways even more menacing, in 1973 Bill Bain, BCG's best salesman ever, had struck off to form his own consulting firm.

What Bill Bain
Wanted

F OR ALL HIS SUCCESS, Bill Bain remains a touch sensitive about his educational credentials. Perhaps surprisingly for a man who founded the second great strategy consulting firm, he has neither an MBA nor an engineering degree, the latter the standard academic credential for the original lords. But absolutely like the rest of them, he was a maverick, a disruptive force, and ultimately someone who insisted on doing things his own way.

Born July 30, 1937, Bain grew up in Johnson City, Tennessee. His father came from a farming family, one of twelve children. While Bain père completed only elementary school, he subsequently worked his way up to become a small wholesale food broker. William Jr. started college at East Tennessee State in his hometown, initially majoring in engineering, but soon, under the spell of a professor who could magically pull together all the elements of the subject, switching to American history.

After two years, he transferred to Vanderbilt—his father cashing in all his insurance policies to pay the additional expense—with the aim of eventually getting a PhD and teaching history. Although he'd won a Woodrow Wilson Fellowship to help finance his graduate studies, he found he quickly tired of doing research filling out three-by-five-inch cards in the library. Bain went back to work for a steel distribution company where he'd held summer jobs, but soon it suffered reverses and he was let go as part of a general cutback.

A friend then suggested that Bain return to Vanderbilt to take up a position in the university's development office. The institution faced an energizing challenge. Vanderbilt was one of five universities to which the Ford Foundation had offered a multimillion-dollar matching grant: if it could raise an equal amount by a certain date, it would get the money; if not, "we got zero," as Bain puts it. In his retrospective view, the foundation initiative in large measure created what was to become common if occasionally wearying practice in the citadels of higher education: the modern capital campaign.

Bain took to the job readily—he became Vanderbilt's director of development at age twenty-six—and from it extracted two lasting lessons. First, he found that he enjoyed and was good at working with senior corporate executives. His fund-raising territory included New York, and he ended up spending considerable time with the heads of Kodak, J.P. Morgan, Chemical Bank, and the Bank of New York. "I was fascinated by how they got there, what they did, how they thought about their jobs," Bain recalls. He discovered that he shared many interests with them: "sports, women, business, competition, goals," as he lists them. "I liked every single one of those guys a lot, and they liked me. I felt very comfortable with them."

He also learned to focus on results. At the end of each week, all the fund-raisers would gather for a team meeting, sharing food and telling tales about what they'd each been up to. While prizing the group's esprit, Bain says he came to realize that at some point in every meeting, he had to ask the question "So, where's the money?" For the rest of his professional life, it was to be his mantra and a watchword of the work his firm performed for clients.

Bruce Henderson was one of the Vanderbilt alumni Bain called on; they met first when Henderson was still at Arthur D. Little. When the university began to explore the idea of starting a business school, Bain went back to Henderson, who had by then founded BCG, and asked him to speak to a small group of businessmen in Nashville looking into the possibility. The lunch went well. Henderson was particularly impressed with how the younger man prepared him for the meeting beforehand—dissecting the motives of each of the participants—and critiqued his performance afterward, including the observation that Henderson had been needlessly curt at times.

The two had dinner that night at Bain's house, and in response to Henderson's questions, Bain described the fund-raising he was doing with executives, how well he got along with them, and what he had learned about how they thought. As Bain recounts the aftermath, the next morning before he left, Henderson said to him, "I need someone very smart, who understands and can work with and motivate senior executives and be respected by them. And I need someone who understands business. Normally I start with very smart people who know about business, not that they really know anything about how business works but they know about business because they've been to business school. You have the other two things but don't have that. But there's no reason why you should be behind anybody from Harvard Business School, because while they're learning how to play nice with others, and how not to be scared to death of chief executives, you can learn some of the rudiments of a business education." He invited Bain up to Boston to meet and be interviewed by others at the firm.

By this time—1967—the Vanderbilt team members were almost sure they were going to hit their fund-raising target. Realizing he'd have to identify his next opportunity, Bain took Henderson up on the invitation. In Boston, he talked with Sy Tilles, Jim Abegglen, and Arthur Contas, the three most senior people at the firm besides Henderson, and with Charles Faris, a rising star among the consultants. After Bain completed the process, Henderson, in a characteristically Hendersonian gesture, gave him copies of the interviewers' evaluations, "all of which damned me with faint praise," Bain says with a laugh. "They certainly didn't see what he saw. They saw a guy who hadn't gone to business school and who was bright enough, but so were a lot of, oh, priests, who you clearly weren't going to hire."

Nonetheless, Henderson offered him a job. "Bruce knew the three things he was looking for," Bain says, "and I had two; lots of people he hired only had one." The proposed compensation was $14,000 a year, the average offer the firm made to graduating Harvard MBAs. The trouble was, Bain had been making $18,000 at Vanderbilt—"I was well paid." The two men negotiated, Henderson upped his offer to $17,000, and Bain agreed to join the firm. "I tell my kids that every job change I ever made, I took a pay cut," Bain volunteers.

He quickly got his business education, including knowledge gained by traveling with Henderson—he recalls one ten-day trip to Europe soon after he joined where he spent "easily two hundred hours talking with Bruce, night and day; he was an insomniac, even if I wasn't"—and working on some of BCG's biggest clients, including General Instruments, Dow Corning, and Texas Instruments. He demonstrated a gift for building and sustaining such relationships. By 1968, spurred by BCG's lack of business, Bain and Henderson had together begun making sales calls on prospective clients, an exercise in attempted teamwork that other colleagues avoided. With repeated coaching from Bain, Henderson even learned to begin the conversation by asking questions rather than just launching into the ideas then most on his mind.

During this period, Henderson's fascination with competition had him looking beyond business to seek the deeper roots of what set one entity against another. Over the 1960s, his reading had landed him on some of the further shores of paleoanthropology. In these realms, thinkers argued that the behavior of modern humans was still shaped by the aggressiveness of their primitive ancestors who hunted in small groups and fought other groups to defend their little patches of ground. Inspired by the works of Robert Ardrey and others—Ardrey published *The Territorial Imperative* in 1966—Henderson divided his firm into competing blue, green, and red minifirms.

To this day, most BCG veterans of that era view the move as a disaster, in part because unintentionally, it laid the foundation for the subsequent formation of Bain & Company. Each group was constituted around two group vice presidents, then the senior position at BCG—equivalent to a senior partner at other firms—and the vice presidents and "managers" who worked with them. The blue group, headed by Bain and Patrick Graham, a cofounder of Bain & Company, included George Bennett, Dick Lochridge, John Halpern, and Ralph Willard, all of whom—except Lochridge—would follow Bain to his new firm.

As we've seen, Bill Bain was the man in charge of many of BCG's biggest client relationships, with Black & Decker and Texas Instruments, among others. After the partition, his blue group easily accounted for a majority of the consulting firm's revenue and profits. In more than one conversation, Bain says, Henderson indicated to him that he would be the natural choice to lead BCG if anything were to happen to its founder.

The Classic Strategy Study Revealed

Bill Bain has his detractors, and over the course of his career he provided colleagues with not a few occasions for distrust and dislike. The first was his departure from BCG in 1973 to found his own firm. It would take pages to rehearse all the reasons different people cite for his striking out on his own—most of them variants on "He wanted to take over BCG and Bruce wouldn't let him." For the purposes of this story, though, what's most valuable is what Bain himself says compelled him to move on, beginning with what he came to see as the flaws in how BCG did business.

Bain notes that in this period, the late 1960s and early 1970s, the typical BCG assignment lasted perhaps six weeks, culminating in a written report to the client.

He became frustrated by the fact that the consultants would hand over the report and then leave, not checking back later to find out if anything came of it. Moreover, in contrast to the corporate planners, the real decision makers seemed to be reading only the executive summaries. He began wondering if the BCG consultants might not be writing up their exquisite reports—rich with surprising insight, supported by terrific data—more with an eye toward impressing colleagues than out of any concern with what the client might do with the findings.

He told friends at the time, "I feel like I'm a consultant on a desert island, writing a report, putting it in bottle, throwing it in the water, then going on to the next one." Today, he recalls his mounting frustration: "I wouldn't know, perhaps ever, how well I did on that study." Which led to his ultimate question: "Do our clients make any more money because of us?"

Nor was the consulting firm making as much money as it might from its existing clients. In fund-raising for Vanderbilt, Bain had learned that it was "always easier to get money from someone who had already written you a check than from someone who'd never written you one." The short-term, usually one-off nature of the assignments that BCG did—at least prior to the growth-share matrix—didn't inherently make for repeat business. Which meant a continuing scramble for new clients and more marketing expenses—more *Perspectives* to be sent out, more conferences staged.

The catalytic realization, he says, and the moment "when Bain & Company actually started"—in his mind at least—occurred as he prepared the proposal for Union Carbide, specifically for Warren Anderson, the head of its biggest division. Impressed with BCG's work on small projects for the company, Anderson invited Bill Bain to come down to the company's Manhattan headquarters for a conversation. Fifteen minutes into it, Anderson called his boss, Perry Wilson, the CEO, and told him this was something the senior man would be interested in. The two were invited up to Wilson's executive aerie.

Bain had fairly recently put together a presentation for a BCG conference in London drawing on his long-standing fascination with chess.

It suggested how, if a competitor was hurting you in one business, you might respond by hurting your adversary in another of its businesses, where it might be more vulnerable. Henderson dubbed the construct "really interesting," and Bain ruminated on how he could incorporate it into his pitch to Union Carbide.

In later years, as Bain & Company hit its stride, both critics and admirers would ascribe much of the enterprise's success to Bill Bain's ability to forge a relationship with the chief executive of a client corporation. Some detractors would even speak darkly of his Svengali effect, like George DuMaurier's fictional hypnotist who took over the tender minds of his victims and bent them to his will. In that light, the seminal conversation at Union Carbide is intriguing. The twin themes are opportunity, including the opportunity for dominance, and the other side of the coin—jeopardy, danger, failure.

"We were sitting at a little table," weirdly "like one you play chess on," in a sprawling office with the light coming in the huge windows but fading with the day over the course of the conversation, which made it "surreal," Bain says.

> I showed them the price experience curves for all their businesses; they were familiar with that. Then I pulled out a notepad, which I always had with me, and started drawing for them what I'd drawn in London, talking about competition and dynamics, and why [the determination of] who makes money ineluctably and properly derives from these dynamics that are part of the capitalist system. Then I added, "Obviously, the real world is much more complex than that"—they nodded—"fortunately for guys like us."
>
> [I told them,] "If you're going to play a game, for your life, with a guy who has an IQ of one hundred and ten, do you want to play tic-tac-toe, or checkers, or chess? It's going to be chess. Now, I'm going to tell you the guy has the same IQ you do, and again, you're playing for your life. How many chess books are you going to look at, how many old master games? Either you're a lot

smarter, or you're a lot better prepared and you think a lot more strategically."

And then, zeroing in,

"Because this is so complex, and because to my knowledge you're the only people of your level at a company of this scale *in the world* who are having this conversation, that gives you a head start. But if tomorrow, another group has this conversation, that's only a day's head start.

"If we get going here and we really try to look at your entire business as an intricate competitive environment where your profits and your security at the end of the day depend on how you wend your way through this three-dimensional bunch of armed robbers out there . . . if we get going, you're going to have a big head start on getting the profits you deserve."

The three men talked for five hours. Both Wilson and Anderson were intrigued; they asked Bain to go back and prepare a written proposal detailing what BCG would do, how long it would take, what it would cost. Says Bain, "Bain & Company was born then in the sense that this was the first liberated discussion about what was the best concept of strategy I could muster that I'd ever had with the number-one and number-two guys of one of the biggest and most important companies of the world, where I described strategy in its most beautiful complexity that I could come up with. And they understood it. And they *loved* it."

The written proposal consisted of a long letter—a form Bain says he learned from Henderson—that began, "Dear Warren," and, after a paragraph of niceties, got going in earnest with the line "The classic strategy study unfolds in the following manner." He proceeded to outline a project that would examine virtually all the division's businesses, apply the most advanced conceptual frameworks to analyzing the findings, and knit the results together into an integrated strategy that would provide competitive advantages unavailable to others in the industry.

Shortly thereafter, Bain showed the proposal to some of his colleagues. Their response, he says, was "peals of laughter." This because there was no such thing as the "classic strategy study," at least not one that BCG had performed. The document represented more his dream of what ought to be done than any existing reality.

Many of the proposal's features posed a sharp break from BCG's standard practices; they were also at the core of the business model for consulting that Bain would perfect at Bain & Company. Theretofore, BCG had, like all traditional consultants, worked on a project-by-project basis. Its relationships with clients were episodic, depending on what came up. And for all the firm's slowly evolving emphasis on strategy, with rare exceptions, like the work for Mead, it hadn't done that many pull-it-all-together-for-the-company assignments.

Bill Bain proposed instead a study so sweeping that he couldn't predict for the client how long it all might take or what exactly the deliverables might be. Instead of fixing a fee for the entire project, he asked Union Carbide for $25,000 a month, a daunting amount at the time—BCG was doing some assignments for $15,000 total—promising not a series of reports along the way but rather a monthly meeting between consultants and clients to agree on what had been done to date and what remained to be done.

The sharpest break with BCG practice was more subtle and would later figure in making Bain & Company's work seem slightly sinister to some. Implicit in BCG's retail marketing of ideas was the notion that these ideas were available to all. Bill Bain, by contrast, wanted his consulting work to result in strategies that were distinctive, proprietary, even secret. One might say that in contrast to most of his colleagues, Bain took the power of strategy and competitive advantage really, really seriously.

It was the general response to his proposal within BCG's senior levels that, he says, convinced Bain he had to leave. Like his audience at Union Carbide, they, too, loved it. Even Bruce admired it. Then, about ten days later, Bain learned that another partner had copied the proposal virtually word for word and used it to pitch another company, one that competed with Union Carbide. Bain was outraged, arguing to Henderson that doing the same work for an industry competitor represented a conflict of interest, at best.

"If you read the proposal," Bain says, "you're talking about someone ending up as the master of a three-dimensional competitive world, and part of that means putting into place each of these other competitors by the action you take, which causes them to do certain things without knowing what they're doing or why they're doing it. You want your client to be the king of that little world, and you want everyone else to be his subjects. You don't start sending the same elixir to all his subjects."

Henderson essentially told Bain to swallow his reservations. Companies were free to hire and fire consultants at will, he argued, and consulting firms couldn't afford to tie themselves up with a single client in an industry. Henderson did agree to let Bain explain BCG's policy to Anderson, which he did.

Rather to Bain's surprise, Union Carbide accepted every aspect of his proposal, including the novel fee arrangement. Bain put together a first-class case team—you could do so for $25,000 a month—and proceeded to "scope out their critical competitors"—eventually including what became the first full-blown growth-share matrices for each. The consultants "highlighted some things it would be important for them to do differently in their businesses," and began to plot the next steps for the company to take, he says.

The study had continued for two or three months when Bain found himself in a BCG officers meeting. His colleagues began asking him questions, slightly critical in tone, about what they regarded as "the problems associated with a client that lasted indefinitely." These allegedly included tying up consultants whose consequent availability for other work would be unknown. Other colleagues worried that the open-ended arrangement was disrupting the schedule of the editing department, which had to book well in advance to prepare final reports. Even Henderson himself, the original disruptive force, seemed ambivalent.

A few months later, in 1973, Bain left to form Bain & Company, taking most of the senior members of the blue team with him.

Greater Taylorism Done Beautifully

For all of Bill Bain's prior ruminations, the new firm spent some months figuring out its own strategy. In its early days, operating out of his Beacon Hill apartment, Bain & Company bet on the notion that it could commercialize the computer models that one of the other founding partners, George Bennett, had developed to do strategic analysis. The models never really worked. Parting on a sour note, Bennett went off to pursue other ventures, which not too much later included founding his own consulting firm, Braxton Associates.

Bill Bain and the others were left to perfect their new type of consulting. The process didn't take long. Measured by the number of professionals it employed, the firm grew 40 percent to 50 percent a year through the 1970s and into the 1980s, even as the rest of the American economy staggered under the blows of oil shocks and repeated recessions.

Not that many outside the industry were aware of this. To the extent that such a thing was possible in working with large, public companies, Bill Bain and his compadres wanted to operate in secret, concealing their efforts on behalf of clients, lest the client's competitors pick up on their presence and guess that new strategic moves were in the offing. In that spirit, for most of the firm's early years, its consultants didn't carry business cards. Rivals joked that Bain & Company was the "KGB of consulting." (Others, in a not-entirely-humorous comparison of Bill Bain's followers to those of the Rev. Sun Myung Moon, tagged the firm's consultants "Bainies.")

But can't KGB's accomplish a lot, sometimes more than rivals operating in the light of day? The way Bain worked with clients may actually have done more to change corporate practice in certain areas than did the ideas being brooded about by others in the late 1970s and early 1980s. This success arose not because of the firm's secretiveness, but because of the duration and depth of its client relationships and the open field they presented for the consultants' emphasis on results as measured in reduced costs, improved profitability, and, ultimately, stock price appreciation exceeding that of competitors.

Steve Schaubert, a long-standing Bain partner, puts it this way: "We wanted to get strategy down to the level where somebody with a wrench in his hands could do something about it." Already by the mid-1970s, voices were beginning to be heard to the effect that it was one thing to make strategy, but quite another to implement or execute it. By virtue of its be-there-with-you-all-the-way approach, Bain & Company stole a march on its competitors in tackling implementation. Effectively, Bain was taking the concepts from the early stages of the strategy revolution and figuring out how to turn them into behavior, in ways that BCG, already moving on to look for the next killer construct, was not.

This approach entailed delivering on the promise of the experience curve. "We recognized that your costs don't *automatically* decline with the experience curve," says Schaubert. "You have to manage them down." The firm may not have blazoned forth what it was doing, but if you want to see how Greater Taylorism was first done best, you need look no further than Bain's work with its clients.

Bain & Company would work for only one company in an industry, or, more precisely, in a competitive set, and only if that company agreed to a continuing, probably multiyear relationship. That kind of commitment and open-endedness made it possible for the firm to spend months gathering data and analyzing it. If necessary, Bain would dispatch large teams of consultants to camp out on the client's premises to do the work.

The product of Bain's efforts was to be not a report or a study— the firm's consultants still drip with disdain at the mention of such things—but rather a strategy and, even more important, *results*—results that you could see first on the bottom line, then in the stock price. Fairly quickly, this value proposition was boiled down to a snappy formulation: "We don't sell advice by the hour; we sell profits at a discount." In practice, this usually meant relentless attention to the three Cs—costs, customers, and competitors—a distillation of the essential elements of strategy that Bainies still ritually invoke. Particularly costs.

Consider, for example, Bain & Company's work for Bausch & Lomb, the contact-lens maker, in the early 1980s. Christopher Zook, who worked on the project as a just-hired consultant and later went on to become head of Bain's strategy practice, describes it as "the most classic piece of work of the decade, the perfect embodiment of everything we did in the eighties."

Founded in 1853, Bausch & Lomb had through most of its history been a maker of lenses, whether for eyeglasses, cameras, or military equipment, and a manufacturer of products that used lenses. In the 1960s, it began to pioneer the development of soft contact lens in the United States. The release of its Softlens contacts in 1971 caused its stock price to take off. The market for soft contacts grew rapidly, attracting new competitors such as Warner-Lambert, but by the end of the decade, Bausch & Lomb still held over 50 percent of the market, and soft lenses accounted for nearly two-thirds of the company's profits.

The man who won much of the credit for this success was Daniel E. Gill, who had been hired from Abbott Laboratories in 1978 to head the soft-lens business. He was promoted to president of Bausch & Lomb in 1980 and then to chairman and CEO the following year. In many respects, he was just the kind of CEO Bain & Company preferred to work with. Some of the firm's older and less politically correct partners still talk of how Bain, in seeking potential clients, likes to look for "our kind of guy" in the head office, "someone radically discontent with the status quo."

Subsequent press accounts described Gill as "tenacious, demanding—and very numbers-oriented." An auditor before he became a marketing executive, CEO Gill worried that his company was still burdened by too many old, inefficient businesses, and he began selling off some of these, including prescription eyeglasses. He also realized that Bausch & Lomb faced increasing competition in its core contact-lens business from the likes of Johnson & Johnson and Ciba-Geigy, both of which were introducing new products such as extended-wear soft lenses and gas-permeable hard lenses, categories in which Bausch & Lomb had either no product advantage or no entry at all. It was in this area where Bain & Company went to work.

"We did an excruciatingly detailed competitive-cost analysis," says Zook, "so much so that to understand the cost structure of a plant that Coopervision [a competitor] had newly built in the south of England, we got a copy of a BBC tape of the Queen Mother touring the plant. We were able to blow up the nameplates on all the machines she pointed at as she walked by, and we then visited every single equipment vendor in the plant, saying 'We might be interested in that type of molding and lathing machine.' We reverse-engineered, by piece of equipment, the exact plant, and used engineers at Bausch & Lomb to figure out exactly what the costs had to be." This phase of the study took about three months.

"Similarly for customers. We went out to personally visit optometrists, opticians, and ophthalmologists all over the country [the United States]. We sat down, talked to them in great detail, and discovered there were only three types of ophthalmologist, four types of opticians, and two types of optometrists, an incredibly intricate understanding of the market." Another three months of work.

In the last phase, Bain used its analysis to develop the list of strategies Bausch & Lomb should pursue and capabilities it should build. The firm recommended that the company get into gas-permeable lenses by making an acquisition, which the lens maker did. The consultants argued that cast molding, as practiced by Coopervision, was a bigger competitive threat than Bausch & Lomb had thought. There were essentially three ways of making contacts: lathing plastic discs for the most complex lens, spin casting—Bausch & Lomb's specialty up until then—and the "ultimate low-cost method," cast molding.

The consultant recommended that Bausch & Lomb get into all three tiers of the market, using the marketing and distribution power it had gained with its original products. Bain found "a couple of companies" that its client could acquire to take it into cast molding to compete with Coopervision, which without such a countermove, would underprice Bausch & Lomb and thus "had to be stopped," says Zook. "We had to let them and all the other companies who might be tempted to get into the business know they weren't going to make a lot of money in it." Bausch & Lomb could then reposition its spin-cast offering as a "higher-premium, more comfortable lens." The consultants also pushed their client to get into more of the related high-end products—lens solutions, so-called cooking machines for lens wearers—for which the company would have a marketing advantage through its strong share of the "three Os" market (ophthalmologists, opticians, and optometrists).

"It was viewed as one of the most successful strategies of the decade," Zook says. "They took over fifty, sixty percent of the market for 'new fits,'" up and down the tiers, "and ended up with a fifty percent competitive cost advantage." Even with Coopervision responding to Bausch & Lomb's moves by starting a price war, Bain's client was able to achieve overall market dominance, at least through the mid-1980s.

Bain & Company would do similarly comprehensive projects for companies such as Baxter International, Dun & Bradstreet, and Monsanto. When Bain went to work for National Steel in 1981, the client's costs to produce cold-rolled steel were the highest for any U.S. manufacturer, and it faced horrendous competition from the Japanese. (U.S. production accounted for well over 50 percent of the world total in 1947, less than 10 percent by 1960.) The company's challenge was a "pure cost problem," Zook observes.

Says another Bain partner who worked on the case, "Most people in business never penetrated their costs to a microeconomic level to

understand how the factors at that level tied in to their performance."
Bain's analysis did just that, leading to recommendations for improving
National Steel's position by way of selling off some assets—including its
entire huge Weirton, West Virginia, division in 1983—adopting new
technologies, including continuous casting, and otherwise tweaking its
operations. By the time Bain was finished, National Steel had the lowest
costs of any U.S. competitor. Greater Taylorism in action.

Looking for the *Best* Best Practices

Even as change—technological, competitive, economic—drove companies into Bain's embrace, the consulting firm continued to refine its
own intellectual technology. By so doing, it was leading the way from
strategy as focused on positioning to a version that subsumed both position and process.

To gauge how a client's costs and ways of doing things (read
"processes") measured up to competitors' processes, Bain developed
successive waves of benchmarking techniques. In its first years, it went
after *best demonstrated practices*. By the late 1970s and early 1980s,
books, articles, and scholarly studies on benchmarking and its application in different industries were becoming more common. What information from the published record might be of use to the client? What
might be replicable and susceptible to being converted into action?

Bain got steadily better at exploiting the Freedom of Information
Act to gather intelligence on competitors from their filings with the
government, as well as at reverse-engineering techniques like those it
used for Bausch & Lomb. The search evolved into one for *best competitive practices*.

Even that focus might be too limiting, though, the consultants gradually concluded. In an era when the boundaries between industries were
becoming increasingly porous, why constrain yourself to looking for
lessons and insights just in the client's industry? Might not a retailing

company, say, have come up with processes—in distribution, perhaps, or customer service—that a client in manufacturing could emulate to its advantage? The aspiration now became to find the *best feasible practices*.

By the early 1980s, the Bain formula was triumphant, at least in the eyes of other strategy consultants. While most consulting firms were built on a model that called for breaking even at 50 percent consultant utilization—you needed to use the other 50 percent of the partners' time to go out and bring in new clients—Bain was getting so much continuing business from existing clients that its paid-for consultant utilization was more like 90 percent. Consequently, large amounts of money fell straight to the bottom line and into the pockets of the small group of Bain founding partners, Bill Bain chief among them.

Along the way, Bain & Company's eye for measurable results became, if anything, keener. Beginning in 1980, at the meetings where partners evaluated each other's efforts for the year—meetings that determined their annual compensation—each partner was required to publicly chart the stock price performance for his or her clients plotted against that of other companies in the industry and the stock market as a whole. Their timing was propitious.

Probably the main reason the pioneers of strategy hadn't focused on their client's stock price as the ultimate measure of success was that throughout the 1970s, not much was happening in the market, and much of what was, was dismal. After a sustained bull market in the 1960s—"the years the market went topless," in one wag's phrase—recessions early and late in the following decade bracketed an ugly bear market. The Dow Jones Industrial Average, charting the performance of thirty big companies' stocks, hit 1,000 for the first time on November 14, 1972; plunged to 577 two years later; and wouldn't crawl back up to 1,000 until the end of 1982. (On an inflation-adjusted basis, it wouldn't get past the 1972 peak until 1992.) Through this period, the eyes of the world became focused not on how companies were faring in the stock market—even some in the Nifty Fifty had by 1974 suffered precipitous declines—but rather how they were holding up under the pressures of inflation and intensifying foreign competition.

That began to change by 1983, by which time Bain felt confident enough in the results it was achieving for clients to go public with the information, or as public as Bain ever got with what it was doing. It began making a chart displaying the stock-appreciation premium those clients attained over their competitors, as attested to by Price Waterhouse, the centerpiece of its marketing pitch to potential clients. No double-dome marketing of ideas for it; this is results we're talking about.

Bain's founding partners, ever entrepreneurial, ever in search of alternative ways of making money, also began to ponder how they might more effectively capitalize on the stock-market success they were helping others achieve. They toyed with the idea of setting up a mutual fund, but concluded that such a move would take them too close to investing directly in their clients, an ethical and practical tar pit for a consultant.

The solution they finally hit upon to satisfy their yen was the creation of Bain Capital, a private equity firm, in 1983. Bain Capital would be separate from the consulting firm. It would raise money from investors, including from Bain & Company partners but not limited to them, and buy businesses, which would then be given the complete Bain performance-improvement treatment, including the practice of adding performance-enhancing debt to the capital structure. After the magic had been worked, the businesses would be taken public or sold to another buyer, ideally at a multiple several times what Bain Capital had originally paid for them. In later chapters, we'll see just how prescient Bain and his partners were in their bet on private equity.

What the consultants didn't foresee was that Bain & Company, at least in its original incarnation under Bill Bain, had just about reached the apogee of its success. By 1986, with around eight hundred professionals and over $90 million in annual revenues, it had overtaken the Boston Consulting Group. But its model—so much strategy from the

CEO's office, so many consultants crawling all over the company's operations—was showing signs of overreaching itself. Moreover, Bain & Company, which prided itself on its superior understanding of the dynamics and tricks of competition, was about to get a more formidable dose from a new quarter. McKinsey, the most famous and prestigious consulting firm in the world, was rousing itself from sleep, woken by the cannon bursts from the strategy revolution.

6.

Waking Up McKinsey

TODAY, FRED GLUCK LIVES in one of the larger houses—8,667 square feet—in Santa Barbara. To reach it, you drive up a private road, check in with the staff on an intercom, wait as the twenty-foot-tall electric gates swing open, and then proceed up the palm-lined drive. At night, specially trained German shepherds patrol the grounds; not too many years ago, Fred and his wife awoke to find two robbers in their bedroom, each holding a gun to their respective heads. The house is named Casa Leo Linda: statuary lions guard the front door; Fred's third wife, Linda, is a former banking executive.

It's quite a distance from the one-bedroom apartment in a Roman Catholic neighborhood of Brooklyn where Frederick W. Gluck grew up with his mother, father, grandmother, and five siblings. (To be sure, Dad was away a lot, working administrative jobs on construction projects everywhere from Greenland to Aruba.) One might understand the trajectory of Gluck's life as another instance of the classic American story, poor boy works hard and makes good, and it is that, of course. But Gluck's tale also presents some variations on the usual drill, intersections between the intellectual and the organizational, that make it an integral part of our narrative. As with Bruce Henderson and Bill Bain, the forces that propelled him were set in motion by the strategy revolution. But unlike those two pioneers, he didn't found his own firm; he did something arguably more difficult. Fred Gluck led a commensurate revolution at McKinsey & Company, the world's most prestigious, accomplished, and self-confident consulting firm.

Even readers who can't overcome their prejudice against consultants may find managerial lessons for the twenty-first century in the story. Wise heads like Dartmouth's James Brian Quinn have argued that if you want to figure out what it will take to run a garden-variety company ten or twenty years from now, you should look at the issues that professional-services firms such as McKinsey wrestle with today. As our narrative unfolds, consider that the leading strategy consulting firms might already represent a model of what corporations will need to become if they're to survive as our century grinds on: realio-trulio global, with talent recruited from around the world and elevated to high position. Based most of all on intellectual capital, in McKinsey's case, the brains of its consultants. And perhaps most surprisingly, effectively democratic. In how many other multibillion enterprises do the senior people elect their leaders?

Stung by the gales of change that animated the strategy revolution, including new competition from the likes of BCG and Bain & Company, McKinsey's survival in the 1970s wasn't guaranteed. The list of consulting firms that didn't survive includes names in their day just as formidable—Arthur D. Little, Cresap McCormick & Paget. What McKinsey had going for it, and the first lesson in organizational adaptiveness, was a culture strong enough to embrace, however reluctantly, even someone as strange by its genteel lights as Fred Gluck.

What Are We Going to Do About Fred?

Nothing about Gluck's early history suggests he would end up as head of one of the whitest of the great white-shoe institutions. His father was an orphan who never went to high school. The son attended Catholic schools and then, working one or two part-time jobs from age seven on, studied electrical engineering at Manhattan College. He did well enough to be able to pursue a PhD in operations research at Columbia—"a lot of statistical theory, linear programming, basically applied math," as he describes it, and to get a job at Bell Laboratories. There he found himself designing guidance systems, and then, in his late twenties, becoming program manager for the Spartan missile and head of a team of engineers on the project. It may not have taken a rocket scientist to accomplish what Gluck did in his career, but as he points out, he was one.

Restless despite his success, pushing thirty, and with a family, Gluck went looking for a new job. He landed one at McKinsey & Company, which he joined in 1967 at age thirty-one. The firm—or as its denizens call it, the Firm—had realized that it lacked the bench strength to work with technology companies, and it was seeking the kind of smarts Gluck brought with him. But seeking them only in limited amounts, as Gluck soon found out.

The McKinsey & Company Gluck arrived at was a somewhat strange beast, albeit a thoroughly august one, at least in its own eyes. When the consultancy was founded in 1926 in Chicago by James O. McKinsey, a professor of accounting, its original business had consisted largely of providing "finance and budgeting services" to clients, typically the bondholder committees of troubled companies looking for assurance that their investments were safe. The mid-twentieth-century firm, though, was largely the creation of Marvin Bower, a corporate lawyer from Cleveland who joined it in 1933, at age thirty-one. After James McKinsey died in 1937, the original entity split up. One-half was to become A.T. Kearney, a consulting firm specializing in operations management for manufacturers. Bower assumed leadership of the other half, which had been the New York office, and kept the McKinsey name.

Bower also moved the Firm away from James McKinsey's original self-definition as "management engineers." It was the "engineers" part of the term he didn't like. With both a law degree and an MBA from

Harvard, Bower worked tirelessly to instill in his colleagues the notion that consulting was a dignified profession, akin to medicine or the law. (In 1989, when told by the editors of *Fortune* that he had been elected to the U.S. Business Hall of Fame—they did the electing—he initially refused the honor, arguing that he wasn't a businessman.) At his firm, the interest of clients would always come first, assignments would be refused if the consultants couldn't add value, and everyone would wear a hat on leaving the office.

But what work, exactly, *was* the Firm to do? McKinsey & Company would address "organization and management issues," it was agreed, but the definition of just which ones changed over time. It dabbled in executive search, aka headhunting, and in advising on executive compensation, but decided those weren't compatible with its larger aspirations. Much of its effort came to focus on the organizational, and in particular in the 1950s and 1960s, on helping large companies shift from a functional model into a divisional one. McKinsey was already becoming a global operator, doing so by installing this American setup, which drew heavily on the work of Alfred Chandler, in corporate behemoths around the world, beginning with Royal Dutch/Shell.

The one element of continuity through all this, dating back to James O. McKinsey, was an instrument called the *general management survey*. The preferred diagnostic of many early consulting firms, it represented a sort of standardized audit of a company's organization, procedures, records and budgets, all supposedly aimed at gauging the effectiveness of the client's management. Bower himself rewrote and updated McKinsey's version and titled it the *General Survey Outline*, and a copy was given to every consultant on the tyro's joining the firm. "Bower's was such a *normative* approach," one of his competitors says today—so lawyerlike, so checklist-y, so "this is what you need to do to conform to good practice." What it clearly wasn't was deeply analytical, outward looking, or calculated to help develop a competitive strategy.

Just as Gluck joined the firm in 1967, Bower was stepping down as managing director—he had served in that role since 1950, built revenues from $2 million a year to $20 million, and was to continue having a voice in McKinsey councils well into the 1980s. The gentlemanly outfit he had created didn't know quite what to do with the flat-topped, Brooklyn-accented engineer and operations research expert. "Although McKinsey had decided they wanted someone with my kind of background," Gluck says, "when I actually showed up there, nobody would take me out on an engagement. And they were right. I didn't know anything about business, zippo, never knew a businessman."

What happened next foreshadows the kind of change Gluck would ultimately work at the Firm. With nothing to do, he grew restless again and worried, complaining to his group manager that he didn't leave a good job at Bell Labs to do nothing at the consulting firm. That manager, Tom Mullaney, who was doing some work for Corning Glass, suggested that while there wasn't an assignment for him, why didn't Gluck conduct a bit of research on "the environmental area" to see if it offered business possibilities the client might become interested in.

A week later, Gluck returned to Mullaney's office with a report and two large volumes of backup material. "Where the hell did this come from?" Mullaney asked, incredulous. Gluck, accustomed to running large projects, explained that he had gone to McKinsey's research department, "gotten them organized," as he describes it, "and we put together a pretty comprehensive thing." About all that Mullaney could mutter in reply was "Jesus Christ."

The Firm promptly put Gluck on the team consulting to Corning. Its leader was Rod Carnegie, an Australian Oxford graduate and oarsman, rumored to have received the highest grades at Harvard Business School since Robert McNamara, and a school friend of Amory Houghton, scion of the family that founded and ran Corning. In a wonderfully characteristic McKinsey touch, Carnegie was actually running the Corning work from the Firm's Australia office, which he had founded. "Oh, you're Gluck," Carnegie responded when his new team member introduced himself, "The Firm made a real mistake hiring anyone dumb enough to spend ten years locked up in an R&D lab."

Carnegie wouldn't allow Gluck any contact with Corning executives. Over the occasional dinner in Painted Post, New York—the town closest to Corning headquarters with a hotel, where the consultants stayed—he would repeatedly explain that it would take two years for Gluck to learn to gather facts, another two to learn to make sense of it, and another two to learn how to present it. "Then we'll talk about you becoming a real consultant." (Rich organizational cultures have their downside.) Gluck replied that he thought he had already acquired those skills.

By the time Gluck was up for his first salary review, he was allowed to sit in the back of the room at some meetings with Corning but not much more, even though in McKinsey's offices, he was continuing to amass carefully sifted piles of information on another industry, electronics, that might represent a strategic opportunity for the client. His new group partner, Archibald Alexander "Arch" Patton, told him not only that he would get no salary increase, but also that "You know, Fred, things are not going the way . . . uh . . . maybe we need to reevaluate." To get past the awkwardness, Patton quickly went on to "By the way, how are things going at Corning?"

"Lightning flashed through my mind," says Gluck. "What do I say to this guy? Do I tell him the truth? But I grew up in a tough neighborhood in Brooklyn, so I said to him, 'I don't think we know what we're doing.'" "*What?*" Patton replied. Gluck elaborated: "We go up there to the client, and we show them a chart that says this is the kind of revenues you need, what we call a *strategic gap analysis*; here's what your projects are going to be, there's a big gap in here. The Corning guy would say back to us, 'Don't worry, we'll fill it with stuff out of our laboratories.' Which means nothing happens." Dismayed, Patton said, "We'll see about this."

Gluck went back to his office and called his team leader on the case, Michael Jordan, who per another fairly standard McKinsey drill would subsequently go on to become CEO of CBS and then EDS (Carnegie would end up head of Rio Tinto, the minerals and metals giant, and would be knighted). After telling Jordan about his ex-change with Patton, Gluck went home and had several martinis. The next morning, he got in early, as usual, to find a handwritten note on his desk—"Dear Fred, please come see me"—from the senior partner in charge of the New York office, Dick Neuschel.

"I went in there," Gluck says, "and he had his silver coffee service out. 'Hello, Fred, good to see you. What's going on? Coffee? Every-thing all right?'" Neuschel reported that he'd been up all night, on the phone with Jordan, Patton, and Carnegie in Australia, and "Well, Fred, we've decided that you're right; the study's not going anywhere. We're going to cancel it and return half of Corning's fees. And we're going to make sure that you get a real chance to see what you can do."

"You can imagine," says Gluck, "the impact that had on my percep-tion of what kind of place McKinsey was." As he also says, the story gets even better. While McKinsey had, and still has, a policy dictating regular performance reviews, Gluck had never received one, leaving him in the dark about the value of his efforts. But when the Firm informed the client of its decision, Corning agreed, saying the study wasn't making much progress, "but we want that guy Gluck to keep doing that study of his on the electronics industry." While he may have been sitting in the back of the room at client meetings, Gluck con-cludes, "they knew who was doing the work."

McKinsey espouses and, at its best, puts into practice a principle it calls the democracy of ideas. The notion, to be commended to any company dependent on the bright minds of its people—which by the middle of the twenty-first century, will be every company—is that an idea or insight should be judged on its content, not on the seniority of its source, or lack thereof. Sounds like motherhood and apple pie, but fiendishly difficult to make work, in part because mother and father seem to hard-wire a degree of hierarchicalism into our human na-tures. Fred Gluck's early survival at McKinsey and his later success there are testimony to the power of disruptive democracy.

Bringing Rocket Science to the Firm

The brief history on McKinsey's Web site describes the 1970s as "our most challenging decade" in the firm's nearly eighty-year history. It goes on to spell out the results of the self-analysis the consultants put themselves through: "We discovered that our growth in the 1960s had threatened a precious commodity: our client relationships. We took a hard look at our processes for selecting and evaluating consultants and at the quality of our knowledge." This is McKinsey-speak for the realization that it had expanded too quickly and promoted people who weren't as sharp as they should be, particularly in the face of mounting worldwide economic troubles and increasing competition from the upstarts at BCG and Bain. Marvin Bower's immediate successors as managing directors were struggling a bit, whittling the firm down—never a happy experience in a partnership—even as they labored in Bower's shadow.

Fred Gluck, by comparison, was doing just fine, elected principal (McKinsey's term for junior partner) in 1972 and a director—or senior partner—in 1976. He worked on assignments for clients such as ABC television—"looking at how we could get some costs out"—AT&T, Western Electric, and Northern Telecom (which would eventually become Nortel Networks). All the while, he resisted being labeled as a technology specialist, but was happy to be identified as an expert on technology-based companies. Gluck had concluded that the heads of functional practices at McKinsey—technology, finance—didn't have much clout because they lacked an assured base of clients. Most of the Firm's partners prided themselves on being generalists.

Gluck continued to build his reputation as a hound for data—on costs, technologies, competitors—and for more in-depth analysis than the firm was accustomed to. "I told my colleagues we can't work with the aggregated information we've been getting"—typically the numbers generated for the usual financial reports—"because what's going on is way beneath that level," he says. As a result, "we really went out and created a lot of data"—dug for it, assembled it—"that wasn't there before." But this wasn't strategy. "At that point, I didn't know what strategy was."

Gluck was also dismayed to find that, to use the phrase that would come to be applied to the problem, McKinsey had no way to systematically capture the knowledge it had gained from each consulting project. Consultants would do an assignment, finish the project, perhaps write a report for the client, and then move on. Except in one or two of the nascent practice areas—consumer products was the best example—there was no effort to formally sit down, distill the generalizable lessons that could be of help in other engagements, and share them across the firm.

Even before he had much formal responsibility in the firm, Gluck began to lobby for changes to build excitement around gathering and sharing information. In the early 1970s, the consultants in the New York office would once a month come in on Saturday for a half-day of refresher training in one subject or another. Like most "refresher training" sessions, these were typically anything but refreshing. The head of the technology practice asked Gluck to make a presentation on the electronics industry for one such occasion. Gluck initially refused, finally acceding to the request only on the condition that the consultants interested in attending be flown to Bermuda to conduct their deliberations. Today, he argues that it was the first of what was to become a grand—in many ways—McKinsey tradition: the off-site retreat to create new knowledge.

The obstreperous, dissatisfied man—Gluck—met the opportune organizational moment in 1976, when McKinsey elected D. Ronald Daniel as managing partner. In many respects, Daniel represented—and still represents—the *beau ideal* of the McKinsey partner: tall, handsome, elegant, he'd gotten his undergraduate degree from Wesleyan in mathematics, served as a naval officer, gone to Harvard Business School, and, in 1957, become among the first of the top-school MBAs whom Bower had begun to recruit for the firm.

Daniel would eventually be elected to four three-year terms as McKinsey's managing partner, presiding over its climb out of the doldrums from the 1970s, launching it on its modern growth trajectory, and making the firm genuinely global. Rather than sending over Americans, he installed locals as the heads of McKinsey offices in Germany, Italy, Japan, and France.

Upon being first elected managing partner, Daniel took a step that exemplified one of the best aspects of the McKinsey culture: its insistence on examining itself. He asked his partners what issues he and they should be addressing. In response, Gluck wrote a memo essentially arguing that the firm was falling behind its competitors on several fronts, particularly in its approach to the subjects of strategy, operations, and organization.

In response, Daniel—using a managerial tactic Gluck himself would often use later: set the person who identifies a problem the task of fixing it—asked Gluck to become head of the firm's strategy practice. Gluck declined the invitation in that form—he hadn't been doing strategy work, after all—but said he would serve as head of a strategic management steering committee, to develop McKinsey's understanding of the subject. (Making him, de facto, the head of the strategy practice.) At the same time, Daniel also launched initiatives aimed at creating organization and operations practices; up until then, McKinsey had no formally constituted specialties in either area. The operations initiative, to help McKinsey improve its service to manufacturing clients, went nowhere. The organization effort led to the work of Tom Peters and Bob Waterman, and a simmering, long-running critique of strategy's weaknesses.

From the Tower of Babel to the Shores of Vevey

Gluck took on the assignment, realizing only as it went forward how much of a challenge the effort represented to McKinsey's norms. Up until then the firm's consultants had been told that if they received an inquiry about strategy, it should be referred to one particular partner, Bill Johnson, who had developed an interest in the subject working with GE. "I thought that was crazy," Gluck says. One of his first steps was to invite thirty "guys from around the firm" to come and spend two days "telling how *they* did strategy." The results weren't encouraging: "I refer to it as the Tower of Babel," he says. "There was no consistency, no definitions; it was all over the goddamn place." In the tumult, certain talents did stand out, though, foremost among them a young Japanese who had joined the firm in 1972 after completing his PhD in nuclear physics at MIT. When Gluck asked each participant to publicly sum up the results of the proceedings, a partner from London declared, "Christians: 0; Lions: 0; Kenichi Ohmae: 100."

Dismayed by the confusion, Gluck decided he needed a small group to spearhead the intellectual initiative. Accordingly, he assembled a cadre of a half-dozen consultants from different offices, including Ohmae; Gluck christened the team, none too diplomatically, the Superteam. The team members began a systematic exploration of strategy, figuring out what they didn't know, gathering insights from both within the firm and outside. "We were making good progress," Gluck recalls, even in the face of intellectual snobbery that, at McKinsey, wasn't directed merely at those outside the firm. One partner told Gluck that so intellectually challenging and important was the task of charting strategy that only ten of the Firm's partners—the brightest and most seasoned, obviously—should be permitted to do consulting in the area. "I thought that was crazy, too," recalls Gluck.

Gluck finally decided that if the strategy effort was to get anywhere, McKinsey needed to educate all its partners in the discipline. With Daniel's backing, he arranged with Harvard Business School to use a facility it had in Vevey, Switzerland, a poshly decorous little town on Lake Geneva, as the site for weeklong seminars the firm would conduct. Those seminars were "really the secret of the development of strategy at McKinsey," Gluck observes. He and his team would bring in groups of fifteen to twenty partners, show them the "primitive materials" they had developed, but—and this proved the key—mostly just provide a forum in which the participants could discuss insights and debate them. "We found we had phenomenal people who really had great ideas about this, and when we pulled them together for a week, the teachers learned what they were teaching from the guys who were doing the work."

Oddly enough—and this theme will run throughout the history of the Firm's slightly perverse relationship to the history of strategy—what strikes an observer today is how eminently forgettable most of the ideas McKinsey developed in those seminars turned out to be. Certainly nothing on the order of the experience curve or the growth-share matrix. Even the closest thing the firm has to a history of its thinking about strategy—a thirty-eight-page 2005 staff paper titled "Perspectives on Strategy" by a long-time leader of its strategy practice, John Stuckey—finds little to mention from before the mid-1980s.

To the retrospective eye, it seems clear that the issues Gluck and McKinsey most closely wrestled with were precisely those you would if you were an established consulting firm with a large client base—in the late 1970s, McKinsey's revenues, at over $100 million a year, were nearly three times those of BCG's—whose clients had come to you and asked, "What is this thing called 'strategy'? How does it relate to our current planning efforts? What should we be doing about it?" It was the Firm's attempt to answer those questions, and in particular its stab at figuring out the relationship between strategy, planning, and the nature of an almost mythic creature named *strategic management*, that *are* worth paying attention to in our intellectual history.

In 1978, Gluck and two members of the Superteam published the first ever McKinsey staff paper, the start of building what he and others still refer to as the "knowledge culture" of the firm. (A cynic might ask what kind of culture they had before.) Its title: "The Evolution of Strategic Management." Of the twenty such papers published through 1981, eleven had the words *strategy*, *strategies*, or *strategic* in their titles.

As we've noted, it's easy to conflate strategy with strategic planning, but it's also dangerous. Especially in the early days of our revolution but still today, there are many more companies that have a plan than there are that have a strategy. Scratch most plans, and you'll find some version of "We're going to keep on doing what we've been doing, but next year, we're going to do it more and/or better." Typically, the planning exercise only gets truly serious when it comes down to determining everyone's budget for the upcoming year. What you won't find in most plans, even ones called strategic, is a serious take on the three Cs.

"The Evolution of Strategic Management" was fostered by recognition on Gluck's part that planning constituted only one source of strategy. Equally important, he argued, indeed maybe more so, were strategic thinking ("creative, entrepreneurial insights") and opportunistic decision making (an "effective response to unexpected opportunities and problems"), with all three sources rooted in "market understanding, competitive analysis," and a grasp of "major environmental trends."

To buttress the argument and point toward what clients should aspire to, Gluck and his coauthors posited four phases or stages in the upward evolution of a company's "strategic decision making," based in part on a survey they had conducted—details not provided—of the planning processes of "a number of large companies" (figure 6-1). The first, primitive phase consisted of mere *financial planning*. Here planning was "viewed as a financial problem" and consisted of little more than the annual budgeting exercise. Rather to their astonishment, the consultants found that "in well over half of the business enterprises surveyed (including a number of highly successful companies), formal planning has never evolved beyond annual budgeting."

The second, Neanderthal phase in the McKinsey schema was *forecast-based planning*. The planners on the corporate staff recognize they need to look further ahead and begin to employ "more sophisticated forecasting tools—trend analysis, regression models, and finally simulation models." It's here that, for the first time, "a creative spark

FIGURE 6-1

The stages of planning

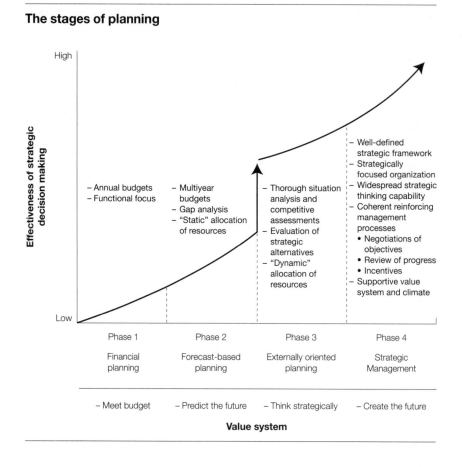

stirs the imagination of the planners, and the first true strategic planning is born." The clouds part, and the planners "suddenly realize
that their responsibility is not so much to chart the future," which is
tough to do, "as it is to lay out for management decision the key issues
that face the company." Lyrically, the McKinsey paper labels this spark
"issue orientation."

From their research, the consultants conclude that the issue that
most companies first grapple with in this second phase is resource allocation, deciding how much capital and other investment each business

should receive. The tool the study finds that most enterprises use to tackle this number one issue is "portfolio analysis, an array of diversified company businesses along two dimensions: competitive strength and market attractiveness." Here you might think *growth-share matrix*, but no, the paper refers instead to the McKinsey variant on same. Its nine-box device plots industry attractiveness (not exactly as precise a measure as industry growth) on the vertical axis, and business strength (again, hardly as sharp-edged as market share) on the horizontal (figure 6-2). (Thirty years later, Gluck would confide that part of his mission, he had concluded at the time, was eventually to "stand down" the nine-box matrix, or at least surround and submerge it with better ideas, in part because the McKinsey construct was so mushily inferior to BCG's.)

FIGURE 6-2

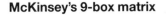

McKinsey's 9-box matrix

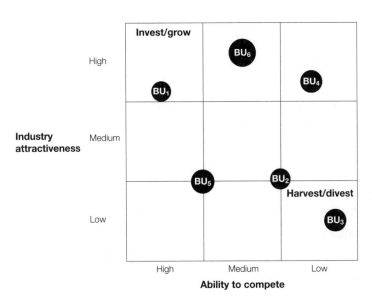

Source: Adapted from McKinsey papers.

McKinsey's third phase, *externally oriented planning*, represented "a great leap forward" in a company's planning capability, the consultants wrote without apologies to Chairman Mao. What most distinguished planning at this Cro-Magnon stage was that it began with "a thorough situation analysis of the business environment, the competitive situation, and competitive strategies," an undertaking that might well include "a wealth of in-depth analysis of the kind that bespeaks many months of effort"—something that the right consultants might help you with enormously, no doubt. Enter, at long last, the three Cs. Your resource allocation became dynamic not static, with opportunities surfaced to "shift the dot" that a business occupied into a more attractive sector, either by creating new capabilities, redefining the market, or changing customers' criteria in buying to better match your strengths.

There was a downside, however. If you truly got the phase three magic working, your planners were likely to "present not one recommended course of action for management, but several." This, the consultants concluded, made it "a very uncomfortable phase for top management." People lower down in the organization, not just planners but managers as well, would be making decisions, even strategic ones, without the participation of those at the top of the hierarchy.

Happily, there was an answer to the dreadful tension that could arise from such topsy-turviness: the company need only ascend into phase four, full *Homo sapiens* status, where it would practice *strategic management*. Unhappily, the odds on your doing this were long, since "No more than a few companies in the world . . . can claim to be strategically managed."

In this corporate empyrean, "strategic management welds strategic planning and management into a single process." There's a widely understood and agreed-to framework for planning tied to an organizational structure rejiggered to fit with the company's strategy. (Once again, as in McKinsey's franchise specialty from the 1950s and 1960s, structure will follow strategy.) The ability to think strategically is widely distributed throughout the company. The planning process entails "a negotiation of objectives based on reasonable alternatives," presumably lightening the burden of a manager running a low-share, low-growth unit.

With "The Evolution of Strategic Management," we've a come a long way from an eight-hundred-word BCG *Perspectives* essay. McKinsey's thinking seems directed as much at planners as at line executives, or maybe even more. It rather quickly plunges the discussion into a concern with process and with that ol' McKinsey touchstone, organization. With the concept of strategic management, the paper begins to sneak up on the issue of how to link the execution of strategy with its conception. And, at least to this observer's eye, along the way some of the clarity around just what constitutes a strategy gets lost: the sharp-edged focus on costs and competitors, the notion that there are imperatives attached to a business's competitive situation.

Whatever the intellectual shortcomings of its approach, many in the Firm caught the strategy fever. Gluck and his team conducted one seminar a month for two years, putting almost all the McKinsey partners from around the world through the exercise. "They were incredible events," Gluck says of the sessions, "drinking, carousing. One night, the disco at the hotel was closed, but our guys managed to open it up on their own," leaving in their wake much disarranged furniture and a woman's stocking draped over a chair. The next morning, when Gluck went to apologize to the hotel manager and offer to pay for damage, the young Swiss replied, "Mr. Gluck, high spirits are not all bad." Indeed, that was part of the point: "We made it fun," says Gluck.

Even more important, clients seemed to love what McKinsey was purveying. By the end of that period, Gluck says, "we were killing BCG." He calculated that by 1979, about 50 percent of the Firm's billings derived from strategy, at least as McKinsey defined the subject, making it bigger in that sphere than either BCG or Bain. Indeed,

Gluck argued to Daniel that striking for a higher figure, say 75 percent, would compromise McKinsey's ability to help clients with problems in other areas, such as operations and organization.

Homage to Bruce Henderson

Not that Fred Gluck's ambitions for McKinsey around strategy were exhausted. In 1979, Daniel asked Gluck to "formulate a program to establish the Firm as 'the recognized leader in strategy consulting.'" The proposal Gluck sent Daniel in response is fascinating, partly for the perspective on how the field had evolved, partly for its recognition of how much more McKinsey needed to do.

Gluck attributed BCG's success to its assembly of a cadre of what he called strategy buffs. He didn't mean the term derisively. Whereas McKinsey had emphasized "the situational nature of strategy development"—as in, "It all depends"—its competitors had developed a systematic approach to the subject and had even gone beyond this to actually demonstrate "a capability to execute it." To Gluck, the buffs were conversant with the state of the art, always debating its fine points, particularly implementation, "supported by standard analytical approaches" and better at empiricism than the Firm, and increasingly "committed to developing the interpersonal skills of client nurturing and development which distinguish us." (The effrontery.)

"The most accomplished 'buff' of all," Gluck went on, "is, of course, Bruce Henderson. Over the last fifteen years, he has established himself as the most thoughtful spokesman on strategy in the world. In fact, he doesn't seem to have a challenger at the moment." Or at least none Gluck knew of. What follows, coming from the head of the Firm's largest practice area and a rising star, is almost breathtaking in its graciousness and un-McKinseylike humility: "The opportunity to dislodge Henderson and his protégés (both within and outside BCG) with a frontal attack on his conceptual leadership was lost a decade ago. His contributions have proved to be of enduring value and the firm he built is strong and capable. We should tip our collective hats in his direction, acknowledge his contribution and do the things that we obviously must to reestablish leadership capability and put the glitter back on our tarnished image."

To counter the interlopers, Gluck outlined a program with several thrusts. They included, first, "strengthening and expanding our arsenal of concepts, techniques, tools, knowledge, practitioners, and spokesmen primarily through intensive internal development programs." Another thrust was in reaching out to others "with additional expertise that we can gain access to from academia"—people such as Harvard's Michael Porter—and other institutions. McKinsey would also adopt "a more expansive and statesmanlike posture externally." In other words, the Firm should suffer itself to enter the retail-marketing wars around ideas.

McKinsey adopted many of the elements of Gluck's proposal. As part of building the "knowledge culture," its consultants began grinding out staff papers—often twenty pages long, based on experience with clients and internal debates, and some suitable for repurposing as *Harvard Business Review* articles. Within five years, they had turned out twenty-three, which bore titles such as "Strategic Market Segmentation," "Competitive Cost Analysis," and even "The Experience Curve as a Strategy Tool." McKinsey named an alter ego for Gluck in the person of Dick Foster to take over running the strategy seminars, and even hired an outside public-relations firm, which didn't work out at all. (Its presiding eminence, a famous PR man, could never "get" McKinsey's ideas, Gluck says.) What did work in that respect was hiring a youngish Harvard MBA, Bill Matassoni, who would serve both as Gluck's right-hand personage and as his foil in midwifing ideas, papers, books, and an entire system for managing and sharing the intellectual property the Firm was amassing.

By the early 1980s, Gluck argues, McKinsey was on its way to becoming a firm of strategy buffs. To be sure, there were still pockets of resistance, or uninterest, mostly growing out of the perceptions of many at the Firm—perceptions that endure to this day—that its greatest asset isn't its ideas, or even its people, but rather its dazzling array of clients and the continuing strength of its relationships with those clients. Nowadays in a given year, some 85 percent of the firm's revenues come from repeat business with existing customers.

From the days of Marvin Bower, McKinsey has prided itself on its "one-firm" model, meaning that there are no separate profit centers and that a consistent organizational culture is maintained worldwide largely by means of recruiting, evaluation, and compensation schemes that work the same way everywhere the Firm operates. Even within this remarkably democratic partnership, though, much power accrues to the innocuously named office manager, the partner in charge of a particular geographical area and all the client relationships based there. Indeed, when I recently asked one of the senior-most partners to rate the clout of different roles within the Firm on an ascending scale from 1 to 10, his assessment was this: office manager 10; head of an industry practice (e.g., pharmaceuticals, or telecommunications) 4 approaching 5; head of functional practice (e.g., corporate finance or, yes, strategy) 1 or 2. He had, of course, built his own grandly successful career as an office manager.

Gluck tells of flying into one of the Firm's U.S. offices to make a presentation on strategy, this three or four years into McKinsey's push to become a "recognized leader" on the subject. The consultants heard him out, but the office manager was dismissive: "Fred, I'm not interested in this crap. Just give me what I need to get the project." Gluck, who was already beginning to formulate a policy of take-it-or-leave-it toward strategy's skeptics—"I wasn't going to force it down anybody's throat"—ended the conversation with a drop of acid: "Well, you might want to know what you're talking about."

He was already busier with larger matters. In 1980, he had been asked to formally oversee virtually all McKinsey's endeavors to systematically build expertise in particular subjects and industries. Soon—and to get slightly ahead of our story—the Firm would be circulating one-page bulletins summing up what had been learned on each engagement. In 1986, after four terms and because of his age, Ron Daniel was barred from running again for managing partner of McKinsey & Company. Rather to Fred Gluck's surprise, he was elected Daniel's successor, to walk in the shoes of Marvin Bower. Gluck had never been an office manager, never headed an industry practice, never done most of the things that traditionally led to the top job. What he had done was establish McKinsey as "a strategy firm," or, by its lights and those of some others, "*the* strategy firm."

And yet, the dismissive comment of the one office manager hangs in the air, framing Gluck's accomplishments and also pointing to both the power and the limitations of McKinsey & Company's contribution to the early intellectual history of strategy. What the Firm found it needed "to get the project" was, precisely, an apparent expertise in the subject, which Gluck and his confreres set about building.

In turn, the fact that the world's most prestigious consulting firm had embraced strategy as a requirement for every company served to confer an almost papal blessing on the emerging paradigm. If McKinsey was pushing strategy, how could anyone deny its centrality? The only higher intellectual authority one might look to was, well, probably the Harvard Business School. After fifteen years of near silence on the subject, that quarter was about to be heard from, in the person of another revolutionary.

7.

Michael Porter Encounters the Surreal

O NE MIGHT HAVE EXPECTED the strategy revolution to have been hatched at one of those institutions whose purpose is to study the management of companies and educate their future leaders—a business school, in other words. To the contrary. Business schools first turned their noses up at evolving modern conceptions of strategy, then seemed to resist their advance. Their disdain extended to scholars who tried to bring the subject into their halls, in particular Michael Porter, who would eventually become the most famous business-school professor of all time. To get there, though, he would have to fight off academic elders who wanted to deny him a job, and then thoroughly disrupt both the curriculum and the pedagogy of the Harvard Business School (HBS).

What Harvard Had Instead of Strategy

Up through the 1970s, the closest approximation HBS had to a course on strategy was a two-semester offering named Business Policy. Required of all students in the second, final year of the MBA program, it was supposed to serve as the capstone of their education, showing them how to integrate the different disciplines they had studied—finance, marketing, accounting—as would the "general manager" of a business, the person with profit-and-loss responsibility for its operations overall.

The principal architects of the modern Business Policy course were Professors Roland "Chris" Christensen, a legendary classroom teacher who wrote barely a word, and certainly not a book, after completing his doctoral dissertation, and Kenneth Andrews, who produced one of the very first books on strategy. Published in 1971, *The Concept of Corporate Strategy* grew out of the effort to provide a framework for the cases taught in Business Policy. It's not unfair to regard it as the standard doctrine on strategy at Harvard Business School until the rise of Michael Porter.

The book reflected the attitude and concerns of its author. Andrews, who died in 2005, was a formidable, multifaceted, occasionally saturnine character. He represents a humanist in all that word's senses—a Phi Beta Kappa graduate of Wesleyan, he had gone on to get a PhD in English, writing his dissertation on Mark Twain. Although in an interview shortly before his death, he jokingly told me that he was "barely numerate," during World War II he had risen from private to major doing work that grew out of his training at the Army Air Force's Statistical Control School, which was run at HBS by its faculty members. After the war, a professor who had taught him lured him back to the business school to teach.

In his nearly forty years as an active faculty member, Andrews would do much distinguished service for Harvard, including a good bit of pioneering. As head of the business school's advanced management programs—the ones for working executives who typically don't have an MBA—he wrote a report that led to the increase in the number of such programs, from two to twelve over the 1970s. He and his wife served as comasters of Harvard's Leverett House during the same turbulent decade, providing hundreds of undergraduates as much *in loco parentis* beneficence as the residents were likely to find in the college's sink-or-swim milieu.

As the editor of *Harvard Business Review* from 1979 to 1985, Andrews would lay the foundations for that publication's modern success as arbiter of the best thinking on management. His essential insight there was to hire as staff editors people who were both excited about ideas and capable of reading, writing, and editing the English language, even if they didn't know much about business. In part through his Leverett House connections, Andrews found some of these rare beings in Harvard's PhD program in the history of American civilization. Included in this cadre were Nan Stone, who would herself become editor of the *Harvard Business Review* in the 1990s, and Alan Kantrow, who would become a partner first at McKinsey, where he edited the *Quarterly* and later at Monitor Company, Michael Porter's consulting firm.

Whatever his other successes, Andrews's place in this history derives principally from his 1971 *summa theologica*. Read today—though few do—*The Concept of Corporate Strategy* stands out mostly as a map of the road, a very high road, not taken by subsequent thinkers on the strategy, including the posse who would later make Harvard Business School the leading source of academic wisdom on the subject.

Andrews got a couple key elements exactly and formatively right. His definition of strategy identifies it as *the* roll-it-all-up-into-this framework by which a company is to determine what the enterprise is and what it wants to be. There's much rolling to be done, though, given the author's prose style, approximately the opposite of Bruce Henderson's. For Andrews, "corporate strategy is the pattern of major

119

objectives, purposes, or goals and essential plans for achieving those goals, stated in such a way as to define what business the company is in or is to be in and the kind of company it is or is to be." Though the thought sometimes seems buried in his verbiage, Andrews also was clear on the proposition that a company's strategy was, within certain constraints, the product of choices made by its leaders—still a surprisingly novel idea in academic circles of that era.

For Andrews, the point had been brought home by the research he'd done on, of all things, the Swiss watch industry. Writing cases that were to be cornerstones for his Business Policy course, Andrews found that contrary to what contemporary economists would have predicted, different companies in that industry actually had different cost structures and different levels of profitability, mostly because competitors pursued different product and sales strategies.

In our conversations, Andrews took pains to describe his conception of strategy as reflecting a general manager's point of view—in contrast to the economist's view, which he had little use for. Economists, he argued, failed to take into account the rich variety of issues that such a manager should consider in charting the company's future, including relating strategy to the needs of society, the environment, and the manager's personal values, and parsing how "organizational processes and behavior" conduced to "the accomplishment of purpose." His was in this sense, and to use a word he might not have approved, a "holistic" paradigm for strategy. The title of his book's first chapter nicely summed up its overall approach: "The Importance of Being General."

It was precisely this multidimensionality that Andrews ultimately believed had been abandoned by those who succeeded him in thinking about the subject, including at HBS. "Economists have been harassing my idea of the concept of competitive strategy ever since," Andrews told me, "in the sense that the human, and the moral, and the ethical dimensions are largely ignored. Michael Porter and that group are working within the concept, but have departed from it—the ethical and moral elements—from sheer lack of interest."

Or, perhaps, from what they deemed its lack of rigor and utility. What Andrews and his colleagues in the Business Policy course resolutely refused to do—and the main reason his ideas largely disappear from the subsequent history of strategy—was to agree that there were standard frameworks or constructs that could be applied to analyzing a business and its competitive situation. Oh, they might allow one, perhaps because they had helped develop it: so-called SWOT analysis, which called for looking at the strengths, weaknesses, opportunities, and threats besetting an enterprise. But nothing more schematic and hard-edged than that. Individual companies and industries were just too idiosyncratic, and the ambitions and values of their managers too rich and varied to be mapped on any single template.

Where the Five Forces Came From

This was the received wisdom Michael Porter encountered when he enrolled in Harvard's MBA program in 1969. Porter's father was a civil engineer and Georgia Tech graduate who had gone on to a career as an army officer. The younger Porter, who inherited a bit of his father's starchiness, majored in aerospace engineering at Princeton, placing first in his college class while also winning a spot on the NCAA championship golf squad. Ask Porter today how he first became interested in competition, and he'll note that "probably my defining activity as I was growing up was sports." He excelled at football, baseball, and basketball.

Porter considered pressing on for a doctorate in engineering, but decided he wanted something "more holistic"—his word—"and managerial." One of his Princeton professors, Burton Malkiel, subsequently to become famous as a champion of the efficient-market hypothesis, "told me I just had to go Harvard Business School," Porter says with a laugh.

Porter did well enough in his first year at business school, but broke through to the absolute top of his class only in the second, under the tutelage of Chris Christensen, who taught him the first semester of Business Policy. The younger man had been hesitant to speak up in class, a prerequisite for success in a place that takes as the high point of its educational experience so-called magic Aldrich moments, when, in the classroom building of that name, students would collectively crack the case under discussion, led, of course, by the brilliant Socratic ministrations of a masterly teacher. (And they were good teachers. In contrast to Harvard College or Law School, no amount of scholarship would get you tenure at HBS unless you could also get the point across in the classroom.) To this day, Porter gets uncharacteristically emotional when he recalls how Christensen sent him a handwritten note that began, "Mr. Porter, you have a lot to contribute in class and I hope you will." There was, and he did.

"The real reason I got interested in strategy was Roland Christensen," says Porter, using his teacher's given name, as few others do. "I found this guy and this subject so compelling; it just ignited a tremendous passion for this holistic, integrated, how-to-get-all-these-pieces-to-come-together" approach. Porter ties the theme in with what became his life's work: "What I've come to see as probably my greatest gift is the ability to take an extraordinary complex, integrated, multidimensional problem and get arms around it conceptually in a way that helps, that informs and empowers practitioners to actually do things."

After his conversion experience with Christensen—"I got turned on; I could talk in class"—the question for Porter became, in his slightly surprising formulation, "how to get trained." The standard route, what he calls "the default," would have been to go after a doctor of business administration degree, or DBA, at HBS. But considering the prospect too repetitive of much of what he was already learning in the MBA program, Porter enrolled instead in the PhD program in business economics jointly offered by HBS and the Economics Department of Harvard's Faculty of Art and Sciences. The decision may seem to turn on the smallest, most academic of distinctions, but it was to have profound implications for the strategy revolution.

One can't get a PhD from the Harvard Business School, only a DBA, for reasons that in some sense go back to the business school's founding in 1908 in part as "a protest against the Harvard economics faculty"—or so Ken Andrews argued—who rather looked down on the intellectual bona fides of an effort to educate young men for business administration. (To be fair, the Faculty of Arts and Sciences doesn't allow any of the university's other schools to grant a PhD, either.) One way Porter later revolutionized HBS was by helping lead the charge to fill faculty positions there with PhDs, many from the business economics program, rather than DBAs, whose credential has been steadily devalued.

As part of his PhD studies, Porter took a course in industrial organization, which was taught by a youngish economics professor named Richard Caves, who later became the third chairman of the program in business economics. Coming from the world of business policy, the industrial organization course proved to be, in Porter's words, a "surreal experience." It was also an experience from which would spring a new perspective on competition and strategy—a perspective radically different from that being developed by the consultants.

Industrial organization (IO) economics is a world of models that depict the effect of forces, at the highest level all purposed at explaining why competition exists in certain industries but not in others, and hence why some industries are more profitable. It had grown out of the work of two other Harvard economists, first Edward Mason in the 1930s and then Joe Bain (no relation to Bill) in the 1950s.

Like most economists, Mason and Bain initially held the assumption that profits were, in some sense, an aberration—or at least profits above the "normal" level, which is low, approximately market participants' cost of capital. In the perfect world dreamed of in their philosophy, the laws of supply and demand should quickly compete away any supernormal profit-making advantage. If this didn't happen, why not? And was something sinister going on? Indeed, much of the thrust of IO economics, particularly as developed by Joe Bain, revolved around whether what was going on in a profitable industry somehow reflected behavior by companies aimed at denying the public the benefits of competition, such as low prices.

The overarching conclusions of the IO economists—and a sense of just how high up they lodged in the stratosphere of abstraction—are sometimes summed up as the *SCP schema*, shorthand for structure, conduct, and performance. Every industry has to cope with different conditions of supply and demand, and from this tussle emerges an industry structure—so many buyers, big and small, so many sellers. Structure in turn shapes the conduct of the players and the choices they make and can make, which in turn determines their performance, not just their profitability but also, as Pankaj Ghemawat points out, their efficiency and innovativeness. IO's stock in trade is concepts like barriers to entry or seller concentration.

If the Business Policy course said no generalizations were possible—and Porter's professor for the second semester of Business Policy had been Ken Andrews—IO seemed like nothing but. Or, to use Porter's more decorous phrase, it was "very stylized." With his usual amazing diligence, Porter set about doing research and writing papers, some with Caves, exploring concepts like barriers to exit and switching costs (calculating how much of an incentive it would take, in theory, to get a company to change to a new supplier).

He also saw his main chance, which was to prove the foundation of his work for the next ten years, he says. He would take the conceptual apparatus of IO, which was about why certain industries were highly competitive and others not at all, and—to use the expression employed by almost everyone who knows this story—"turn it on its head," focusing instead on what structural factors created opportunities in an industry that a company could exploit to its competitive advantage. He would carry that apparatus back to the business school, where its discipline would bring much-needed rigor, he believed, to the school's thinking about companies and what they should do.

"That was the radical that I was," Porter says. "To this day, I completely accept the premise that every company is different, that every company is unique." But he also thought "there was a framework or structure for thinking about competition from which we can generalize. The radical in me said, 'Look, we can believe in the core ideas of Chris and Ken, but that doesn't mean you can't strive for analytical frameworks that will add horsepower and insight to that quest for this unique strategy.' That's what we [meaning 'I'] set out to do."

Importing the concepts of IO back into strategy proved to be tougher than he originally expected, particularly as he attempted to break the concepts down to a level of detail useful to a real live company. At that stage in IO's history, he says, the view of industry structure was "overwhelmingly dominated by just two factors: seller concentration [what percentage of the market did the top four or top eight command] and barriers to entry," of which three or four types were posited, such as scale. "When I put that next to the industry studies I had looked at in the business school, I said, 'No. Fails. Not enough. Too stylized.'" He became an even more avid student of business school case studies of individual industries and companies, as well as articles from magazines such as *Fortune* and *Forbes*. "I just read and read and read and read."

From the effort to make IO models detailed and nuanced enough to explain the situation of particular companies came the first set of ideas Porter was to become famous for, the five-forces framework for looking at an industry. ("Framework" not "model," reflecting a deliberate choice; Porter wanted to stress the practicality of his conceptual scheme and its comparative lack of theoretical pretensions.) His overall premise, as later captured in the first sentence of the first chapter of his 1980 book, *Competitive Strategy*, was that "the essence of formulating competitive strategy is relating a company to its environment," and that the "key aspect" of that environment was the industry it found itself in and that industry's structure.

The framework posited five factors essential to determining how profitable an industry could be for its players and where and how within it a company might have room to compete. At the center of a diagram of the forces was the competitive rivalry between "firms" (the economists' term for "companies") (figure 7-1). Arrayed around this rivalry and helping determine its intensity were the other forces: the bargaining power of suppliers, the bargaining power of buyers, the threat of new entrants, and the threat of substitute offerings. In his book, Porter goes on to detail under each force a seemingly exhaustive list of sources and factors that he believed had to be considered in determining the forces' strength in a given industry.

The standard criticism of the five-forces framework, particularly from consultants, is that it's static, that unlike the experience curve, say, it doesn't help predict how the competitive situation in an industry will evolve or how the positions of the different players shape up or shake out. Porter doesn't buy that. "The five forces is a system that's in motion at all times, and industry, technology, and consumer forces and all these outside forces are always acting on the five. At any point in time, you can use the framework to explain the current profitability of the industry. There's nothing in the industry-industry structure work that says the structure is fixed." Which isn't necessarily quite what the consultants were getting at.

The framework would also eventually provoke a measure of skepticism from IO scholars, which may reflect nothing so much as Porter's originality in trying to bridge the worlds of economics and business practice. As Ghemawat observes in his invaluable article on strategy's history, "In the case of the five forces, a survey of empirical literature in the late 1980s—more than a decade after Porter first developed his framework—revealed that only a few points were strongly supported by the empirical literature generated by the IO field."

None of the criticisms, though, were to prevent the five-forces framework from being taken up and applied by legions of consultants, students, and businesspeople seeking to forge strategies for their enterprises. It might have lacked the hard-edged quantification of a growth-share matrix, but with its long list of factors to be considered, the framework gave users a feeling of gratifying thoroughness.

FIGURE 7-1

The five-forces framework

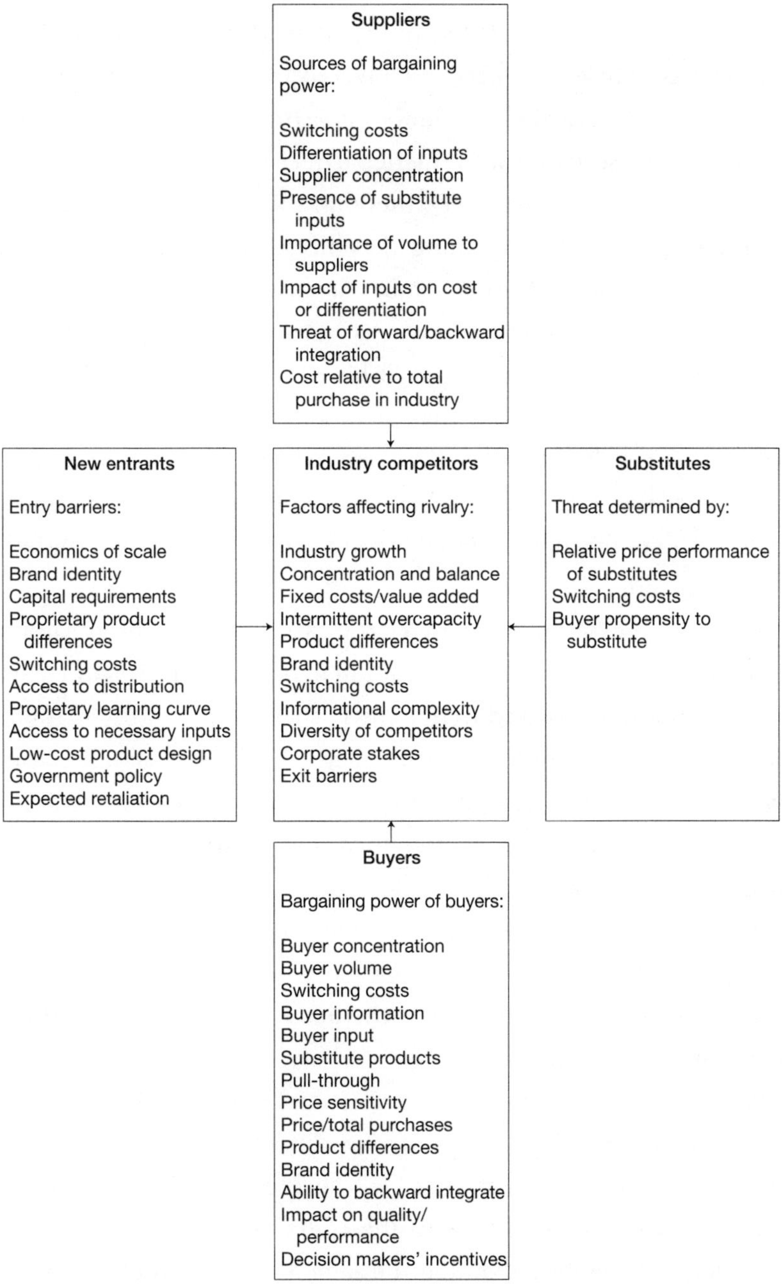

Suppliers

Sources of bargaining power:

Switching costs
Differentiation of inputs
Supplier concentration
Presence of substitute inputs
Importance of volume to suppliers
Impact of inputs on cost or differentiation
Threat of forward/backward integration
Cost relative to total purchase in industry

New entrants

Entry barriers:

Economics of scale
Brand identity
Capital requirements
Proprietary product differences
Switching costs
Access to distribution
Propietary learning curve
Access to necessary inputs
Low-cost product design
Government policy
Expected retaliation

Industry competitors

Factors affecting rivalry:

Industry growth
Concentration and balance
Fixed costs/value added
Intermittent overcapacity
Product differences
Brand identity
Switching costs
Informational complexity
Diversity of competitors
Corporate stakes
Exit barriers

Substitutes

Threat determined by:

Relative price performance of substitutes
Switching costs
Buyer propensity to substitute

Buyers

Bargaining power of buyers:

Buyer concentration
Buyer volume
Switching costs
Buyer information
Buyer input
Substitute products
Pull-through
Price sensitivity
Price/total purchases
Product differences
Brand identity
Ability to backward integrate
Impact on quality/ performance
Decision makers' incentives

Pushback Across the Charles

You would not have predicted the framework's success from the reception that Porter's efforts initially received back at the business school. While Harvard's Economics Department had loved his work—his doctoral dissertation won the department's Wells Prize as the best of the year—across the river "there was a tremendous pushback" against it, Porter says. Meaning they hated it? "They hated it," he agrees. Or at least the Business Policy faculty did.

Porter had returned there as an assistant professor in 1973, teaching Business Policy and trying to fit his efforts in the classroom to the department's iron discipline that everyone teach the same case on the same day conveying the same set of agreed-upon insights. In building his pedagogical skills Porter got abundant, generous help from Christensen, who to this day is remembered at HBS as a paragon of the art of case teaching.

Starting even before he completed his dissertation, Porter sat in on the hours of preparation his mentor put in before each class discussion, observed the sessions, and frequently hashed over with the master afterward the how-to of the Socratic magic he'd witnessed. The pupil would go on to eventually put on wildly popular courses himself—and routinely command fees in the high five figures for speeches to business audiences—but he still doesn't rank his teaching abilities as high as he rates Christensen's. "I consider myself an excellent teacher," Porter says, "but I don't rise to his level. Where I fail is on the human dimension—I wonder sometimes whether I would have noticed Mike Porter sitting in the room."

Porter remains conspicuously grateful for the support Christensen gave him. Nevertheless, Porter says, "I don't know that he ever quite understood the elegance of what I was able to do, which is that I could actually have both"—be true to the tradition that Christensen and Andrews had established and at the same time have frameworks that could be readily applied across a range of industries and companies. (Obviously, Andrews never quite got the elegance, either, even though Porter says that he, like Christensen, was supportive of the younger scholar's work.)

By the early 1970s, Christensen and Andrews were increasingly giving over the teaching of the Business Policy course to a younger generation of faculty. Christensen spent more of his time sharing his insights on case teaching to audiences beyond the business school. Five years after publishing *The Concept of Corporate Strategy* in 1971, Andrews gave up teaching Business Policy to MBAs altogether to focus instead on the *Harvard Business Review*.

Meanwhile, Porter continued his work in economics, trying to translate it back into business-school language, most notably in a 1975 "note"—the closest thing HBS then had to a research paper—titled "The Structural Analysis of Industries," which laid out the five-forces framework. A senior business-school professor told him it was "a noble experiment that failed." When Porter came up for a vote on whether he should be promoted to associate professor, all but one member of the faculty who taught Business Policy voted against him.

Becoming an Unstoppable Force

His career was saved by wiser heads, mainly that of John McArthur, soon to become dean of the school. McArthur suggested that the faculty table the decision for a year, in the meantime moving Porter out of Business Policy and into teaching in one of the nondegree programs where he could try his ideas out on practicing managers. In the Program for Management Development, Porter was freed from the doctrinal and pedagogical rigidities of Business Policy. Younger than most of his students in the program, he says he learned from listening to them, shifting his focus slightly from industries to individual companies and their plight.

Porter used this painful time out of the HBS mainstream—he admits he suffered "discouraging moments"—to complete two large, ultimately triumphant projects. He developed for the MBA curriculum an elective course that he introduced there in 1978 under the title "Industry and Competitive Analysis," or ICA. It was an immediate hit—oversubscribed, students clamoring to get in, additional faculty brought in to teach under Porter's direction the extra sections that had to be added to meet demand. "Two things win you status among your colleagues here," another HBS professor says, "creating a hugely popular billboard course and which corporate boards you serve on." Porter had done the first. "It was really ICA that silenced the doubters" among his colleagues, Porter says. "It was at that point that the powers that be said, 'This is an unstoppable force. We ought to just embrace it.'"

With the new course he had also, as he put it in a 2002 interview, "begun a pedagogical battle around the school that has largely been won." Students were provided not just cases to analyze but also conceptual notes and frameworks to use on them, a handout for almost every class. Porter admits that he even lectured a bit at the end of some sessions, coming out from behind the Socratic mask. His students ate it up, new-style intellectualization breaking through the primordial, each-case-is-different mist: instead of walking away from class discussion wondering what they were supposed to have learned, they came away with charts, templates, lists that they could apply to the next strategic problem thrown at them. "Tons of takeaways," as Porter describes them.

In the process, he was of course laying down the academic substrate for the principle that a well-educated manager, armed with the right analytical techniques, could chart strategy even without a wealth of experience. "It allowed people who weren't geniuses and hadn't been doing it all their lives to do it," he says. "Another problem with the old way of teaching strategy"—Christensen's and Andrews'—"was that unless you were lucky, you were reinventing the wheel every time."

During his time in the wilderness, Porter had also completed the work for his 1980 book, *Competitive Strategy: Techniques for Analyzing Industries and Competitors*, today in its sixtieth printing. *Competitive Strategy* has become the most attended-to treatise ever written on the subject—the only possible rival for that crown would be Porter's next book, *Competitive Advantage*, published in 1985—and it and its successor volume have made its author famous and celebrated. He heads the list of authors most frequently cited in the academic literature on strategic management and, since Peter Drucker's death in 2005, of popular ratings of the most influential management guru. Which only makes more arresting certain of the book's slightly odd qualities that jump out when you read it in the context of the history of strategy.

For starters, there's the way examples are used. If the consultants were devising concepts to help them solve their clients' problems, Porter seems clearly to start with the theory—mostly his considerable refinements on IO economics—and then to survey the literature (cases, magazine articles) for examples of companies whose experience illustrates the workings of the principles he has identified. Few of his discussions of a particular company run to more than a sentence or two; they can come across as bolted on after the theoretical assertion.

In the next chapter, we'll look a bit more deeply at the question of intentionality in strategy. For our purposes here, though, it's enough to observe that Porter's use of examples raises a question that should haunt readers of business literature whenever they encounter an author using a company example to illustrate a point about strategy—or about change management or leadership, for that matter. Namely, "Is that what the company thought it was doing? Did it know that it was performing this alleged act of strategy?"

The bigger oddity about *Competitive Strategy* for our history is that most of it, fifteen out of its sixteen chapters, isn't actually about strategy. Rather, it's about industries and how to analyze their structure, as Porter readily admits: "The *Competitive Strategy* book is basically a book about industries, because that's what I'd worked with."

The standout exception to the industry focus of *Competitive Strategy* is chapter 2, the last chapter he wrote. In writing the book, he had gone over and expanded on the five-forces model, but then, close to the last moment, Porter decided that he "needed to say something about positioning," about how a company should seek to locate itself within an industry, given the array of those forces. "Having taught cases, I knew that one had to have something to say about the firm, and firms are all different."

In a 2002 interview published in the *Academy of Management Executive*, Porter summarized how his thinking unfolded: "Fundamental to any theory of positioning had to be superior profitability. That in turn required competitive advantage, and fundamental to any thinking about competitive advantage was scope, or the breadth of the company's strategic target. That led to the generic strategies," the subject of his chapter 2 and the other big idea that the book became famous for. There were essentially three strategies a company could choose, he posited: low-cost leadership (beloved of fans of the experience curve), product differentiation (making your offering so distinctive that you could charge more for it), or market specialization (pick a niche and dominate it).

As we will see, by the mid- and late 1970s, even the intellectual bravos at the Boston Consulting Group had started to explore the idea that a low-cost, experience-curve-driven strategy was not, perhaps, the only alternative available to a company. But no one else had delimited the possible choices of strategy quite as starkly as Porter had done. Making the list even more memorable, he added an ominous observation, suggesting you'd damn well better pick one and stick to it.

A company that is "stuck in the middle," as he put it, that has failed "to develop its strategy in at least one of the three directions . . . is in an extremely poor strategic situation . . . almost guaranteed low profitability." It will either lose high-volume customers looking for the best price, because it won't have the share to keep driving costs down, or it will lose the high-margin customers, which are courted by others willing to invest in delivering a higher-value product. The theme that strategy is about choice, that a company must pick a strategy that distinguishes it from its competitors, was to become a constant in Porter's work over the decades that followed. It would secure him the place as head of the "strategy as positioning" school.

For all the niggles one may have with it, *Competitive Strategy* did more than any other book to consolidate the advances of the strategy revolution, bring scholarly respectability to its subject matter, and brand the paradigm as one that needed to be at the center of both corporate deliberation and business school education. About the only regret registered by the consultants at BCG in their invention of the retail marketing of business ideas was that they never published a sum-it-all-up book such as Porter's.

Not that he did sum up the entirety of what they had done. But his suggestions for industry analysis were so exhaustive and so seemingly practical—the book ends with a fourteen-page appendix, "How to Conduct an Industry Analysis"—that even if you haven't figured out a strategy for your company by the time you finished the process, you would feel as if you had. Porter suggests as much in the book's other appendix, a curt six-page critique and dismissal of BCG's growth-share matrix and McKinsey's nine-box counterpart.

He might dismiss their work, but—to pile trope on trope to the point of toppling over into silliness—it was the consultants' shoulders Porter stood on to catch the lightning he bottled in *Competitive Strategy*. It was they, particularly at BCG, who over the course of the prior fifteen years had pushed both the concept and the word *strategy* into the corporate consciousness. (If Porter's book had been titled *Competitive Industry Analysis*, would it be in its sixtieth printing today?) With devices such as the experience curve and the growth-share matrix, the consultants had pioneered the use of readily understandable concepts—what the late Sy Tilles of BCG would describe to

Pankaj Ghemawat as "powerful oversimplifications"—as the building blocks for strategy, paving the way for Porter's more elaborate set of templates.

Like the other original lords, Michael Porter consistently displayed indefatigable energy and the courage not to be daunted by rejection. More than most of the others, though, his timing was superb. By the late 1970s, strategy was in the air. Even the press was beginning to notice. *BusinessWeek* was running a regular department under the heading "Corporate Strategies" and conducting conferences where people would pay to hear consultants discuss their latest ideas. Porter's 1979 *Harvard Business Review* piece, "How Competitive Forces Shape Strategy," had won the publication's McKinsey Award as the best article of that year.

In 1981, shortly after the publication of Porter's book, *Fortune* did a series of four articles on the key concepts of strategy; one article centered on the generic strategies he posited. It was accompanied by a photograph of Porter looking like a young god in tortoiseshell glasses, someone out of an F. Scott Fitzgerald novel by way of an Arrow-collar-man advertisement. He continued to look like that, and still does. Six years later, in 1987, *Fortune* would put the by-then-celebrated professor on its cover, accompanying a cover story on changes at the Harvard Business School.

Under Fred Gluck, McKinsey was beginning to put its august authority into ratifying the importance of strategy. Meanwhile, BCG's luster had begun to fade a bit, its formative concepts losing their novelty, its practice buffeted by competition from both McKinsey and Bain & Company. As we will see, too, just as Porter burst on the scene with his book, Bruce Henderson, the leading "strategy buff" of the preceding generation, was being kicked upstairs by his partners, out of the leadership suite and off to an increasingly withdrawn and irascible semiretirement. Henderson, never as photogenic or articulate in person as the younger man, was to surrender his role as the public face of strategy to Porter, who has held it ever since.

On to Revolutionizing HBS

The clamorous success of Porter's Industry and Competitive Analysis course and his growing reputation beyond HBS had made him "bulletproof" to further faculty sniping, a colleague recalls, and a shoo-in for tenure, which he duly achieved in 1982 "by acclamation," he says. Up through 1986, nearly 2,700 students would take the ICA elective as taught by Porter and his disciples, amounting to about half the school's graduating MBAs.

In a turn of the wheel that still resonates at the business school, in 1979 the traditional year-long Business Policy course was turned into two courses: Business Policy I, a semester on the formulation of strategy, was taught in the first year and drew increasingly on Porter's work. Business Policy II, supposedly on the implementation of strategy, was the only course required of all MBAs in their second year. It was the beginning, John McArthur says, of the "disassembly" of Business Policy. Porter was named to head Business Policy I in 1983, and since then, no one has ever figured out how to make Business Policy II successful, as each of the few professors who tried to create a version of the course admits. Which is to say that other than the teaching of strategy, over the past twenty-five years, Harvard Business School has never figured out exactly what it wants to teach by way of its "capstone" course on general management. (The most recent attempt, focused on entrepreneurship, is taken up in chapter 15.) Strategy formulation had eclipsed all the other functions expected of a well-educated executive.

As head of Business Policy I, Porter began introducing his frameworks and takeaways into the curriculum that all MBA students were required to take. Partly in recognition of this, in 1986, the course's name was changed to Competition and Strategy. As course head, too, Porter could spearhead the other critical sally in his "pedagogical battle," importing PhDs as faculty members at the expense of DBAs trained up in the school's own doctoral program.

In his commanding history of business schools and their purpose, *From Higher Aims to Hired Guns*, HBS professor Rakesh Khurana points out that by the 1960s and 1970s, the business school had already begun to hire more nonbusiness doctorates than before, partially as a response to calls for greater academic rigor in business education. But Porter markedly accelerated the process, at least to hear him tell it.

"Before me, everybody had a DBA," he says. "After me . . . I wouldn't hire you in my group unless you had either business economics or some economics training. We were going to bring a new level of rigor in. I think I started this at the school; I was the one who got the PhD, business economics, hire-from-the-outside thing really going, because of my case." He points out that Harvard's PhD program in business economics has become a disproportionately rich source of eminent HBS professors, not just in the strategy but also in areas such as finance, entrepreneurial management, and negotiations.

Maybe too much so. These days, he fears, the school may have pushed too far in the direction of pure academe. "Now that we've gone to any random PhD from any other great school, we are at risk, frankly—our focus on practice. The core of this school is really about problems and practice, and we use analytics and academic horsepower to approach them. Whereas so many of our colleagues now are about the literature, they're academics, that's what gets them turned on. [For them] it's the paper, the publication, not the problem."

That Pesky Question About People

By 1981, Michael Porter was well and truly launched. In the next few years, he would start up a consulting firm, Monitor Company, and publish a successor 1985 book, *Competitive Advantage*. By the end of the decade, having settled most questions of strategy to his own satisfaction, he would move on to study and write on the competitiveness of nations. He returned to the fray, and our narrative, in the mid-1990s, when he came to believe strategy was beginning to get a bad name.

Part of the case against it, dating almost from its inception and steadily building after the publication of *Competitive Advantage*, was that strategists, including Porter, had thoroughly neglected the dimension of the human, the capabilities and desires of the individuals who turn strategy from concept into reality. One of the few questions that seems to make the Bishop William Lawrence University Professor—as he now is—slightly defensive is the pesky query we've encountered before: "Where are the people in a Michael Porter strategy?" He says:

"I think it's important to understand that all of my work is positive," he says, "in the sense that it tries to say, 'Here's how the world works.' Then the question of how it actually happens, and whether it's conscious or unconscious, and what role various people play in making it happen—that's all really important stuff. But it's not what this work is trying to do.

"We did provide a clear understanding, particularly in the work on competitor analysis, that there are human beings here, and people had values and egos and emotions, and sometimes that distorts what actually gets done away from what you might call the economically rational point of view. But the people who say it's process versus position"—actually, they'd describe the debate as strategy-as-learning versus strategy-as-position—"that's just so ludicrous. You need to have both. You need to understand the [underlying] economic logic so you don't have to reinvent the wheel every time. And that's my job, my business. There's all this stuff about how do you create an organization that can both understand and go through the process of doing this, and implement it well, and commit to it, and all that is really, really important stuff. But that's complimentary" to his own efforts.

Within a year or two of Porter's initial triumph, it was to become startlingly apparent just how really, really important—and popular—the human stuff actually was.

The Human Stain

8.

Y OU WILL ALMOST NEVER see the following question raised explicitly, but it rumbles beneath most debates between strategy and its critics: What is the best way to define the consciousness of a company? To capture it as a purposeful entity? Corporations aren't conscious beings, of course, but are legal constructs that are also agglomerations of individuals, each with his or her own mind, bound together by agreement, law, and custom. But if it were in your interest, perhaps because you were running one, to get your mind around the company as something akin to a person, self-aware, with aspirations and fears, capable of conceiving action and taking it, what would be the most useful framework, model, or construct to adopt?

Businesspeople don't spend a lot of time thinking about such questions but a review of the management literature of the second half of the twentieth century suggests that at least three possibilities contended for their attention. The first chronologically dates from Peter Drucker's 1946 book *Concept of the Corporation*, whose title suggests he thought the world needed one. In the preface to the 1993 edition, he observed that his was not a book about "business," but rather that it was "the first book that looked upon 'business' as an 'organization' that is, as a social structure that brings together human beings in order to satisfy economic needs and wants of a community." He also proclaimed that "it was altogether the very first book that looked at 'management' as a specific organ doing a specific kind of work and having specific responsibilities." So a company was an organization, and management was its brain.

While Drucker goes on to modestly allow that "*Concept of the Corporation* is credited with having established management as a discipline and a field of study," what strikes this observer is how few organized legions march in his name, even in and out of the halls of academe. Almost every thoughtful executive at some point discovers Drucker's sagacity, the power of his insights. But giant consulting firms have not grown up around his work, or even, truth be told, that many academic departments. Rooted in his education as a sociologist, Drucker's output was so rich, wide-ranging, and ever-renewed with fresh observations that it somehow didn't come across as systematic, at least not in the sense that could be built upon by a social scientist looking to get tenure at a business school. He certainly didn't do matrices or cost curves.

By contrast, the early champions of corporate strategy didn't write much about sociology or community. Implicit in their thinking was a concept of the company more like that of economists, but less passive, more the master of its own destiny than the pawn of market forces. If the economists posited a sort of corporate version of their famous fiction, *homo economicus*, the consultants endowed it with certain qualities of an army—always in a fight (competition), led from the top, its sense of itself built around its strategy. Nevertheless, and surprisingly for people who worked every day with real companies, the consultants could be as oblivious as the most theory-ridden economist when it came to gauging the role of people in making a company work. In explaining the dynamics of the experience curve at BCG conferences, Henderson would toss off as a given, "Assumes standard good operating management." Over the next forty years, he and his colleagues would learn just how unwarranted that assumption usually was.

The third contender for how to think about a company or about how a company thinks had a more distinguished academic pedigree than either of the others. Its intellectual god was and remains Herbert Simon, a polymath—cognitive psychology, computer science, public administration, sociology—and professor who in 1978 won the Nobel Memorial Prize in Economics for his work on, as the citation read, "decision making within economic organizations." Probably his most memorable finding was that those organizations didn't abide by theories of rational decision making. Instead of choosing the path that economists would say leads to the best possible result, they will often pick an option that keeps contending internal factions at peace, "satisficing," to use the word Simon coined, rather than optimizing.

In contrast to Drucker's work, Simon's helped spark the research of many who were to become renowned experts on how organizations make decisions. Renowned at least within academe, these experts included Richard Cyert ("the behavioral theory of the firm"), Karl Weick ("collective sense-making under pressure"), Henry Mintzberg (four books on strategy), and Stanford's James March. Simon's findings also inspired a doctoral student of March's, one Thomas Jacob Peters. To page through Peters's 1971 copy of March and Simon's book *Organizations* is to follow the smoke trail of a mind on fire: underlining everywhere, marginal notes, words circled, arrows linking one passage with another.

The Origins of *Excellence*

Tom Peters was born in Baltimore in 1942, the only child of a father whose career with Baltimore Gas & Electric lasted forty-one years— "a bit of a Prussian," according to the son—and a schoolteacher mother, "a talker who raised a talker," he wrote in dedicating a book to her. For college, he went to Cornell on a navy ROTC scholarship, starting in architecture but eventually majoring in civil engineering. He went on to study for a masters in the subject, writing his thesis on "combining probabilistic time distributions in multitask Program Evaluation and Review Technique design," for which he claims to have designed the world's most complex PERT chart.

After four years in the navy, which he loved—two tours with the Seabees in Vietnam building bridges and airstrips, and a stint at the Pentagon—Peters worked a quick bit for Peat Marwick and then decided, without giving it much thought, to seek an MBA. After a year in the program at Stanford, his curiosity prompted him to simultaneously go after a PhD in organizational behavior.

The title of the dissertation that would eventually win him that degree in 1977 shows just how inclined he was even then to pursue themes that later infused his best-sellers: "Patterns of Winning and Losing: Effects of Approach and Avoidance by Friends and Enemies." The dissertation also reflects the fact—one that might surprise readers of his business best-sellers—that, as Peters described it to me in an interview, "I get off on statistical analysis. If you look at my dissertation, it is loaded to the gills with *fabulously* beautiful statistical analyses with strange measures of distribution—they're just fun to me." About 370 pages worth of fun, to be precise, in a 380-page bound text.

Having completed his course work at Stanford and earned his MBA, he continued to toil on the dissertation even as he took a job as assistant to the director of the federal Office of Management and Budget, where, he told a biographer, he became "completely and hopelessly fascinated by complex organizations. I watched people being vilified by bureaucracies." Then, in the winter of 1974, after several attempts, he managed to get himself hired by the San Francisco office of McKinsey & Company.

His timing was propitious. A little more than a year after he arrived, McKinsey's new managing director, Ron Daniel, launched the initiatives to build up the Firm's intellection on strategy, organization, and operations. While the big bet was on strategy, McKinsey's richer tradition of doing corporate reorganizations meant that it could hardly walk away from that area. A partner, Jim Bennett, was named to head the effort to figure out the best thinking on what made organizations effective. He quickly enlisted Peters to survey the literature and, even better, to go around the world looking at real live companies and their operations, the start of the work that was to lead to *In Search of Excellence*.

Peters found that much of the wisdom McKinsey had on his subject, whether homegrown or borrowed, didn't go very far, particularly when measured against the Simonian thinking on organizations he'd been steeped in at Stanford. The Firm had built much of its reputation translating into client practice Chandler's observation that structure follows strategy. Over time, somewhat weirdly but also perhaps inevitably, this morphed into an impression in certain McKinsey minds that in effect, a company's strategy *was* its structure.

Strategy and structure, Bennett and Peters quickly concluded, weren't by themselves nearly sufficient to explain what goes into making a company effective. Over the course of the year 1977, they cast about looking for other factors. Peters presented his preliminary thinking to McKinsey's leadership, which was mildly intrigued but not enough to do anything except let the project putter along, with Peters returning to normal consulting duties.

McKinsey did promote Bennett, though, and, to replace him as head of the organization initiative, in early 1978 installed an august, if still youthful presence within the firm, Robert H. Waterman Jr. A graduate of the Colorado School of Mines—another engineer, he writes computer code for fun when he's not painting with oils or watercolor—and a Stanford MBA, Waterman had been with McKinsey since 1963. Rising through the ranks to partner, he had turned around its Australian operations and was beloved by clients, even if he did take a year off in part to teach at a business school in Switzerland.

He quickly brought order and purpose to the team's deliberations, which were now being run out of San Francisco, where he and Peters had their offices. But the effort still struggled a bit to define what it meant to be an effective organization. Waterman and Peters were tempted by the thought that they were actually looking for the most innovative companies, anticipating by about twenty years an entire genre of business books. Then, "hastily," they say, they put together what they called a "thought starter" with the one-word title "Excellence." Under that name, the work rapidly gained momentum and increasing visibility—articles in *BusinessWeek* and the *Wall Street Journal* in 1980 and some forty presentations to senior management audiences. (Lew Young, the editor of *BusinessWeek*, would be one of five people to whom the ensuing best-seller was dedicated.)

Part of the reason for the work's resonance, and a major factor in the success of the book that came out of it, was that in an era when it sometimes seemed all the business press could talk about was the superiority of the Japanese, the McKinsey study purported to show that some forty-three big American companies had attributes or inclinations that made them as well-managed as any other company in the world. (This at a time when the U.S. unemployment rate was 10 percent.) Almost anyone who has read *In Search of Excellence* can probably still remember a few of the defining qualities of these paragons. The complete list comprises a bias for action; closeness to the customer; autonomy and entrepreneurship; productivity through people; a hands-on, value-driven emphasis; stick-to-the-knitting persistence; simple form, lean staff; and simultaneous loose-tight properties.

To this day, Peters and Waterman remain proud of the fact that in the face of much advice to the contrary, they insisted on putting up front in the book what they thought of as the theory they had evolved to explain their findings. They captured this theory in a framework they labeled the seven S's, which were pictured as a sort of molecule linking the factors that made for corporate excellence. Each factor conveniently began with an *s*, as in skills, staff, style, systems, structure, shared values, and, oh yes, no bigger or smaller than any of the others, strategy (figure 8-1).

FIGURE 8-1

McKinsey's 7-S framework

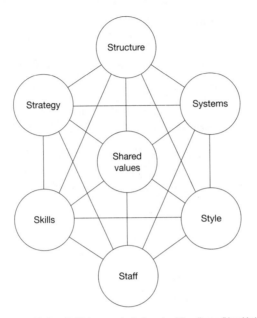

Source: Thomas J. Peters and Robert H. Waterman, Jr., *In Search of Excellence* (New York: Grand Central Publishing, 1988).

The issues raised by Peters and Waterman didn't fit easily into the calculations of strategy consultants. How do you quantify the costs and benefits of sticking to one's knitting, or staying close to the customer? Where does that fit on a matrix?

The difficulty was reflected in McKinsey's response to the success of *In Search of Excellence*. Peters actually left the Firm in December 1981, eight months before the book was published, ostensibly to finish work on it. Others said he was shown the door because the public success of the research was making him too obstreperous for McKinsey's we-are-all-one-in-service-to-the-client-and-the-firm culture. Even by the fairly liberal standards of McKinsey's northern California outpost—"The reason we got away with murder was that we were the weirdos in the

San Francisco office," Peters says, adding that if the excellence work "had happened in New York, it would have been totally put aside and dead in a year"—the emerging evangelist was too wild a presence.

Probably more telling was what happened to Waterman, by then an eighteen-year veteran of the firm. As early as October 1978, even before the excellence research, he had begun to think that McKinsey needed to redo its organization practice. The new aim, he argued in a prescient memo to the firm's leadership, should be to help clients "realistically enrich capabilities." ("Capabilities" were to become *the* hot thing ten years later.) He applauded McKinsey's increasing empiricism, noting that up until the 1970s, "we were essentially prescriptive . . . we had a reasonably fixed notion of what organizations should look like and our time was spent understanding our clients well enough to custom tailor that suit." But—and a fairly revolutionary admission— "[we were] perhaps not always problem solvers."

To correct that deficiency and bring the organization practice in line with the rest of McKinsey's new push for a "knowledge culture," Waterman recommended studies that, like those done by the strategists, might be broken down into three phases—diagnostic, problem-solving ("crack the case"), and implementation. His ambitions were large, even heroic, like someone setting out to be the best social scientist ever.

And it was all, largely, to come to naught. While Waterman gathered around him a team of McKinsey consultants interested in furthering the work on organizations, with periodic retreats in places like a dude ranch near Cody, Wyoming, much of the effort went into pulling the book together for publication. *In Search of Excellence* was finally published in October 1982, to modest expectations on the part of the McKinsey firm. Partners were told it was so unlikely that the book would sell that they should use copies primarily as Christmas gifts to clients.

The book reached the *New York Times* best-seller list the following April and remained there for two years, the first business book ever to occupy the number-one position. Peters was already creating a market for speeches and videos on the lessons of excellence, but soon Waterman, too, though vastly more reserved, found himself "giving a speech every single day," as he recalls.

This mass-market success didn't sit well with Waterman's partners—he tells of reading in a memo from one of them the phrase "Once we get past the *Excellence* problem"—and their unhappiness was aggravated by unpleasantness around royalties: Waterman had gotten Peters a going-away package that included a split of the proceeds from the book after the first hundred thousand copies, though he himself got none. Given the book's blinding success, and the fact that Waterman was getting no share of it, when Bantam approached him with a lucrative deal for a second and third book and McKinsey replied, in his words "it all belongs to us," he felt he had to leave the firm, which he did in 1985.

His departure wasn't just about money, though. Waterman had been vocal in sharing with his partners his worry that the Firm, fueled by its success in strategy consulting, was growing too fast, that the quality of its people and its work might be in jeopardy. Nor did he see the same kind of institutional energy going into the organization practice. McKinsey was doing splendidly, thank you very much, tilling the fields of strategy and Greater Taylorism, and this human element, by comparison, just seemed so hard to get a proper model around.

The Case Against Strategy

Strategy purists still heap derision on the seven-S framework. Bill Bain almost cackles when he remembers how "I had *so* much fun talking to people about the seven S's," pointing out their lack of quantitative underpinnings, looseness of definition, questionable interrelationship of the factors, and all-around failure of rigor, at least in his eyes. As if to confirm the point, in a much-remarked-on 1984 *BusinessWeek* cover story titled "Oops," John Byrne pointed out that something like a third of the original excellent companies seemed to have hit the skids since the book had come out.

For the history of strategy, what stands out in hindsight initially is the powerful critique of purely rational strategy making—as its proponents thought of it—that Peters and Waterman's work aimed at being. The first paragraph of the first chapter of *In Search of Excellence* launches the attack: "An organization chart is not a company, nor a new strategy an automatic answer to corporate grief. We all know this; but like as not, when trouble lurks, we call for a new strategy and probably reorganize." Not that either move will avail much, for "eventually the old culture will prevail. Old habit patterns persist. Moreover"—and here they were to send up rockets in a debate that still goes on—"the crucial problems in strategy were most often those of execution and continuous adaptation: getting it done, staying flexible." (Or, as Jack Welch approximated the point more pungently in his 2005 book *Winning*, "In real life, strategy is actually very straightforward. You pick a general direction and implement like hell.")

For all their book's optimism—you too can be excellent if you'll just adopt some of these good corporate habits—Peters and Waterman continually pointed up where the typical, not-so-excellent company fell short: in its flawed decision making, distrust of its people, inattention to customers, and exaggerated focus on the bottom line. Peters sees an irony to the at-last-some-Americans-are-winners element in the book's reception: "We were actually talking about how shitty the management of most other American companies was."

None of Peters and Waterman's conclusions would have surprised Herbert Simon or his other disciples. And just as the organizational decision-making research had prefigured much of the *Excellence* findings on the down side, so it also foreshadowed their main affirmative thrust, namely, productivity through people. In their subsequent books, Peters and Waterman would each return again and again to the centrality of people to a company's success—employees as the source of innovation, well-executed service, and continued corporate learning, customers as people whose wishes must be understood, honored, and if possible exceeded. It is in this sense that Waterman, in a 2002 interview, argued that "with a lot of the organizations I've written about, in a very important sense the strategy is the organization."

If strategy was elitist, it had fostered in the work of Peters and Waterman a countervailing populism. And Tom Peters was to be its William Jennings Bryan. But it was not a brand of populism that triumphed in the corporate mind.

The Mysterious Sources of Honda's Strategy

In Search of Excellence would go on to sell upward of five million copies, lifting business books for the first time into a front-of-the-store category. In the spring of 1984, the *California Management Review*, with less than twenty thousand subscribers, published an even more devastating attack on the strategy-as-a-rationally-chosen-position school of thought: "Perspectives on Strategy: The Real Story Behind Honda's Success." While the article's readership may have been minuscule, its impact was to be large and disquieting.

The article's author was Richard T. Pascale, who then combined teaching part-time at the Stanford business school—he had an MBA and a DBA from Harvard—with writing and consulting. He had been a White House Fellow, a special assistant to two secretaries of labor, and had served four years in the navy reserve. In the late 1970s, his interest had turned toward Japanese companies, which he studied just as they were coming to be perceived as major threats to American industry. To this day, you can pick up a whiff of the Mysterious East emanating from Pascale, a hint of Zen spirituality, an appreciation of the power of silence. Born Richard Johnson, he changed his last name in 1978 at the age of forty, after learning of his un-Anglicized patrimony; friends took it as a measure of the man's authenticity.

Peters and Waterman had enlisted Pascale's help, along with that of HBS professor Tony Athos, in developing what eventually became the seven-S framework. The first publication of the framework to receive much notice came in a 1981 book by Pascale and Athos, *The Art of Japanese Management*, one of the better—and better-selling—works of the genre then emerging on what we should learn from Nippon. Twenty-five years later, Peters is still angry that Pascale published the framework first, in contravention of what he thought they had agreed on.

Pascale began his article on what he termed "the Honda effect" by noting that "strategy," while seemingly "an innocent noun," had come, for "a vast and influential population of executives, planners, academics, and consultants," to embody "an implicit model of how organizations should be guided." For these folks, the basis of what he described as "a $500-million-a-year 'strategy' industry" in the United States and Europe, the characteristic elements of strategy formulation were that it was "generally assumed to be driven by senior management whom we expect to set the strategic direction," that it had been "extensively influenced by empirical models and concepts," and that it was "often associated with a laborious strategic planning process that, in some companies, has produced more paper than insight."

The Japanese viewed this emphasis on strategy as strange, Pascale argued, much "as we might regard their enthusiasm for Kabuki or sumo wrestling." In their superior wisdom, they saw such a single-minded focus as limiting the "peripheral vision" they deemed critical to spotting changes in customers, technology, or the competitive landscape.

What truly makes the "Honda effect" article memorable, though, are the different narratives Pascale offered up around the same episode, the company's dazzlingly successful entry into the U.S. motorcycle market. Honda had established its first beachhead in 1959. By 1966, it had a 63 percent share of the U.S. market for lightweight motorcycles. How did this happen?

First, Pascale quoted a 1975 report from the Boston Consulting Group, the fruits of a study it had conducted for the British government on the competitiveness of that country's beleaguered motorcycle industry. The report attributed Honda's success to the growth of the domestic market for motorcycles in Japan in the 1950s, which permitted the company to develop "huge production volumes in small motorcycles," with the attendant "volume-related cost reductions" that an experience-curve analysis would lead you to expect. It was this "highly competitive cost position which the Japanese had used as a springboard for penetration of world markets in the early 1960s," the consultants concluded.

With a nod to the increasing uptake of the consultants' thinking in the business-school community, Pascale then noted that case writers at HBS, University of California–Los Angeles, and the University of Virginia had leaped on and adapted the BCG report for use in class, particularly in first-term business-policy courses, the very one that Porter was revolutionizing at Harvard. Indeed, theirs were precisely the kind of "industry notes" that Porter sought to have accompany most case discussions.

Pascale quoted extensively from what he termed "the Harvard Business School" rendition" of the BCG study, on how "Honda started its push in the U.S. market with the smallest, lightweight motorcycles." This to take advantage of the Honda machines' cost advantage over bigger American and British motorcycles—the small Honda bikes selling for $250 at retail, compared with competitors' price tags of $1,000 to $1,500—which in turn reflected that by 1960, Honda, with its big domestic market, was already the largest manufacturer of motorcycles in the world. The rendition further recounted how the Japanese company had "followed a policy of developing the market region by region," rolling eastward from a base on the West Coast.

To close out the consultant-academic account of Honda's success, Pascale quoted the UCLA teaching note on the case written by Richard

Rumelt, another Harvard DBA, who by this time had made a reputation for himself as an academic heavyweight on the subject: "The fundamental contribution of BCG is not the experience curve per se, but the ever-present assumption that differences in cost (or efficiency) are the fundamental components of strategy."

Then Pascale sprung his intellectual trap. His stroke of genius—or at least of great cleverness and cunning—was to go to Japan and interview the six Japanese executives who had actually been in charge of Honda's entry into the U.S. motorcycle market. Three of the men were retired, all were in their sixties. The strange story they told provides probably the best available single-snapshot comparison of the strategy-as-learning school with its strategy-as-positioning adversary.

You had to begin by understanding the company's founder, Pascale argued. Sochiro Honda "was an inventive genius with a large ego and mercurial temperament." Fortunately, he had a more sober-sided business partner in the person of Takeo Fujisawa. Fujisawa pressed Honda to channel his inventive energies into improving motorcycle engine technology, which led to a revolutionary design of the four-stroke engines that were gradually replacing their noisy two-stroke predecessors. The company built on this success to become one of the industry leaders in Japan.

But the innovation that was to prove central, however inadvertently, to the company's entry in the United States came from an entirely different market segment. Fujisawa had noticed that many small Japanese businesses still used bicycles for deliveries and other errands and that, as Pascale wrote, the "purse strings of these small enterprises were controlled by the Japanese wife—who resisted buying conventional motorcycles because they were expensive, dangerous, and hard to handle. Fujisawa challenged Honda: Can you use what you've learned from racing to come up with an inexpensive, safe-looking motorcycle that can be driven with one hand (to facilitate carrying packages)[?]"

The result, in 1958, was the Honda 50cc Supercub, "with an automatic clutch, three-speed transmission, automatic starter, and the safe, friendly look of a bicycle." It proved an instant success, with the company scrambling to finance new manufacturing facilities to meet demand. As Pascale noted, by the end of 1959, Honda was the largest manufacturer of motorcycles in Japan. Of its total sales of 285,000 machines that year, Supercubs represented 168,000.

But that success wasn't the impetus behind Honda's entry into the United States, the article found. Here Pascale began quoting Kihachiro Kawashima, who started scouting the U.S. market in 1958 and not too soon thereafter became president of American Honda Motor Co., Inc. After getting over his first reaction to seeing the United States—"How could we have been so stupid as to start a war with such a vast and wealthy country!"—Kawashima registered dismay at the sad state of motorcycle sales in the United States: almost everyone seemed to have a car; of three thousand motorcycle dealers, only a thousand were open five days a week, the rest being night and weekend operations.

Kawashima did note that about sixty thousand European machines were sold in the United States each year, a little less than 15 percent of the total sold, and concluded that it didn't seem unreasonable to shoot for 10 percent of the import market. He returned with that "seat-of-the-pants target"—his words—to Fujisawa, who, without much further thought, allocated a million dollars for the initiative. "He didn't probe the target quantitatively. We did not discuss profits or deadlines for breakeven." In fact, Kawishima said, "we had no strategy other than the idea of seeing if we could sell something in the United States."

Founder Honda was particularly confident that his company's bigger bikes would do well in the United States—"The shape of the handlebar on these larger machines looked like the eyebrow of Buddha, which he felt was a strong selling point"—so the initial inventory allocation was 25 percent each of 305cc, 250cc, 125cc, and 50cc Supercub machines. Japan's Ministry of Finance permitted Honda to invest a mere $250,000 in the venture, only $110,000 of which could be in cash. Partly as a result, the Honda team lived frugally, sharing a furnished apartment in Los Angeles—where at least there was a large

Japanese community—two of them sleeping on the floor. They rented warehouse space in a "run-down section of the city," where they stacked motorcycle crates by hand, swept the floors themselves, and kept up the parts bin.

Even though Kawashima and his colleagues had known no better than to time their entrance to coincide with the end of the April-to-August sales season, they gradually recruited about forty dealers, and by the spring of 1960, a few of the 250cc and 305cc models had begun selling. But then, as described by Kawashima, "disaster struck." The larger Honda motorcycles, pushed to higher speeds over longer distances than they had encountered in Japan, began to break down, their clutches failing, their engines leaking oil. The team had to use its cash reserves to air-freight the defective bikes back to Japan for testing. The Honda labs there worked overtime and, in less than a month, had a new head gasket and clutch spring redesigned to address the problem.

By that time, though, "events had taken a surprising turn." The Honda team had been riding Supercubs around Los Angeles to run errands, drawing a lot of attention, including that of a buyer from Sears. The Japanese had held back from pushing the smaller motorcycle from fear of alienating their potential customers and dealers—"a macho market," according to Kawashima. But with their bigger bikes breaking down, what else could they do? Sales of the Supercubs took off, with many customers coming from beyond the ranks of motorcycle enthusiasts. Another surprise ensued: the outlets that lined up to sell the Supercubs were sporting-goods stores, not traditional motorcycle dealers.

Pascale then went on to complete his tale of, in his words, "miscalculation, serendipity, and organizational learning." In 1963, a UCLA undergraduate majoring in advertising, as part of a course assignment, turned in a model campaign for Honda bearing the theme "You Meet the Nicest People on a Honda." Grey Advertising bought it and then pitched the concept to Honda's U.S. team. Over some opposition, its proponents won out, the campaign became famous, further accelerating sales growth. "By 1964," Pascale noted, finishing his story with a flourish, "nearly one out of every two motorcycles sold was a Honda."

Not that Pascale was finished with his argument. The "Honda effect" was only the first of three takes his article offered on strategy, accounting for less than half of a twenty-five-page article. The last of these argued that since strategy and the "analytic and microeconomic tools" to make it were no longer adequate to the competitive task at hand, a broader framework should be employed, one that included at least six perspectives. Strategy was merely one of the six. The others consisted of our old friends from the seven-S framework—organizational structure, systems, style, staff, and shared values. Skills get a mention, but apparently don't qualify for full-perspective status.

In 1996, twelve years after the publication of the original article, *California Management Review* would bring it out again, this time in the context of what it labeled a forum, assembled and introduced by Henry Mintzberg. In his introduction, Mintzberg praises the original: "Perhaps no other article published in the management literature has had quite the impact of Richard Pascale's article on the 'Honda effect.'" In his follow-on piece, Pascale modestly confesses: "Little did I realize that this small foundation of anecdote would find itself at the epicenter of tectonic debates between the 'design'" (as in, you can choose your position and design your strategy) "and the 'emergent'" (as in, it emerges from what you learn when you try to do something in the world) "schools of strategy." Tellingly though, in the forum version, the original article has been edited down just to the Honda stories, completely leaving out Pascale's other two grand perspectives.

So mesmerizing is the story told by the Honda executives and so gleefully sharp its suggestion that the consultants didn't know what they were talking about that one almost forgets to ask questions about its larger import. Questions such as, Would the let's-give-it-a-try-and-just-find-out model in the Honda example have worked as well in a long-established company as it did in one still fired with the founders' entrepreneurialism? Wasn't it in fact Honda's dominance in small mo-torcycles back home, much of it in accordance with classical principles of strategy, that permitted the company to fund and experiment with the push into the United States? Was there really much evidence that Honda had been paying any more attention to Pascale's six of the seven S's than it had to experience curves or portfolio analysis? (Stu-dents of the consulting industry might add, "If Honda was so purely intuitive, why did it subsequently become a client of the Boston Con-sulting Group?")

In his follow-on piece of the package, Richard Rumelt helpfully sought to clarify what the positioning school was up to: "A 'strategy' explanation of events is not always about intentionality, but is some-times simply about the forces at work that permit sustained asymmet-ric positions to be maintained."

Stories like the Honda effect, though seldom as memorable, were to become a staple in the discourse of those criticizing classical strategy for its neglect of the human. Asked to explain the success of *In Search of Excellence*, Peters cites, besides other factors, the book's abundance of exemplary tales. This was a first among business books, he maintains, arguing—mostly accurately—that "Peter Drucker doesn't tell stories."

The ability to tell a story well, one rooted in the frustrations and occasional epiphanies in corporate life, launched Peters into celebrity on a circuit that steadily grew on the pattern of his success, that of the management author cum speaker. Readers of the guru's book could be enticed to hear its author, often at an event sponsored by a company seeking to inspire employees or by an outfit putting on a conference in the hope of drawing paying attendees. Admirers of the speech would swell the audience for the author's next tome, the research for which— if there were any—would be underwritten by generous speaker's fees.

Most readers' familiarity with at least some of the following names is testimony to the house that Tom Peters built, or whose construction he at least started: Jim Collins (*Built to Last, From Good to Great*), Charles Handy (*The Age of Unreason*), Gary Hamel (*Competing for the Future*),

Rosabeth Moss Kanter (*The Change Masters*, *When Giants Learn to Dance*), John Kotter (*Leading Change*).

Their writings and speeches have inspired hundreds of thousands. Their insights no doubt contributed to better practice at innumerable organizations. What they haven't managed to do is come up with a paradigm that can hold its own with strategy, or with strategy's off-spring, Greater Taylorism.

9.

The Paradigm
That Failed?

THERE ARE OBSERVERS WHO maintain that much of what goes on in business organizations comes down to a struggle between those who see the enterprise largely through the lens of the numbers—sales figures, costs, budgets—and those who focus instead primarily on people, their energies, ambitions, and limitations. A gross oversimplification, of course, but one that approximates the argument between the two schools of strategy.

To see how and why the numbers people won out—at least until recently—we need to kick the debate even higher, to the level of competing paradigms. The concept of a paradigm was originally enunciated by the late Thomas Kuhn in his 1962 book, *The Structure of Scientific Revolutions*. In fields like physics or chemistry, Kuhn argued, scientists will converge on a single unifying explanation of what they see—for instance, that the sun, planets, and stars revolve around the earth. Succeeding generations of scientists will premise their research on that paradigm.

Over time, however, sometimes thanks to new tools or ways of measuring, observations accumulate that can't be explained by the dominant construct and, indeed, seem out of whack with it. The puzzled will begin to try to construct an alternative grand explanation—it helps here to have a Copernicus or an Einstein—and a new paradigm will emerge.

This book has attempted to make the case for strategy as the paradigm by which people in business have come to organize their understanding of what a company wants to do. We've seen how successive thinkers built on an original construct that integrated calculations of cost, competition, and customers. Michael Porter may have ended up dismissing some of the consultants' early concepts, but not because the ideas were utterly wrong. Rather, he thought he could offer a more complete framework that took the concepts into account but also overcame their limitations.

It is harder to show how experts failed to come up with a competing paradigm, one that would have put people at the core of an enterprise's success. What we would be looking for in an alternative to the strategy model—a unified theory of management, if you will—would be a construct addressing each of the issues a company faces in dealing with people: how they were to be selected, trained, disciplined, compensated, motivated, managed, and led (if you admit a distinction between the last two). The unified theory would demonstrate how each of these elements related to one another, in ways that could be both predicted and controlled, how they could be measured, and how their combined effect determined the fate of the organization, preferably in dollar-and-cents terms that would satisfy the most exacting chief financial officer. In the world of this paradigm's triumph, no CEO would dream of standing before an audience without a detailed explanation of how his or her company was exploiting the principles of the unified theory to achieve competitive success.

In arguing for the absence of anything like a unified theory, I'd point to four sources of supporting testimony. First, ask almost any human-resources executive, most of whom wish there were such a construct. In discussions I've had with scores of HR leaders over the past five years, I've asked them about the most pressing issue they faced. Almost unvaryingly, their response came back, "Trying to get line management to pay attention to—understand, appropriately value, direct resources toward—our company's employees and what I and the people who work for me do." I've yet to encounter an HR executive who says he or she is satisfied with the metrics available to demonstrate the contribution people make to the organization's success.

Next, look to the consulting industry. We've seen how McKinsey & Company mostly declined to take up the opportunity offered by Bob Waterman and the excellence work. Over the course of the 1980s and 1990s, the Boston Consulting Group and Bain & Company, while tussling with implementation, would also make occasional forays into the dimension of the human—BCG in its work on integrating operations at global companies that had merged and in Jeanie Duck's studies of the management of change, Bain with Fred Reichheld's explorations of corporate loyalty. But all three outfits proudly cling to the appellation "strategy firm," which sets them in a tier above all other consulting firms, as reflected in their higher per-partner revenues.

Other consultancies grew up to help clients address issues that would have been subsumed in a unified theory. Some firms were specifically created to provide a consulting platform for authors celebrated for their insights in this realm. Waterman had his own outfit, Rosabeth Moss Kanter her Goodmeasure Inc., Gary Hamel his Strategos. But none of these enterprises would develop anything approaching the size, reputation, or clout of the strategy firms. Consultancies that did concentrate on human resources (the Hay Group, Mercer, Towers Perrin, Watson Wyatt) might grow large, but their practices would remain rooted in their traditional specialties, namely, compensation, benefits, performance-appraisal systems, and "workforce planning." They might have the ear of the client's HR chief, but not necessarily the CEO's.

Academics, probably the only subgroup actually comfortable talking about paradigms, provide the most explicit testimony on the failure of one to form around the human. Perhaps the clearest voice on the issue comes from Stanford professor Jeffrey Pfeffer, who is to the field of organizational behavior what Porter is to strategy, at least in the eyes of many. In a 1993 *Academy of Management Review* article, "Barriers to the Advance of Organizational Science: Paradigm Development as a Dependent Variable," Pfeffer marshals a stunning case on the benefits to a scholarly field of having a strong paradigm, and how and why the social sciences, organizational studies in particular, lag well behind on that score.

Organization studies displayed "a fairly low level of paradigm development, particularly as compared to some adjacent social sciences such as psychology, economics, and even political science." Scholars in the field couldn't agree on the important topics for further research—a survey of 105 of these experts produced 146 suggestions, 106 of which were unique—and the relationship between the topics they were pursuing was "getting weaker over time." It all amounted to what other commentators had labeled "pre-paradigmatic state," a field that was "more fragmented and diverse than it had ever been."

Why was this so? In some sense, Pfeffer argued, people in the area wanted it that way, "less elitist and more egalitarian." He cited a recent special issue of the *Academy of Management Review*, making the point that "the field not only has, to use the current political parlance, a very large 'tent' but a tent in which fundamentally any theoretical or methodological approach is as valid as any other." In his peroration, Pfeffer noted that he had said much the same thing ten years before, in 1982—the same year *In Search of Excellence* was published

In his history of management education in the twentieth century, Rakesh Khurana teases out the implications of organizational science's failure for business schools, setting it in the context of larger trends that look suspiciously like the triumph of those with a paradigm over those without. In reaction to the Ford Foundation's 1959 report decrying business schools' lack of rigor, more and more of the institutions had added so-called discipline-based scholars—that is, people with PhDs in respectable subjects such as economics, sociology, or psychology—to their faculties.

Khurana points out that two areas in particular developed rapidly to the extent of even "affecting managerial practice." The first was strategy, as developed by Porter; the second was finance, which coalesced around our old friend—and a paradigm for sure—the efficient-market hypothesis. Of all the discipline-based scholars, it was economists, once comparative strangers to the halls of business schools, who were winning the competition to fill faculty positions.

As Khurana notes, the disarray in organizational science—he himself is a professor of organizational behavior at HBS—merely made it easier for strategy and finance to gain primacy. Perhaps the only field in worse shape, judged by academic standards, was the study of leadership, as Khurana wickedly demonstrates. Even organization-science scholars looked down their noses on academic colleagues trying to plow that furrow, or rather countless and meandering furrows, since the leadership field seemed to have no agreed-upon premises or research base. What made this particularly ironic was that over the course of the 1990s, an increasing number of business schools, including Harvard, would declare that their mission was "educating leaders."

In his book, Khurana has another quote from Jeffrey Pfeffer and colleagues in a 1997 work that can be taken, I'd argue, as a fair summing-up of where academics would come out on the question of strategy versus the paradigm that wasn't: "There is little doubt that economics has won the battle for theoretical hegemony in academia and society as a whole, and that such dominance becomes stronger every year." In matters of scholarly citation and research on organizations, "one is hard pressed to think of many substantive models . . . providing an alternative hypothesis."

The final source of evidence for the failure of a people-first paradigm comes from the authors of that school themselves. One of the hallmarks of a healthy paradigm is that once it has been established, subsequent studies refer to it, build on and elaborate the framework it provides. In this regard, it's instructive to see what became of the seven S's, the closest thing to an organizing paradigm to be found in

THE LORDS OF STRATEGY

In Search of Excellence. In the subsequent writings of the framework's inventors, the seven-S framework virtually disappears.

You'll look in vain for any mention of it in Peters's next two books, *A Passion for Excellence* (1985, coauthored by Nancy Austin) and *Thriving on Chaos* (1987). It does reappear in *Liberation Management* (1992), but only for a fleeting moment of three pages in an 834-page work. In Bob Waterman's next book, *The Renewal Factor* (1987), he does return to the seven-S framework, but, this time, mostly to propose that its "happy atom" needs to be linked with another framework, that embodying the seven Cs—chance and information, communication, causes and commitment, crisis points, control, and culture, all arrayed around capability in the nucleus.

Richard Pascale, having first flown the seven-S flag in *The Art of Japanese Management*, keeps it flying a bit longer. In *Surfing the Edge of Chaos* (2000), there are two brief mentions. But in 1996, when the *California Management Review* revisited "the Honda effect," Pascale's original discussion of the seven S's was excised entirely, replaced in his new companion piece by a disquisition on "organizational agility," which now apparently explained Honda's success.

What was the poor reader of management literature to do, particularly the reader looking to maintain the importance of people to organizations even as the chariot of strategy bears down on him or her? New banners to march under were offered at a pace both exhilarating and confusing—culture, chaos, renewal, agility, revolution. What didn't seem to be much in evidence were abiding truths to hold on to.

The Myth That Readers Most Frequently Fall For

Before we escape the realm of the human and plunge back into the world of economics and consulting, we need to consider the most ineffable factor underlying how strategy eclipsed other constructs. This takes us to perhaps the most common, thoroughly understandable mistake made by readers of management literature: they fall for what I call the myth of corporate persistence.

What do most readers remember about *In Search of Excellence*, besides a few of the managerial lessons? Probably that, as first proclaimed by *Business Week*, about a third of the companies on the original list of forty-three almost immediately fell off, no longer meeting the book's criteria for excellence. Fifteen years later, in *Surfing on the Edge of Chaos*, Pascale argued that Peters and Waterman were really writing more about managing for equilibrium, an equilibrium that couldn't survive the tempests of modernity. With a touch of superiority, he notes that within five years of their book's publication, "half of the forty-three companies were in trouble. At present, all but five have fallen from grace."

He then goes on in his own book to hold up and explore in great detail the examples of six organizations whose "living systems" approach to management is allegedly more suited to our chaotic times: British Petroleum, Hewlett-Packard, Monsanto, Royal Dutch/Shell, Sears, and the U.S. Army. Each of which would find its own way to fall from grace in the years since *Surfing on the Edge of Chaos* was published in 2000.

The ever-shifting sands of modern management literature are littered with the wrecks of corporate examples that seemed to founder. So the books' authors got it wrong, did they? Of course they did, at least partly; their choice of form dictated that this be so. If Peters, Waterman, and their successors imported the story into management literature, they were hoist with both the exaltations and the limitations of that particular petard. Scholars such as Charles Tilly have pointed out that as an explanatory mechanism, the story form typically elevates the role of the individual or individuals at the expense of other, complicating factors, this in service to building a memorable narrative.

Think about your own experience of organizations. How often did the actions of just one person or a small team adequately account for all that went on there? Could their story alone possibly explain all the energies, ambitions, tensions, and adaptation that permitted—or failed to permit—the organization to cope with changes in its environment? Henry Mintzberg makes the point wonderfully in his rejoinder to accounts of how this CEO or that one "turned around his company": "Did he do it all by himself?"

The problems weren't just with the story form. Raising companies up as examples, whether in *In Search of Excellence* or any of its hortatory successors, draws much of its power from the expectations readers bring to the tale, what they want to believe. Business readers, ever practical, want lessons they can put to use, examples backed up by the assurance that these lessons reflect the experience of practitioners like themselves.

But from layers below their conscious practicality, readers also seem to bring other wishes and hopes to their experience of examples. There's the search for an inspiring ideal—excellence, an art of management, heroic organizational performance—that transcends anything most of us encounter in our lives within companies. But more subtly and more dangerously, we also import a kind of stickiness to how we think about a company, a usually unconscious sense that once we know what it's like, we can pretty much count on it to remain that way. "Exxon, that's a great company," we say, "always has been." As we did of Wal-Mart (through the 1990s), IBM (until the early 1980s), and General Motors (from the 1920s until the 1970s).

The problem is that the myth of persistence no longer comports with the facts, and less so all the time. Certainly this is true when it comes to superior financial performance. One management author after another—McKinsey's Dick Foster in *Creative Destruction*, Bain's Chris Zook in *Profit from the Core*, to name just two—demonstrates that only a tiny minority of large corporations actually outperform the overall market over time, if they manage to survive at all. As Foster notes, of the five hundred companies on the original S&P 500 in 1957, only seventy-four survived on the list until 1998—most who disappeared were merged out of existence, not victims of bankruptcy—and the stocks of only twelve outperformed the S&P index itself over that period.

Foster in particular bangs away at the point: "McKinsey's long-term studies of corporate birth, survival, and death in America clearly show that the corporate equivalent of El Dorado, the golden company that continually performs better than the markets, *has never existed*. It is a myth. Managing for survival, even among the best and most revered corporations, does not guarantee strong long-term performance for shareholders. In fact, just the opposite is true. In the long run, markets always win."

And yet we cling to the myth of persistence, reflexively imbuing companies with an assumption of excellence or permanence that the facts belie. We see enduring monuments, edifices we can count on, rather than flowers that bloom, then wither.

Even before Foster and his coauthor Sarah Kaplan published *Creative Destruction* in 2001, other management authors, including Peters and Pascale, had begun to pick up on the increasingly transitory nature of corporate success—an evanescence that they typically attributed to ever-greater "chaos" in the world of business: increased competition, new players, rapidly changing technology. Peters began *Thriving on Chaos* (1987) with the declaration "There are no excellent companies," which was accompanied by the observation that "excellent firms of tomorrow will cherish impermanence."

Even this would not be enough to satisfy some students of corporate performance. In 2005, in their best-seller *Blue Ocean Strategy*, INSEAD professors W. Chan Kim and Renée Mauborgne argued that companies were better served trying to invent new markets ("the blue ocean") rather than fighting it out on seas already beset and bleeding with established competitors ("the red ocean"). Their research on successful blue-ocean moves took them through the work of Foster and others and led them to conclude, with wonderful audacity, that if "there is no perpetually high-performing company and if the same company can be brilliant one moment and wrongheaded at another, it appears that the company is not the appropriate unit of analysis in exploring the roots of high performance and blue oceans."

The unit of analysis that they recommended be adopted in its stead, somewhat self-servingly, was "the strategic move"—"the set of managerial actions and decisions involved in making a major market-creating business offering." As if we all could agree on what constituted one of those.

The final, head-spinning irony underlying the myth of persistence—taking us back to why strategy triumphed—is that there is an element of truth to it. Certain powerful aspects of a corporation do endure over time. Quite often, these are the same factors that prevent the company from adapting quickly enough to changed economic circumstances. They're human factors, ingrained norms and behaviors that make up what in the late 1970s came to be summed up in the term *corporate culture*. Changing your company's strategy almost always proves tougher than you thought it would. But it's inevitably easier than changing your culture.

For me, the first glimmers of this apparently immutable truth came, oddly enough, from Peters and Waterman. Interviewing them before their book came out, when they were still working with a set of sixty-two companies, I asked how the exemplars had become excellent, a question almost entirely unaddressed in their subsequent best-seller. They didn't much want to answer. Finally, they allowed that in all but a half dozen cases, the enterprise had been set up that way in the first place. Subsequent generations of management merely had the good sense not to mess with what, say, Messrs. Procter and Gamble had wrought.

Twenty-five years later, Peters—PhD in organizational behavior, avid student of James March and Herbert Simon—seems only to have confirmed his belief on this point: "I desperately believe that virtually all the behavior of an enterprise is a pretty much direct inheritance of its gene pool. Whatever it was, it will stay. Microsoft is a centralized, personality-driven company, and that's what it will always be. Many of the companies we looked at—Hewlett-Packard, 3M—were decentralized from the start"—all the better for "loose-tight properties" and "autonomy and entrepreneurship."

A bit later, still in the early 1980s, I commissioned a *Fortune* article by Pascale on the importance of organizational culture. (In it, he described strategy as "firewater," something intoxicating the minds of too many corporate chieftains.) Only after it had been published did I have the wit to ask him how many large companies had actually succeeded in fundamentally changing their cultures. He could think of only two—Ford Motor Company and Shell, as I recall—and the process had taken years.

Foster's first book, in 1986, was *Innovation: The Attacker's Advantage*. By the time he coauthored *Creative Destruction*, he was even clearer on the chief impediment to innovation or adaptation: what he called "cultural lock-in." Such lock-in, embodied in a company's "rules of thumb for decision making, its control processes, and the information it used for decision making," kept it from recognizing changes in its environment, left it unable to "shed operations with a less-exciting future," and ultimately signaled "the corporation's inexorable decline into inferior performance."

Even if you wanted to avoid lock-in, who could totally grasp all the squishy variables entailed in analyzing, much less changing, a culture? Strategy at least offered top management the prospect of clear analysis, clean decision making, and choice. Or so it seemed.

10.

Struggling to Make Something Actually Happen

B Y THE EARLY 1980s, the glorious phase of the strategy revolution was drawing to a close. The original lords had largely completed their foundational work. The essential paradigm had been created, widely installed, and rendered preeminent in the sense that every self-respecting corporation by this time knew it had to have a strategy. The consulting firms and academic departments that were to dominate the field had been established.

What happened next was what one would expect by way of a second, consolidating phase. Its unfolding proceeded simultaneously along two occasionally intersecting lines. The thrust of the first was carrying the gospel further into the world, to where it could change behavior; that of the second, taken up in the next chapter, refining the gospel.

With the new set of principles revealed and its detractors in disarray, the revolutionaries and their public found themselves increasingly grappling with the question of how to translate concepts into corporate practice. Or, as it was commonly put, how to implement strategy—or execute it, if you prefer (*implement* from the Latin "to fulfill," *execute* from "follow to the end"). This was not something the consultants had been much inclined to think about; it lacked the flash and crisp bite of a fresh idea or analytic breakthrough. To help their clients address the issue, as the consultants were dragged into doing, the firms—and in particular BCG—would have to devise radically new ways of working, and not just with the top echelons.

Flying Beyond the Seagull and Pushing Henderson Out

Like many other journalists, I'm skeptical about the power of the press. It often seems we write articles and send them out into the void, and the void eats them with nary a burp. It surprised me, then, when BCG's Alan Zakon recalled of a 1982 *Fortune* piece of mine, "That article *really* hurt us."

Titled "Corporate Strategists Under Fire," the story was mostly about how companies had embraced strategy and the conceptual tools it brought with it but now were struggling with implementation, so much so that a modest backlash had set in. At places such as General Electric, corporate planning staffs were being cut back. In the article, I also drew the conclusion from the following exchange, a version of which I had with every single consulting firm I interviewed:

"How many of your clients have strategies?"
"If they're our client, they have a strategy by now."
"How many can effectively implement those strategies?"
"Uhhh," long pause, much visible reluctance. "This is not for attribution, right?"
"Right. Is it fifty percent?"
"Oh no, not fifty percent."

"Thirty percent?"

"Um, no."

After a little more back-and-forth, the final estimate would emerge: fewer than 10 percent of their clients, in the consultants' judgment, were fully successful at putting their corporate strategies to work.

But that wasn't the element of the article that caused the most damage, in BCG's view. What bothered the firm more was the following passage, about the then-dominant practice in the business: "It was, according to the industry joke, the seagull model of consulting. You flew out from Boston, made a couple of circles around the client's head, dropped a strategy on him, and flew back."

The early 1980s were proving to be a painful time for the Boston Consulting Group, what John Clarkeson, Zakon's successor as head of the firm, would later describe as the most difficult period in its history. The reasons for this went well beyond what Zakon called bad PR. For starters, it wasn't just public relations—as one of his partners acknowledges, "We *were* seagull consultants."

Paradoxically, the very success of strategy represented a challenge. Any company not brain-dead knew it had to have a strategy; the concepts with which to conduct the requisite analysis were widely available, with lots of consultants competing to help you use them. To use Zakon's term, strategy had suffered commoditization. (But then, as a McKinsey partner said to me, "Our strategy *was* to commoditize what BCG was doing.") Moreover, as the article reported, once you had been "BCGed"—as the phrase was then—why do it again anytime soon? George Bennett—BCG alumnus, cofounder of Bain & Company, by this time head of his own consulting firm, Braxton Associates—summed up the situation even more colorfully: "When you subtract the companies [that] have been chewed up, and the hardcore no-buys, there aren't many virgins left. Every time I go in to sell an assignment, I find five or six firms there competing for it. You didn't used to see that."

All this was playing out against a background of worsening economic conditions. The second half of the 1970s had battered BCG's still largely industrial clientele, with oil shocks first in 1973 and then in 1979 helping create the plight dubbed "stagflation"—slow growth painfully accompanied by high inflation. Costs, particularly the cost of raw materials, were not behaving the way experience curves suggested they should.

Efforts by the federal government to stem the inflationary tide— President Gerald Ford's hapless "Whip Inflation Now" campaign, President Jimmy Carter's voluntary wage and price guidelines—were unavailing. Another response to inflation, the deregulation of industries such as airlines, trucking, and railroads, would have more significant and longer-term effects, particularly after the unshackling was extended to banking and long-distance telephone service in the 1980s. The combination of deregulation and the invasion of one U.S. market after another by the Japanese and Europeans opened ever-wider reaches of the economy to the forces of competition.

Pankaj Ghemawat cites the estimate by economist William Shepherd that these forces, together with antitrust actions by the government, had served to increase the portion of the U.S. economy "subject to effective competition from 56 percent in 1958 to 77 percent by 1980." These numbers say volumes about why strategy had come to be in demand. This hadn't translated into a commensurate increase in the demand for BCG's services, however. McKinsey had woken up and was piling into the market. The consulting community in Boston whispered that Bain & Company had discovered the right model—multiyear, all-enveloping engagements with only one company per industry—even as BCG clung to its traditional drill of smaller, if exquisitely brilliant projects, sometimes of a seagullish nature.

The confluence of these woes, abetted by irritations more personal, in 1980 led to Bruce Henderson's being fired still one more time—the final time. Or more precisely, to his being kicked upstairs. Back in 1975, as a means of buying the firm from its parent, the Boston

Company, BCG had essentially sold itself to its employees via one of the first employee stock ownership plans, or ESOPs. Henderson, who at the time was granted a ten-year contract to serve as either CEO or chairman of the board, still commands the admiration of some at the firm for this, which they regard as a consummate act of generosity. In 1977, on the way to completing the buyout in 1979, all vice presidents— there were then close to thirty—were made directors of the firm and trustees of the ESOP.

In 1979, the U.S. Federal Reserve, under Paul Volcker, finally took the steps that would eventually rein in inflation, ratcheting up interest rates dramatically. One immediate effect was to tip the economy into recession the following year.

At a board meeting on May 1, 1980, BCG's recently enfranchised directors, having tired of the leadership of their mercurial founder, voted to establish a management committee of four to run the firm— Henderson conspicuously excluded—and named one of its members, Alan Zakon, to a three-year term as CEO. Henderson became chairman of the board of directors, a position he held until his contract ran out in 1985, when he retired from BCG.

In one sense, Henderson's ouster can be understood as a culmination of the management ethos he had put in place; in another sense, as the failure of that ethos to keep up with new challenges confronting his firm. Besides its other manifestations, the founder's belief in competition had translated into what some participants still call a "brutally free market" within BCG for allocating and accounting for the work done by its professionals. In the firm's early years, a tally of each consultant's "billability," the percentage of the person's time billed out to clients, was posted every month on the back of a door of a coat closet that everyone could visit, all the better to compare your percentage with others'. Consultants in charge of client engagements would pick the people they wanted to staff their teams, and if you found yourself passed over too often and not kept busy, soon there would be no place for you in the firm. But the free market's reach seemed to stop at the pay window: Henderson kept most decisions on compensation in his own hands, including compensation for his most senior colleagues. To this day, some of them still mutter about bonuses that had been promised but were never paid.

By 1980, too, Henderson's entrepreneurial expansiveness increasingly looked like something BCG might not be able to afford. In his president's letter of 1979, he conceded that the prior year had been one of "extraordinary prosperity"—as it turned out, BCG wouldn't be that profitable again for more than a decade—and that the kind of growth the firm had enjoyed couldn't continue. Nonetheless, BCG had opened an office in Chicago in 1979—its seventh around the world and as expensive an undertaking as ever—with many of Henderson's fellow officers wondering why.

Oversimplifying the matter, Henderson's senior colleagues believed that the firm he had founded seventeen years before had to change and that he was neither capable of nor disposed to charting a new course. Soon after taking over, Zakon would adopt a rallying cry for the firm—it was inscribed on campaign buttons. The new motto subtly suggests an element of spin-your-wheels intellection that BCG may have been trying to put behind itself, along with Bruce Henderson: "Make It Happen."

What You Can Learn from Your Mother

When it came to making strategy happen, as in implementing it, the obstacles for BCG began with its officers' attitude: they weren't merely uninterested in the effort, they were almost disdainful toward it. A story told by Zakon nicely if unintentionally captures the air of condescension that could accompany this mind-set.

One of BCG's clients was Clark Equipment, a manufacturer of forklifts and other materials-handling equipment. In the 1970s, the company found itself faced with heightened competition, particularly from the Japanese, who were finding a market for forklifts less complex and less expensive than Clark's. After thoroughly studying Clark's costs and its competitors', BCG came in with an elegantly complete strategy recommendation that Clark build a new, more streamlined facility to produce a competitive offering, a forklift that would offer fewer features than Clark's regular models but cost significantly less. Clark, its culture still largely in the grip of engineers who delighted in devising the next bell and whistle, promptly went out and did just the opposite, constructing a factory to build an even costlier, feature-laden product. The experience, Zakon told his colleagues, had been like "giving a ray gun to a caveman."

The BCG consultant who probably did more than any other to teach the caveman how to use the ray gun, even to help design it, was David Hall. He represents a complementary strain in BCG's history— even oppositional at times—to the likes of a Zakon, George Bennett, or Dick Lochridge, men whose brilliance epitomized what the firm most valued in its early days. In his twenty-seven years at BCG, Hall never wrote a *Perspectives* essay nor headed an office (even if he did end up on the executive committee for two terms). What he did instead was pioneer a new way of working with clients, one that can serve as model of fruitful interaction. As an outgrowth of that, almost an extension of it, he also led the development of the firm's practice in the financial services area, helping banks and insurance companies. When he began that effort in the mid-1980s, clients from financial services represented perhaps 2 or 3 percent of BCG's revenues; today, their share is upward of 25 percent.

A Briton, Hall joined BCG in 1973, after studying economics at Cambridge University for three years and then earning a master's degree from London Business School. From 1975 until 1981 he worked out of the Boston office, where he participated in the collective endeavor, "pushing the boundaries of microeconomic analysis," as he describes it. In that regard, he recalls plotting an experience curve for

General Foods' Kool-Aid. The analysis called for twenty years of economic data and traced all the formula changes in the product, the better to detect how changing costs for, say, Red Dye No. 2 affected overall costs. He also noticed a clear-cut pattern among his colleagues: "Given a choice between a project for a new client in a new industry or grinding away to make sure something actually happened at a client, we would all run off to the new client, it was just so interesting and exciting."

By the time he returned to the London office in 1981, he was growing dismayed. "I observed Bain having phenomenal success," he says, with its promise that a legion of Bainies would be there to help the client for as long as it took to turn strategy into results. Also, he says, "I was beginning to get frustrated at all my terrific output . . . It certainly shaped people's thinking, but I was troubled by the amount that was fully implemented. It began to burn me up, quite significantly, I would say." Hall's British understatement hardly conceals the recalled turmoil. As with many of us in times of suffering, his thoughts turned to his mother.

"My mother was a counselor cum therapist. I was talking with her about the therapeutic model then in place. What I took from that conversation was that what a counselor actually did was help the client understand their own issues and work out their own solutions. The counselor was a facilitator, a structurer of the problem, a prober of questions, but never provided the answer. That was up to the client." Aha, thought Hall.

He had already developed a consulting relationship with the Fläkt Group, a Swedish company that specialized in "environmental control technology," more commonly known as heating and ventilation systems. In 1983, it got a new CEO in the person of Björn Stigson, who was in his early thirties and interested in doing an analysis of all the businesses in Fläkt's portfolio. Hall went to him with a novel proposition.

"I told him, 'We've all had experience of consulting projects that didn't have the impact we hoped for,'" Hall says. "BCG's key skills are around pattern recognition, around understanding second- and third-order impacts [of actions you might take], about drawing analogies from other industries, about rigorous understanding of the microeconomics, and experience working with multiple, different organizations. In some ways, the actual doing of the analysis and collecting of the data is something you the client can do."

"Why don't we adopt a very different model here?" Hall suggested. "Why don't you the client take complete responsibility for that piece of work, and we the consultants will support you, facilitate you in the framing of the analysis, in doing the analysis, in coming up with the conclusions and the implementation plan and processes." But how was that to work, practically? "Why don't you allocate somebody from your organization who you can see five or ten years from now being CEO or a CEO candidate," and put that person in charge? he proposed to Stigson. "Why don't you create the team drawn from the different businesses, a mixture of analysts and project leaders, and BCG will support them in doing the sort of work we ourselves would do in a more traditional consulting relationship?"

Finally, Hall ticked off what he saw as major benefits Fläkt could derive from the new model. "I argued that by doing that, you [the client] will gain from intellectual learning, your managerial and analytical capability will increase. You're going to have far more ownership of the thinking that's been done leading to the recommendation. And you'll have people in place who will have the organizational credibility to lead the implementation process."

The pitch worked. "Maybe because he was Swedish," Hall speculates, "or maybe because he was young, or that we were about the same age." The reaction back at BCG was less sanguine: "It didn't feel to me like a big risk," Hall says, "but everyone else was pretty horrified that I'd gone to that extreme. But I was fed up with the old model." Intellectual and emotional discontent, the engine behind so much of the strategy revolution, strikes again. In the next breath, Hall pays tribute to the freedom "you had as a partner to pursue your own dream." His colleagues also realized that this might be a way to meet the "Bain implementation challenge," he says, even though he thought his approach "couldn't be further from Bain's. The Bain model was much more 'We will deliver this amount of profit improvement to you.' I said, 'We're not going to deliver anything to you. You guys are going to deliver these benefits.'"

The Fläkt engagement proved a success. Stigson got a firm grasp of the diverse set of businesses in his charge and a clear view into their leadership down to the middle-management level. Adjustments were made to the portfolio. "Some parts of the business got fixed," Hall says, "some didn't. But do I feel comfortable that it was a real step forward in getting change to happen? Absolutely." In 1991, Fläkt was in sufficiently good shape to be acquired by ABB Asea Brown Boveri, the global power-equipment company, where Stigson became an executive vice president.

Zakon was impressed enough with Hall's new consulting approach to have him present it to a worldwide partners' meeting. What may have most seized their attention was a slide at the end on which Hall charted revenues from the client, first from the days when he was doing old-style, project-by-project consulting for Fläkt—the proceeds bounced up and down—and then with the new model, when "revenues had gone through the roof," Hall says. "As opposed to it reducing the firm's revenue potential, it actually created a much stronger set of relationships, which increased the demand for our services."

In a *Perspectives* piece, Anthony Habgood, one of Hall's partners in London, summarized the essence of the new approach as "discovered logic," wherein client and consultant together descry the inevitable path forward to be taken. In 1985, Hall decided to try to put the approach to work in financial services, an industry where BCG hadn't had much luck.

Again, he was bucking conventional opinion within the firm. "There was a feeling in the U.S. that strategy was less relevant to financial services," he recalls, "and that bankers were boring." Fueling this

view was a perception—an accurate one—that the typical large banking or insurance company was a complex bureaucracy, where costs
were shared across product lines and tricky issues of allocation
abounded. Such an institution typically lacked the sharp, hierarchical
lines of decision-making authority to be found in a client running, say,
chemical plants or forklift-manufacturing facilities. Besides, McKinsey
seemed to have a lock on the business, dating back, some BCG partners argued, to a bankers' conference in the early 1980s, when the
Firm's Lowell Bryan had first proclaimed the importance of strategy
to the industry.

For his part, Hall saw in the sector's complicated, process- and
committee-driven decision making a good fit with his emerging, more
collaborative consulting approach. He also noted that financial-services
companies, with the progress of deregulation, were beginning to be
freed to compete in new ways and new markets. Many were still fat
from their traditional businesses, though, and brought to the exploration of new possibilities some whopping budgets for consulting.
Confronted with such abundance, and with a clear set of client targets,
Hall was quite willing to pitch BCG's services in competition with
McKinsey's.

He won his first such bake-off with the Bank of Ireland in 1985.
("The Irish are like the Australians," he says. "They're both small
countries, so they're always trawling the world for the best ideas.")
With teams from the bank, BCG did a fairly classic segmentation of the
consumer market for banking services in the United Kingdom, with a
microeconomic analysis of each segment to ascertain its attractiveness,
eventually identifying nine segments. This presaged the course BCG
would take as it pressed further into the industry, concentrating on the
retail side, where the consulting firm's ability to gather and analyze
large collections of data could be most effective. "I stayed as far away as
possible from corporate banking," Hall says, and the merchant and investment varieties, the areas "where you actually had to know something about the banking business."

With the results of the work in hand, the Bank of Ireland launched itself successfully into new businesses—life insurance, mortgages, private banking (to what the industry variously terms "substantial" or "high net-worth" individuals). Hall had also observed what he thought was a tendency among financial-services executives to chat with one another across company lines—an inclination that exceeded what you'd find between competitors in other businesses. The grapevine was soon working in BCG's favor. Soon the firm landed Royal Insurance as a client, BCG's first in that industry. By the end of the 1980s, it was doing work on private banking for the Bank of America and Citigroup, both traditional McKinsey clients. In 1987, John Clarkeson, by then the Boston Consulting Group's chief executive, commissioned Hall to form a "practice area" in financial services, one of six industry-specialized practices launched partly in response to Hall's success.

In its ideal form, Hall's new model of consulting would take an iterative, semi-Socratic dynamic all the way through the project to what might seem its conclusion. There, he put in place another radical innovation, one totally consistent with his philosophy: when the results of the study jointly performed by BCG and the client team were finally presented to senior management or the board, Hall insisted that the presentation be conducted entirely by the client's people (even if the consultants might have written much of it).

Over the next twenty years, as they wrestled with implementation, more consulting firms would adopt some version of working with teams from the client. But the question "Who will make the final presentation?" remains a wonderful test of how seriously they take the idea. Hall, for his part, believed that the answer could become a major source of differentiation between BCG and its principal rivals. "McKinsey will talk about client teams," he argues, "but when push comes to shove, the McKinsey director will be at the board doing a presentation. When push comes to shove, Bain will say *we* are going to improve your profits by a hundred million quid, and you're only going to have to spend seven or eight million quid with us to achieve that." He thinks the cultural difference between the three firms persists to this day. It's a variant on a theme one hears from many quarters. Tom Peters, McKinsey alumnus and he of the belief that 95 percent of a company's behavior derives from its original genetic configuration, maintains that the essence of the Firm's genetic endowment is its image of itself as "counselor to the CEO."

For those favorably inclined toward the democratic, it would be inspiring to be told that David Hall's model swept through BCG and was universally adopted as the right way to work with clients. Inspiring but untrue, given that the very notion runs afoul of the democracy of ideas and entrepreneurship that obtained at the firm, precisely the democracy that allowed Hall to pursue his alternative vision. (Among the reasons he developed it, he told me, was that he "never liked being told what to do." It's a theme so constant among partners of consulting firms as to be almost universal, as commonly voiced as the near-allied "I don't want to be managed" and "I never wanted to have a boss.")

Hall's model was available to his colleagues, and with time, he was given ever-wider and ever-higher platforms from which to commend it, first as head of the financial-services practice area, then as partner in charge of overseeing all the firm's practice areas, then in the 1990s, for two three-year terms as a member of BCG's executive committee. But while the full extent of its reach may not be precisely measurable, what Hall's modus operandi clearly did for BCG was to provide a handhold into a future where client relationships wouldn't be merely project to project, but instead could endure for years.

11.

Breaking the World
into Finer Pieces

IMPLEMENTATION WAS NOT THE only problem dogging the
strategy revolution as it tried to consolidate its gains. The tools
had to be continually sharpened, if not discarded altogether
for something else, as began to become apparent in the 1970s and
by the 1980s was glaringly obvious. The experience curve in particular
needed reexamination. To their surprise, consultants were also
discovering that there appeared to be industries for which low cost
was no guarantee of competitive advantage. Enter the possibilities for
differentiation.

For all that, the bulk of the consultants' work under the banner of
strategy was still about costs, mostly about how to reduce them. With
Michael Porter's introduction of the "value chain" in the mid-1980s,
the necessary intellectual tools would finally be at hand to break down
what a company did, from the purchase of raw materials to delivery of
the finished product, into smaller and smaller pieces, each susceptible
to being costed out and judged on its competitiveness.

THE LORDS OF STRATEGY

Finding the Limits of the
Experience Curve

As a BCG consultant who started at the firm in 1979 observed, "When I joined, virtually all our focus was on the cost side." There was much work to be done in that neighborhood. Early on in their push for more and better data from clients, the consultants had discovered what in retrospect seems a fairly startling fact: almost without exception clients didn't know their own costs, certainly not in enough detail to allow them to accurately allocate a particular cost or share of an overall corporate cost to a particular product. This had the dismal-for-strategy effect of making it impossible to be certain which products were profitable, which not. In the late 1970s, I was told by virtually every consultant I asked that inevitably the first thing that had to be done in any engagement was to recalculate all the client's costs. (Thirty-five years later, some said they were surprised by how often they *still* had to do it.)

Blame this sad state of affairs not on the consultants or management but on the accounting profession. Two heavyweights from the field, professors H. Thomas Johnson and Robert S. Kaplan, provide the best history of its dereliction in their 1987 book *Relevance Lost: The Rise and Fall of Management Accounting*, a critique so dead-on it won an award from the American Accounting Association. The essence of their case was that while accountants and their systems may have provided information useful to those trying to manage the growing industrial giants of the 1920s and 1930s, by the postwar period, their thinking was lagging behind changing realities. The profession's focus had turned almost entirely to analysis for the purposes of financial reporting—making sure their clients' income statements and balance sheets conformed to auditing standards. This meant a neglect of cost accounting—except in the academy, where advances were, well, academic—and a failure to keep up with the information that managers truly needed to make decisions, including decisions on strategy.

By the 1960s and 1970s, it had fallen to the strategy consultants to deliver the probing cost analysis that companies under increasing competitive pressure required. Kaplan, today an even more celebrated member of the HBS faculty, says as much: "In the 1970s, the strategy consulting firms *were* the cost-accounting firms. They succeeded by bypassing the standard costing systems, or lack of costing systems. There's no question that was the origin of activity-based costing"—determining the cost of a product by adding up the costs of each of the activities that actually went in to making it.

By piercing the fog created by traditional accounting, BCG was able to begin looking harder at its own concepts, in particular the experience curve, and at why its consultants couldn't adequately explain what clients were encountering. Harvard Business School's Clayton Christensen, who himself worked at BCG in the early 1980s, studied the evolution of their thinking.

He dates the first wrinkle on the experience curve to the late 1960s, when in a project for a large petrochemical company the consultants found that the most direct casual factor behind cost reductions wasn't accumulating experience per se, but rather an increase in the minimum efficient plant scale as the overall market expanded. A competitor that could afford to build one of the new larger plants could in effect "buy" the experience of the market leader and match its costs.

In the early 1970s, working with clients in the paper and textile industries, the consultants stumbled on an anomaly even more upsetting to the BCG experience-curve orthodoxy: in those domains, there didn't appear to be *any* correlation between market share and lower costs and higher profitability. The explanation turned out to be another variation on scale economies, namely, that in certain industries, no economies were to be gained beyond a certain minimum efficient scale, which could be embodied in, say, a single machine. These were likely to be huge machines, mind you—a papermaking machine whose capacity by itself could account for 1 percent to 2 percent of the market demand—but if you could afford one, you'd be completely cost-competitive with the industry giants. Adding another such machine would only replicate your current cost position, not reduce it any further.

Christensen describes how the BCG consultants built on this insight to develop what they termed the "industry supply curve." The curves, reflecting the difference between the latest entrant's cost and those of established suppliers, were much steeper in some businesses than in others. This helped the consultants explain why in industries where scale didn't confer much advantage—paper, aluminum—companies would sometimes build crackerjack new plants, expecting returns on their investment to exceed 20 to 30 percent, but would see the actual return come in no better than 6 to 8 percent.

The glitch, it turned out, was that prices in such an industry would typically reflect what it took to keep the oldest, highest-cost plants in business running—prices high enough to persuade the plants' owners to keep operating the facilities. The industry's overall profitability would depend on how considerable the cost difference between these marginal plants and those of the lowest-cost manufacturers, presumably the ones with the most current technology and scale. If a competitor added enough new low-cost capacity to drive a couple of the marginal plants out of business, a surprising thing happened: prices collapsed, and those projections of return on investment for the new plants proved hopelessly overoptimistic.

For BCG, the even more worldview-shaking implication of all the anomalies surrounding the experience curve lay in the realization that in assessing the competitive situation of their clients, not all industries were alike. The original, unitary paradigm of strategy, built on the nexus of costs as determined by experience and market share, turned out to obtain in some industries, but not in all. In those where it didn't, participants would have to seek new sources of competitive advantage.

The conceptual device that best captured this realization was another matrix created by Dick Lochridge, which he devised at his breakfast table one morning, he says. It charts what BCG termed

FIGURE 11-1

BCG's competitive environments matrix

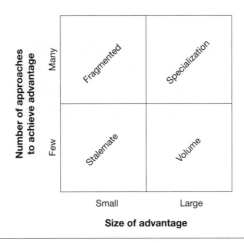

"competitive environments" (figure 11-1) and in some ways echoes the thinking on differentiation Michael Porter laid out in *Competitive Strategy*.

The vertical dimension measures the number of approaches a participant could use to achieve advantage in an industry, from few to many. The horizontal records the size of the advantage that can be achieved, from small to large. The lower right-hand quadrant, where the advantage can be large but the ways to gain it few, represents *volume* industries, those in which gaining "experience" and driving down the curve is still likely to work as a strategy. Automobiles would be an example. In the upper right-hand quadrant, the province of *specialization*, companies can succeed by tailoring their products more precisely to a particular customer segment's needs, and thrive even if they aren't the largest in the business. Think cosmetics.

Either quadrant on the right of the matrix is preferable to the two on the left. A wag might describe the dismal lower-left quadrant, where *stalemate* presided, as the graveyard for companies that might have tried BCG's original ideas and found they didn't work. As in much of the paper business. In this sector, many competitors reached the requisite economies of scale and nobody made much money. *Fragmented* environments were slightly better; you could seek competitive cover in a variety of ways, but none afforded much success. Restaurants were traditionally a fragmented industry, at least before McDonald's turned the low-end stratum into a volume affair.

In a 1981 *Perspectives* piece titled "Strategy in the 1980s"—published a year after Porter's book—Lochridge set out the matrix as part of the argument that the rules of the strategy game had changed. While in the 1960s "increased competition and the internationalization of many industries made cost efficiency and market share critical determinants of success," the 1970s, with high inflation, low growth, and still more internationalization, found that market-share, low-cost strategies "met unexpected difficulty as segment specialists arose and multiple competitors reached economies of scale." In the future, "no simple, monolithic set of rules or strategy imperatives will point automatically to the right course." The growth-share matrix, which Lochridge had helped perfect, had made a "major contribution to strategic thought," but had become "misused and overexposed"—read "commoditized"—sometimes still useful but also potentially "misleading, or worse, a straitjacket."

The trunk of strategy was beginning to send out branches, many of them specific to a particular type of industry. Partly in response, as the 1980s progressed the strategy firms would increasingly build and tout their industry practices, the claim that they already had seen oh-so-many times the competitive ground you were fighting on. We've come a considerable distance from the days when Bruce Henderson would proclaim almost the opposite: that he and his legions, masters of some almost universal truths of microeconomics, were valuable to you precisely because they brought a fresh eye and radical empiricism to your situation.

A bit of something valuable may have been lost along the way, as at least a few veterans of BCG's early days will concede. Call it, as they never would, the consultants' role as flaming sword of the truth, prepared, even eager, to cut through the usual corporate badinage to tell you the facts of your situation, however devastating those might prove to the continuing relationship with the truth bearer.

Alan Zakon proudly tells of what may have been BCG's shortest client engagement. The firm had been retained by Schlitz to help figure out what was going wrong with the brewer's business. Driven by the belief that becoming a low-cost manufacturer was going to be critical to his company's success, the company's CEO had invested millions in plants to in effect industrialize the making of beer, taking the carbonation out at one stage, putting it back in at another. The result wasn't proving popular in the marketplace, though, even at a low price.

The consultants launched their analysis and, with the competitive-environments matrix at hand, quickly reached an unpropitious conclusion. The beer industry of yore, their analysis indicated, had been fragmented, with lots of local breweries serving regional markets. But with the 1950s and 1960s, big competitors like Anheuser-Busch and Schlitz had bought up many of the small operators on the way to turning the industry into a volume business. But now, volume was turning into stalemate, and the future lay with imports and craft beers that would thrive in a milieu of specialists. As the consultants told the CEO, Schlitz's millions of dollars of investment to industrialize beer had been completely ill timed and would never pay out. End of consulting engagement, in a total of something like twenty-eight days.

McKinsey Assembles to Disassemble

Dick Cavanagh, for many years a McKinsey partner before he became head of The Conference Board, puts the matter a little more baldly than most of his erstwhile colleagues would: "McKinsey was always interested in helping our clients figure out ways they could raise prices. I'm not sure that BCG, with its focus on costs, had the same emphasis." Cavanagh's observation raises a distinction, or more precisely a pull between two directions, that we'll see in the evolution of strategy from the 1980s on. On the one hand was the imperative to cut costs now and forever—an imperative born of the experience curve. On the other was the tantalizing prospect of somehow "creating value" for the customer, developing an offering that because of its novelty, special features, or appeal, can command a higher price than the commodity version. Some aspect of creating value lies at the heart of any strategy based on differentiation or specialization.

But can't a company pursue a strategy aimed at creating value and practice ruthless discipline toward costs at the same time? Perhaps some enterprises can—Toyota?—but traditionally, few were as good at both as they were at one or the other. Companies that garner the most public attention often inhabit the extremes of either dimension—a Dell or Wal-Mart among the cost cutters, an Apple or a Whole Foods among the creators of value (and price). Part of the challenge is that value creation, whether in the form of innovation or growth, has never proven as susceptible to systematization as has cost reduction. Ask its champions whether they've succeeded in finding the processes to make innovation a predictable, replicable corporate skill, and they'll generally answer, "Not quite yet." Meanwhile, the engines of Greater Taylorism, with forty years of perfecting the machinery behind them, roll ahead.

McKinsey's slightly wider outlook was reinforced by the nature of its client base, which featured more financial-service and consumer-products companies than did BCG's. A client in that area, then known as the National Association of Food Chains, harbored a belief that manufacturers and distributors, rather than fighting each other, should be finding ways to work together more closely for reasons that, as one partner wryly puts it, Wal-Mart's subsequent success demonstrated. This led to a series of projects that led McKinsey to explore what the consultants came to call the "business system" of the industry.

It's telling that one of the first public expositions of the concept came in a 1980 McKinsey staff paper, "Competitive Cost Analysis." In the paper, the authors proclaimed the importance of trying to figure out your competitor's costs, hardly news to anyone who had been listening to BCG or Bain. What was news was the framework proposed to conduct this analysis.

The McKinsey consultants argued that you needed to identify all the elements that made up the "product delivery system," that is, each component and step that went into making a product and finally getting it to the customer. In a diagram charting these elements, the boffins arrayed them according to what would seem to be their chronological order (figure 11-2).

FIGURE 11-2

McKinsey's business system

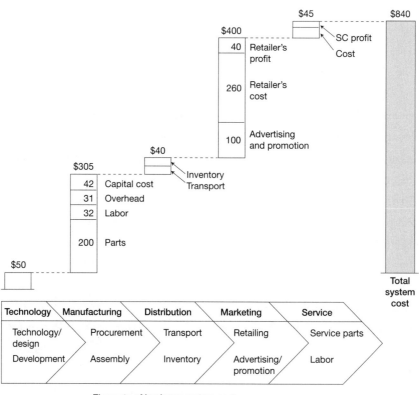

Elements of business system cost

As the consultants outlined it, the business-system framework offered a step-by-step procedure for conducting the analysis required for making a strategy. First, you isolated the costs for each element in the system; this step lets you determine which factors contributed most to the overall cost of the product. You could then contemplate alternative ways to get the work done at each step and how their adoption might change the cost picture.

Such issues were to become the grist of the consultants' mill, even at McKinsey. As one partner describes it, "Ours wasn't a strategy practice in the eighties; it was a microeconomics practice." He distills much of what the Firm did then and still does under the name of strategy as "largely efficiency-based things, broadly about increasing the output per dollar of cost." In other words, Greater Taylorism.

Michael Porter Forges the Value Chain

As Michael Porter's star rose, McKinsey sought a way to put him on its payroll—not to have him leave his teaching position, mind you, but instead to have some sort of continuing relationship for the sharing of ideas and insights. Porter wouldn't bite, though. While he had many discussions about concepts with strategy consultants—not just with the Firm but also with BCG and Strategic Planning Associates—Porter had his eye on a grander platform. In 1983, the same year he won tenure at the HBS, he founded his own consulting firm, Monitor Company, in alliance with five other entrepreneurial types, including brothers Joseph and Mark Fuller. Mark had been an assistant professor at Harvard, teaching some of the overflow sections of Porter's course on strategy. It was at the New Hampshire home of the Fullers' parents that Porter had written the last, crucial chapter of *Competitive Strategy*. The avowed purpose of Monitor was to capitalize on Porter's ideas.

In a magisterial McKinsey staff paper, "Perspectives on Strategy," John Stuckey, for two decades a leader of the Firm's practice in that area, makes an observation fundamental to the issue of implementation. Once you have designed your strategy, he writes, and aligned your organization around it, "the task of executing the strategy remains," obviously. He goes on, in words that probably should be framed and hung on the wall of every corporate conference room where these matters are deliberated: "This means more than just running the business: It generally means changing the business."

It was precisely the question of how to do this that Monitor tackled in its earliest days. The firm's partners saw the effort as an extension of Porter's work on positioning. "You have to mirror those choices you made about positioning into specific actions at the activity level," Joe Fuller says. "The value chain [Porter's second great contribution to strategy] and value system [the broader context for the chain] are frameworks for understanding how those activities have to change in a cost-based strategy or a differentiation strategy in order to implement the strategy you derived from your discussion of the market."

In 1985, using in part the work he had done with his Monitor colleagues, Porter published *Competitive Advantage*, which was significantly subtitled *Creating and Sustaining Superior Performance*. It was to prove another landmark in the history of strategy. As he wrote in an introduction to the 1998 edition, at the heart of the book is its conception of a company as consisting of all the "discrete activities" it performs—"processing orders, calling on customers, assembling products, and training employees"—activities more sharply defined than traditional "functions" like marketing or R&D "are what generate cost and create value for buyers; they are the basic units of competitive advantage."

In a footnote nodding at the craze for business-process reengineering (a craze that had come, and largely gone, since the publication of the first edition), Porter said that "processes" were sometimes a synonym for "activities." Thus, if activity-based analysis is the first step toward begetting change, which in turn is the key to implementing strategy, then the publication of *Competitive Advantage* clearly marks the handoff from strategy's first phase, about positioning, to its second, focused on processes.

Thinking about your business as the sum of its disparate activities might seem a recipe for madness. What gave Porter's book its punch and its wonderful utility—fodder for innumerable PowerPoint presentations, one probably being conducted near you right now—was the organizing principle it supplied for all these goings-on, namely, the value chain. The concept, *mirabile dictu*, arrays all the activities by which you create value in roughly the order that you do them (figure 11-3).

Even the not-especially-attentive reader may by this point have been reminded of the McKinsey business system (and perhaps, slightly, of Adam Smith). If there were an award for the most famous footnote in management literature, a strong candidate would be the first one in chapter 2 of Porter's book. Among McKinsey veterans, mere mention of it still causes certain sets of teeth to grind. In this footnote, the professor acknowledged that the business-system concept "captures the

FIGURE 11-3

Porter's value chain

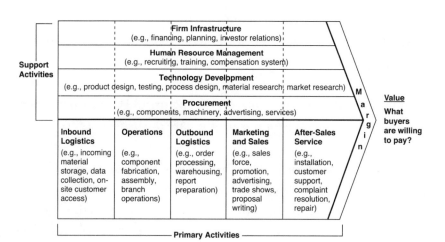

Source: Michael E. Porter, *On Competition, Updated and Expanded Edition* (Boston: Harvard Business School Press, 2008).

idea that a firm is a series of functions (e.g., R&D, manufacturing, channels), and that analyzing how each is performed relative to competitors can provide useful insights." He also conceded that McKinsey "stresses the power of redefining the business system to gain competitive advantage, an important idea."

But then, in two quick sentences, Porter contrasted the system to his own ideas and dismissed its relevance to the rest of his discussion, which would go on for five hundred pages: "The business system concept addresses broad functions rather than activities"—McKinsey hadn't chopped the pieces small enough, apparently—"and does not distinguish among types of activities or show how they're related." Really?

McKinsey's lingering dismay may reflect nothing so much as the unarguable truth that today, any literate businessperson is familiar with the concept of the value chain, while few beyond its original partisans recall the business system. But then, McKinsey didn't provide the lavish, detailed, and exhaustive exposition of its idea that Porter did of his. The value chain, with its supporting analytic apparatus, may be the last central, universal concept in the intellectual history of strategy, at least as of this writing, in the sense that it has to be taken into account in any company's deliberations on what it should be doing. *Competitive Advantage*, far more than Porter's earlier book, *Competitive Strategy*, represents a compendium almost breathtaking in its reach of the best thinking on strategy up until then, as well as a brilliant anticipation of many of the issues that would engage and challenge practitioners in the decades that followed. It provides the intellectual template for the age of breaking the world into pieces.

Just by putting the notion of creating value at the center of his argument, Porter helped yank discourse on strategy up from its nose-to-the-descending-curve focus on costs. In addition to its treatment of cost advantage as a strategy, with lists of lots of ways to achieve it, the book fleshes out the second generic strategy identified in *Competitive Strategy*, differentiation. Along the way it consigns focus, the other generic strategy mentioned there, to a subset of differentiation aimed at a particular set of "buyer needs." As Porter defines it, differentiation represents both a fairly baggy catchall and a residual: "A firm differentiates itself from its competitors when it provides something unique that is valuable to buyers beyond simply offering a low price." Such a strategy might enable you to charge a higher price for your product—for example, McKinsey's Golconda—or sell more than others, or garner greater loyalty from your customers.

What gives the value-chain concept power beyond the clouds of lists it comes trailing is the invitation it provides to think about the links, the different activities that make it up, in isolation or in wider combinations. How did your company's performance of activity X measure up to your competitors' in terms of cost or value delivered?

We've already encountered Bain & Company's ever-more-aggressive pursuit of best practices—from best demonstrated practices to best competitive practices to best feasible practices. For aficionados of best practices—and their ranks grew steadily throughout the 1980s—the value chain is heaven. At last, a framing device by which they could isolate every single component activity that went into the making of a product, breaking up the overall process into "best-practice-able" units, if you will, ones that could be benchmarked against other divisions, other companies, even other industries, that were performing the same activity.

In this respect, the value chain lined up perfectly with the quality movement, which took off in the 1980s as American companies found themselves bested by Japanese competitors and turned for help to the likes of W. Edwards Deming and Joseph Juran. By the end of the decade, organizations such as the American Productivity and Quality Center were offering huge libraries of best practices elicited from their member companies.

Competitive Advantage was prescient in devoting an entire chapter to technology and how changes in it could alter the activities that made up a company's value chain and determined its competitive position. By the early 1980s, the subject loomed ever larger in the corporate consciousness. In the 1960s and 1970s, minicomputers from the likes of Digital Equipment Corporation had supplanted many a mainframe; now, networks of personal computers—a device named *Time* magazine's Person of the Year for 1982—were supplanting them. Porter noted that information technology figured particularly large in value chains since each step along the way both used and created information. But he also pointed to the disruptive effects new technology could have on manufacturing as well as on transportation and logistics, prefiguring the way in which supply-chain management would insinuate itself into more and more discussions of strategy.

Porter was timely, too, in raising the point that for a competitive advantage to lead to corporate performance better than the norm, it had to be sustainable. He doesn't do much with this notion, but others, principally Pankaj Ghemawat, would go on to explore in illuminating detail the importance of sustainability. First in a 1986 *Harvard Business Review* article and then in his 1991 book, *Commitment*, Ghemawat reported just how fleeting advantage typically was, much more so than its proprietors imagined. His study of nine hundred business units showed that "nine-tenths of the profitability differential between businesses that were initially above average and those that were initially below average vanished over a ten-year period." The question of what made this so took on all the more urgency as, in the opinion of most experts who studied the question, advantage was being competed away ever more quickly, the useful life of a strategy declining markedly with changes in the economy. Capitalism was becoming fiercer.

Perhaps the most threatening of the changes under way, at least to the chief executives, was the steadily building pressure on companies to do something to raise the price of their stock. As became ever more evident as the 1980s turned into the 1990s, if the CEOs didn't, someone else would step in to do the job in their place. As part of its fiercening, capitalism was setting up a struggle to see who was prepared to do the tough work of strategy—selling off underperforming businesses, taking on debt, cutting costs.

12.

The Wizards of Finance Disclose Strategy's True Purpose

WHAT IS A COMPANY FOR? To what end do we create and toil in such entities? Nowadays, for most who give any thought to the matter, the answer seems boringly obvious: the purpose of a corporation is to enrich its owners, usually its shareholders. But in fact, agreement on this point has been arrived at only recently, starting in the 1980s largely as the product of newly discovered opportunities to make money. The strategy revolution in itself didn't lead to the triumph of shareholder capitalism, but those leading its charge seized on strategy's tenets as precisely the intellectual underpinnings they needed for their battle plans. In particular, they loved Greater Taylorism. The resultant combination has been the biggest single force making for the fiercening of capitalism.

Getting one's mind straight on these matters requires dispensing with illusions, including some best-sellers. As we've seen, McKinsey's

Dick Foster, coauthor of *Creative Destruction*, doesn't much believe in the idea of excellent companies. Having thought on the subject for over two decades, including his time counseling Enron's board and helping start the Firm's practice advising private equity outfits, he worries that the very hypothesis can lead to confusion about the ultimate purpose of strategy: "The thought of corporate strategy presumes some sort of strategy to do what, and that's a harder question than people have given it credit for. There are two ways of thinking about the objective of strategy. One [coming from those still in search of excellence] is that this company is going to be a great place, and it's going to produce these great products, and suppliers are going to love dealing with it, and it's going to spin off economic value, but basically, this is going to be a great and enduring institution." Foster immediately dismisses this as "a wistful notion"—sweet, sentimental, and completely wrongheaded.

"The other approach," he says, "is, 'To hell with all that. I just want it to produce money for shareholders. This is capitalism, and in capitalism, the shareholder is at the top of the evolutionary tree, and we should return profits to shareholders.'" Foster grinds the point in: "Is that the same as running this excellent, enduring institution that has white Doric columns out front? I don't think it is." In the course of the 1980s, most of the rest of the world, at least the parts that controlled investment dollars, came to agree with his preference for the uncolumned alternative.

In retrospect, it's remarkable how little attention strategy paid to shareholders in its first twenty years. Comb through the early BCG *Perspectives*, for example, and you'll find barely a nod to them. If pressed for an answer to Foster's question—"Strategy to do what?"—most consultants and practitioners would probably have sputtered a bit and then answered, "Well, to achieve competitive advantage, of course."

Today, there are still those who argue that the single-minded focus on the shareholder need not have prevailed, indeed should not have prevailed. The recent global financial crisis has added to their ranks, though for how long remains unclear. This school of thought sees shareholder capitalism as short-sighted, smacking of greed, and in the end unrealistic in that it fails to take into account other constituencies or—the preferred term—stakeholders that a corporation's actions necessarily touch, namely, the company's employees, customers, suppliers, and home communities. While this broader view continues to have adherents, mainly outside the United States—in Germany, for example, it's enshrined in corporate law—over the long pull their number dwindled as strategy spread its reach. (Even if market collapses like those of 2008 give temporary cheer to the revanchists.) The first part of this chapter will seek to explain why and how the shareholder's interest became dominant in calculations of corporate strategy.

The rest will trace out the surprisingly mixed fortunes of the consultants who took the gospel of shareholder wealth most to heart. New firms grew up with alarming lessons to impart, only to find that sounding one note, albeit a terrifying bass note, wasn't enough to sustain them. Bain & Company, the strategy firm most avid in pursuing stock-price-improving "results" for its clients, would grow wildly with the trend, overtaking BCG. Then, through overreaching by both clients and consultants, the firm would almost go out of business.

Making a Market in Corporate Control

Why didn't strategy focus more on shareholder wealth before the early 1980s? Foster provides the best single-sentence answer: "Because before then, there wasn't any shareholder wealth." He exaggerates, but not by much. As we noted earlier in the book, after a glorious bull-market run in the 1960s, the Dow Jones Industrial Average finally reached 1,000 in 1972 and then promptly collapsed, not to return to that high until 1982. From then, though, after climbing out of the deep recession of 1981–1982, stocks would begin a surprisingly steady ascent to the breathtaking, if wobbly, heights of the past few years.

As sharp-eyed types increasingly realized, there was money to be made in owning stocks and perhaps even more in taking over companies, knocking them into strategic shape, and then scooping up the rewards.

At least a half a dozen forces converged to make this possible, freeing a tide of money to flow into the stock market and creating a market in corporate control. Among the first was an innovation that squarely addressed a problem that had constrained strategy for years, namely, how a company was to finance its strategic initiatives. Think of the growth-share matrix and its premise that most companies would need to balance their portfolio of businesses, using the cash thrown off by some businesses to fund others. Though this assumption was once perhaps reasonable, it was markedly less so in the late 1970s, after the creation of the modern less-than-investment-grade high-yield corporate security, that is, the junk bond.

There's so much so-called junk out there currently—by one estimate, the bonds of 95 percent of U.S. companies with annual revenues north of $35 million are rated below investment grade—we may too easily forget how few companies were able to sell their debt to the public before its advent. The small market that existed for less-than-investment-grade bonds was confined to "fallen angels," securities whose ratings had seen better days. Even those companies that did command a triple-A rating were often constrained by born-of-the-Depression notions that borrowing was somehow suspect. IBM made its first public offering of debt only in 1979.

All this began to change in the late 1970s when some of the smaller, more venturesome investment-banking firms began underwriting original issues of junk bonds. First Bear Stearns and then, famously, Drexel Burnham and its wonder boy, Michael Milken, convinced investors—insurance companies, the savings-and-loan industry—that the risk of default from such securities wasn't that high, particularly when measured against the superior rates of return they offered. The total size of the junk bond market in the United States mushroomed from around $30 billion in 1980, to $136 billion in 1986, to $242 billion in 1989.

Issuers found many uses for the money raised by the sale of their bonds—some uses of greater respectability than others, but all making for a more competitive world. Entrepreneurial upstarts such as Compaq Computer Corporation, McCaw Cellular, MCI, and Turner Broadcasting used them to fund their growth and a pop-you-with-a-new-technology competitive threat posed to the likes of IBM, AT&T, and the broadcast networks. But the most famous role for junk bonds, and the biggest source of their raffish reputation—even if it represented only about 10 percent of the total volume issued—was in funding takeovers, attempted takeovers, and leveraged buyouts.

For our story, what's striking about the merger wave of the 1980s is how much of it was carried out in keeping with the basic principles of strategy, specifically, its emphases on treating your company as a portfolio of businesses that might be bought or sold, placing your bets where you had a competitive advantage, and using debt to finance the effort. Conglomerates fell out of favor in the quest for greater focus.

The level of activity in the buying and selling of companies was extraordinary, more than ten thousand deals between 1982 and 1988. These aggregate numbers don't do justice, though, to how terrifyingly large the threat of takeover loomed in many executive suites, or how much incentive it provided for companies to finally carry out the dictates of strategy. For that, you need the figures calculated by professors Andrei Shleifer and Robert Vishny: "Of the 500 largest industrial corporations in the U.S. in 1980"—the *Fortune* 500, in other words—"at least 143 or 28 percent had been acquired by 1989."

Working both sides of that street and contributing to the menace but also providing a buyer for businesses that might be dragging the company down was another relatively new player on the scene, the leveraged-buyout (LBO) firm, precursors of today's private equity outfits. People such as Jerry Kohlberg had been doing so-called bootstrap deals at least since the 1960s, borrowing the money to purchase an unwanted business from a willing corporate seller; giving the management big financial incentives, including an ownership share, to make the operation more profitable; and then selling it off after a few years, either to the public or to what became known as a "strategic buyer," a company that thought the operation would complement its own existing businesses. By the late 1970s, individuals who had been doing such deals found enough lender and investor support to constitute themselves as firms dedicated to the LBO business. Kohlberg Kravis Roberts (KKR) was founded in 1976, Forstmann Little in 1978, and Clayton Dubilier concentrated its efforts on LBOs in the same year.

The creators of the LBO movement were predominantly financiers, not experts on strategy—the conspicuous exception being Bain Capital, which raised its first fund in 1984—but the push they gave to the work of strategy earns them a place in our history. At the most basic level, their efforts demonstrated that there was significant value to be wrung out of underappreciated corporate assets. Their focus on cash as the key indicator to watch in assessing a business was, of course, an idea the lords of strategy had been championing since the 1960s.

And if Bruce Henderson had inveighed that companies should take on more debt than did their competitors, the success of the LBO outfits finally proved the point: they were all about debt; that's why their undertaking had *leveraged* as its first name. To acquire a business, firms such as KKR would put in a small amount of their own money and their investors', borrow lots more from banks—Bankers Trust was a favorite lender—and then finance the rest through the sale of junk bonds, typically with the help of Drexel Burnham. Institutional investors didn't seem to mind the fees charged by LBO artists, given the returns the investors were earning. Many swarmed to take part in the successive funds the LBO firms raised—pools of money for investment, usually with a time horizon of five to seven years for returns to be realized.

Their participation reflected a broader trend, what some have called the institutionalization of the stock market. Increasingly, the owners of stocks would be not individuals but institutions—insurance companies, banks, pension funds, and a relatively new phenomenon, mutual funds—so much so that by 2003, institutional investors would own almost 60 percent of outstanding equities.

Such investors differed from mom-and-pop types, many of whom had been washed out of the market by its dismal performance after 1972. The new investors' money was run by professional managers, often business-school graduates armed with the latest analytical techniques, whose compensation and continued employment depended on the financial success of the portfolios they oversaw. Such big investors suffered some constraints not afflicting Mom and Pop. For example, if their holdings in a particular company became sufficiently large, and if that company's stock-price performance proved disappointing, it was difficult for them to just sell their shares and skulk away without having a nasty effect on their portfolio's value.

Over time, this led some to become activist investors—while *active* is almost always judged as better than *passive*, the label *activist* usually means that somebody thinks you're going too far—lobbying for better corporate governance and, slightly less overtly, an improved stock price. The California Public Employees Retirement System (CalPERS) is the most famous example; by 1990, it was targeting firms for criticism specifically for substandard market performance. More pressure on management.

The spectacular returns rung up by the LBO outfits attracted the attention of not only institutional investors but also—in what may have been the weirdest turn in the story—the companies' incumbent management, which decided that it too deserved a shot at the riches to be achieved through restructuring. In 1985, Ed Finklestein, the CEO of the Macy's department store chain (and a Harvard MBA), decided that the company's prospects of continuing as a public company weren't sufficiently lucrative apparently, and he worked a deal to buy the company and take it private for $4.5 billion. Fred Eckert, then head of LBO activity at Goldman Sachs, said of the knock-on effect of the deal: "Suddenly, every CEO looked at what Ed Finklestein stood to

THE LORDS OF STRATEGY

make on the transaction and what it had done to his organization to spread stock around to 300 executives, and all those CEOs said, 'I want to get in on this.' Then we had the start of a runaway train."

The usual explanation, or cover story, proffered by the CEO went something like this: "The stock market doesn't understand us. To unleash the value latent in the company, we need to free ourselves from its scrutiny, constraints, and short-term pressure while at the same time providing our managers with greater incentives more closely tied to increasing the value of our assets." A cynic might have trouble distinguishing this from the assertion "We need to be paid more and to be given a greater ownership stake, to do the things that we already knew we ought to do to increase the value of the company, in part thanks to the insights of strategy, but found just too unpleasant, or tough, to contemplate."

In a backhanded way, both versions of this notion found support in academic quarters. Trained at the University of Chicago and to an extent walking in the shoes of its famous son Milton Friedman, economists such as Eugene Fama, William Meckling, and, most notably, Michael Jensen revived what was known as agency theory. Starting from the premise that the purpose of a company was to maximize value for its shareholders, they argued that managers, particularly those without large ownership stakes in the corporation, often had motives and interests different from those of shareholders. (For a list of same, you need only consult Ken Andrews's *Concept of Corporate Strategy*.) Such managers needed the discipline imposed by an active market for corporate control, including the threat of takeover, to keep their unsteady gaze fixed on the main chance, that is, the pocketbooks of their shareholders.

Jensen raised a storm, making this case in a *Harvard Business Review* article in 1984. Then, just as the LBO movement was peaking in 1989, he upped the intellectual ante even further in another *HBR* piece, "The Eclipse of the Public Corporation." As summarized by the publisher's blurb, it maintained that the "publicly held corporation had outlived its usefulness in many sectors of the economy," a change manifested by the growing number of "takeovers, leveraged buyouts, and other going-private transactions." Jensen's article won the McKinsey Award for best article of the year. LBO firms celebrated his work and handed out copies, just as he had celebrated theirs. In 1985, Jensen joined the faculty of Harvard Business School. With his new colleagues, there he established an elective course, The Coordination and Control of Markets and Organizations. Incorporating his ideas about corporate purpose, the course was to rival Porter's strategy offerings in its popularity. Thus was the twig of the modern Harvard MBA bent.

As matters turned out, just about the same time Jensen published his second *HBR* article, it was the LBO, not the public corporation, that was proving to have outlived its usefulness, at least until its revival a decade later under the name of private equity. The LBO's high-water mark was the fight for RJR Nabisco at the end of 1988, pitting a management group led by CEO Ross Johnson against KKR, which ultimately prevailed with a bid of $24.7 billion. The very fact that LBO deals had grown so mammoth pointed at some of the problems that eventually undercut their success: many of the smaller, higher-quality LBO possibilities had already been exhausted, competition for deals had intensified, and as one expert observed, the junk-bond market had finally begun "to sag under its own weight." As interest rates rose and the likelihood of refinancing troubled LBOs diminished, pressures increased to break up acquired companies as quickly as possible to capture the value from the resale of their assets.

After wobbling in 1988, the wheels began to come off both the LBO and the junk-bond juggernauts in 1989. After being tarred by scandals attending some individual rascals—Dennis Levine, Marty Siegel, Ivan Boesky—Drexel Burnham agreed late in 1988 to pay a $650 million fine to settle charges against the firm. Michael Milken was indicted in March 1989, pleading guilty the following year to six felony charges in a plea bargain, this only a couple months after Drexel declared bankruptcy. Even worse for investors in LBOs, some deals had begun to go seriously bad, unable to restructure the debt they owed and forced into bankruptcy, including the KKR-engineered purchase of the assets of Jim Walter Corp. Finklestein's Macy's would follow a bit later, declaring bankruptcy in 1992.

But if the danger of a hostile takeover by some junk-bond-fueled buccaneer had abated by the end of the decade, the work of installing shareholder wealth as the ultimate desideratum for all corporate activity—including strategy—was largely complete. In his book *From Higher Aims to Hired Hands*, Harvard's Rakesh Khurana provides an eloquent account of how managerial capitalism was supplanted by investor capitalism starting in the 1980s. The former had at its apex a cadre of managers running large organizations. According to the ideal, they were respected by the public, concerned with the wider good—including the multiple constituencies of their corporations—and sometimes possessed of the aspiration that management could constitute a profession much like medicine or law. The latter saw the only goal of the corporation as increasing shareholder wealth.

I wish I could agree with Khurana on how close management ever came to being a profession, or how susceptible it is to professionalization. (The field has always been too open to untrained upstarts, and always should be.) But his evidence for the triumph of shareholder capitalism seems unequivocal. In particular, he quotes two contrasting statements from the Business Roundtable, an organization of the CEOs of the largest U.S. companies; its members' pronouncements carry the heaviest of weight on matters of corporate policy and governance. In 1990, the Roundtable, admittedly still a bit behind the sharpies on Wall Street, intoned that "corporations are chartered to serve both the shareholders and society as a whole" and then proceeded to list the other stakeholders whose interests needed to be considered. By 1997, the tune had changed: "In the Business Roundtable's view, the paramount duty of management and of boards of directors is to the corporation's stockholders," in the same statement detailing the weakness of the stakeholder model, principally the "absence of an overall objective function"—something nice and concrete like, say, the company's stock price—with which to weigh trade-offs between stakeholders.

The killer argument for shareholder primacy, still capable of ending discussions of the matter, is, of course, property rights. As in, "But wait a minute, who *owns* the company?" In corners like the editorial pages of the *Wall Street Journal*, voices began to be heard trumpeting the new, more broad-based version of shareholder capitalism, in which companies were owned not just by top-hat-wearing plutocrats but by the vast reaches of the middle class. The story was true on one level—by 2006, nearly half of U.S. households owned mutual funds, with the majority of their holdings in equity funds, compared with less than 6 percent in 1980.

But the picture became more complicated once you got beneath the image of the happy, sweater-clad family sitting around the hearth contemplating their latest funds statement. Most households held some or all of their funds through 401(k) retirement plans. And whether the money was being run by a mutual fund, by a retirement fund, or through layers of both, it was in the hands of those professional managers whose inclination was less and less to buy, sit cozily by the fire, and hold. In his 1996 book, *The Loyalty Effect*, Bain's Fred Reichheld lamented that investor loyalty, measured by how long owners held on to a stock, was dropping precipitously. In 1960, he observed, a typical share on the New York Stock Exchange would have traded once in seven years; by the mid-1990s, that figure was down to two years, with the average publicly held company in the United States experiencing "investor churn" of more than 50 percent a year. Nowadays, the average holding period for a NASDAQ stock is less than six months.

The goal for corporate managers had become clear—to increase the value of the company, as reflected in its stock price—and fast. Strategy was taking on ever greater urgency.

Prophets of Destruction

The increasing clarity around strategy's purpose did not work a revolution in what most consulting firms did from day to day. The inertia was a measure of both how entrenched traditional conceptions of strategy had become among their clientele and of how unmessianic and comfortable they themselves had grown, helping familiar clients with the Big Problem du jour (so what if it fell a bit short of strategic?).

But new firms were started up with the explicit goal of helping companies increase the value of their stock—Marakon Associates in 1978, the Alcar Consulting Group in 1979, Stern Stewart & Co. in 1982. Unlike BCG or Bain, their work was rooted not in a probe of the client's competitive situation, but rather in a long crawl down through its finances, akin to the bankerly credit analysis some of these firms' founders had conducted before becoming consultants, but deeper. Much of what they concluded tallied with what the strategy outfits had been preaching. On four fronts, though, the newcomers did enlarge the discussion.

First, when others weren't doing so, the new arrivals banged the drum for the proposition that management's focus had to be on building value for shareholders, arguing that most companies were missing this point as the ever-more-active market for corporate control demonstrated. Their mantra was value-based management, or VBM. Second, they pushed further the argument that stock prices were largely determined by cash flows investors expected from the company, not by reported earnings.

Their third, and perhaps most eye-catching point was their explication of the idea that while some of a company's businesses served to increase its stock price, others might actually be dragging the price down, or, in the ominous phrase the consultants used, "destroying value." This alarming possibility derived from finance theory, specifically from the concepts of economic profits or residual income. Boiled down, the assertion was that to arrive at a true estimate of a business's profitability, you had to deduct from its revenues not just the usual costs, but also a charge for the capital tied up in the business.

What gave this proposition much of its oomph was the granularity with which the consultants proposed to pursue it, that is, their claim that they could calculate the economic profit for each of the client's businesses, not just the company overall. To figure out the true cost of capital for your wing-nut division, for example, you might try to benchmark it against others in the business, including so-called pure players who produced nothing else.

What you might find to your horror—and the consultants claimed they often did find—was that while you had four divisions that were producing economic profit, you had three others that, when measured properly (that is, with a consultant's help), were not. And while these unprofitable divisions were failing to earn their cost of capital, they were also eating up corporate investment dollars that should have gone into the profitable businesses that were propping up your stock price. Foolish you had, in fact, been trying to grow the turkeys according to the conventionally calculated earnings their proud managers reported.

No, the consultants counseled, sell off the turkeys and you may see something of a miracle: even as your company grows smaller, as measured by its revenues, your stock price will increase. In the businesses you retain, to further boost your stock price—and the fourth of the value consultants' innovative emphases—tie managers' compensation explicitly to how much economic profit their operations generate and to increases in that profit.

Some traditional strategy consultants would deride the VBM approach as little more than elaborate financial benchmarking. It might show you how the economic profit earned by your businesses measured up to competitors' profit, they said, but it didn't tell you anything about how to improve that profit beyond the obvious suggestion that it might help to cut your costs. Occasionally acidulous Gary Hamel, whose star would rise over the 1990s, declared much of the work that went on under the VBM banner merely "teaching remedial math to middle managers."

But a number of large companies embraced the gospel, a few quite publicly. Probably the most celebrated was Coca-Cola, a sometime client of Marakon's, whose CEO Roberto Goizueta would tell *Fortune* in 1990 that he pondered how to improve value for shareholders "from the time I get up in the morning to the time I go to bed. I even think about it when I'm shaving." After becoming chief executive in 1981, Goizueta and his team moved to increase market share and beverage sales, introducing new products and accelerating Coke's overseas sales push. He sold off most of the company's nonbeverage businesses, which seemed to have the smell of turkey about them, to concentrate on soft drinks, with their high margins and returns, and he scoured operations for productivity improvements. Coca-Cola's market value, $4.3 billion on Goizueta's ascension to the top job, soared to $59.3 billion by the end of 1992, making the Cuban-born patrician a celebrity whose face on the cover of a business magazine would sell thousands of extra copies.

Value-based metrics themselves burst brightest onto the public consciousness in a 1993 *Fortune* cover story touting the virtues of EVA, or economic value added, the version of economic profit that served as the centerpiece for the Stern Stewart firm's share-price-building methodology (so much so that it trademarked the acronym, as it relentlessly reminded every journalist who used the three letters without proper notation). As Michael Jensen would later note, "The *Fortune* story really put EVA on the map as the leading management tool." Ironically, though, even before the *Fortune* article, some of the original consultant advocates of VBM were bumping up against the limits of their frameworks.

In its brief online history of itself, Marakon talks about how in the late 1980s, its partners realized that while their metrics "unlocked enormous value," they weren't much help with "forward-looking investments"—presumably the best kind—so they needed to broaden their practice. By the early 1990s, Marakon decided that increasing value required new information, including the "best available market, competitor, and profitability data"—precisely the fodder of traditional strategy consulting—so it broadened its practice some more. By subsequently adding an "organizational component" to tackle issues such as executive compensation and then "leadership" to make sure the firm was working at the appropriate executive level, by the end of the decade Marakon had built itself into "one of the world's premier strategy consulting firms," albeit one about a twentieth the size of McKinsey. Meanwhile, in 1992, competitor Alcar had been folded into LEK, a consultancy founded in the early 1980s by three refugees from Bain & Company. For its part, Stern Stewart, the masters of EVA, would tell *Fortune* in a 1998 article that it was basically a financial advisory firm and that it had decided not to engage in "strategy consulting."

Bain & Company Flies Too Close to the Sun

There is a theory—Canadian scholar Danny Miller lays it out nicely in a 1991 book, *The Icarus Paradox*—that when companies truly get into the deepest trouble, it's usually not because of their weaknesses but rather because of their strengths. Or more specifically, it's because they tend to overdo the very energies, inclinations, and expertise that brought them success. Think of Enron and its manic quest to introduce markets, deal making, and new financial instruments to one sector of the energy business after another.

Ever since its founding, Bain & Company gloried in getting results, not writing reports. From the early 1980s on, the firm took as the principal measure of its success on this front—and the one touted loudest to potential customers—the degree to which its clients' stock-price appreciation exceeded that of other companies in the industry and the market overall: a perfect message for the 1980s, in other words, and one that BCG and McKinsey couldn't or wouldn't quite match.

As part of its MO of working with just one competitor in an industry, but doing so for years potentially, Bain also had a tendency to insert many teams and many people into a client company, so much so that the boundary between employee and consultant sometimes became unclear. As one early partner recalls proudly of his engagement with a major client, "They treated me as if I were a member of senior management."

Both of these tendencies were on display conspicuously in Bain's work with Guinness, an assignment that Bill Bain describes in many respects as the best piece of consulting that his firm did in its first fifteen years. It was also the consulting engagement that would nearly cause the demise of Bain & Company and help precipitate the ouster of its founder.[1]

In 1981, a veteran executive named Ernest Saunders had been recruited from Nestlé to become managing director of Guinness, a publicly traded company still dominated by the Guinness family. What he found as he moved into the top job was a dog's breakfast of a company, and an ailing dog at that: a spree of acquisitions had left Guinness owning some 250 businesses, but with no one at headquarters and no centralized management accounting system capable of telling the new chief which businesses were doing well and which were not. Guinness was still brewing up the stout for which it was best known, but even sales of that were declining and the company's stock price had bumped down the stairs to reach a low of fifty pence per share. Saunders went shopping for a consultant to help him out and, after auditioning a few others, approached Bain & Company—not the other way around, as the firm takes pains to point out.

In many respects, Saunders and his company represented an ideal client for Bain. He was clearly what Bain called "our kind of guy," in the consultants' estimation a smart, experienced, self-confident executive ambitious to work major change and unencumbered by any prior history with the company he headed. He presided over a bewildering portfolio of businesses. And, for all the fame of its St. James Gate Brewery in Dublin, his company was headquartered in London, where Bain & Company had just opened an office, part of a very tentative initial push to explore the possibility of becoming more global.

Saunders hired Bain, and soon the consultants had him up on the mountaintop, showing him the vast landscape of what they could do for his company. One of the first points they agreed on was that Guinness sorely needed a management-accounting system and people to run it, which talent would be hard to attract, given Guinness's less-than-effervescent reputation. In a departure from the firm's normal practice, Bain allowed Saunders to install one of Bain's own consultants, a young Frenchman named Olivier Roux, in the role of comptroller, overseeing the company's accounting, even as Roux remained on the Bain payroll. Roux took on the job and, over the next four years, as the work that Guinness and Bain did together succeeded mightily, moved into ever-more-important executive roles within the company, overseeing its finances and eventually taking a seat on its board of directors.

Ask Bill Bain today what he might have done different over the course of his career, and few possibilities occur to him, only one in connection with Guinness: he would not have seconded—he's careful to use the British pronunciation for this use of the term—Roux to hold an official position at the client company. He says he thought the move acceptable in part because of an encounter with a McKinsey consultant who told of being seconded to a New York City agency the firm was doing work for. And Saunders, harried and working extraordinary hours, had been persistent, almost desperate in his pleas to Bain for the help.

More than one Bain partner has said that the key to making one's name at the firm was to build up a client relationship until it represented many millions of dollars a year in revenues. (Not that this hurts your chances at BCG or McKinsey, either.) While Olivier Roux wasn't even the senior-most Bain consultant working with Guinness, his presence within the client did nothing to restrain the size of the engagement. By 1986, Bain was billing Guinness up to $2 million a month, with seventy to eighty consultants working at the client. That year, Roux's own compensation from Bain totaled $650,000, more than that of Saunders, who was by then chairman and CEO of his company. In describing why the consulting engagement with Guinness proved such a success, Bill Bain notes that in most instances, the client at some point cites "the budget"—what it's prepared to spend on consulting— as a constraint on what might be undertaken. At Guinness, he says, that never happened.

Judged by the increase in its stock price, Guinness more than got its money's worth. Within months of coming aboard, Bain had helped Saunders develop a three-phase strategy for righting his company. First, cut costs, staunch the bleeding from current operations, and look to rationalize the portfolio. Then, restore the brewing business. Finally, begin to grow again through acquisitions. As reported in a 1987 *Fortune* article, the effort stepped off smartly: "Within two years of retaining Bain, Guinness had sold off 150 companies, imposed one of the tightest financial control systems in Britain, and revitalized Guinness stout."

By 1984, Guinness was ready to start making acquisitions, in part driven by fear that in the merger-crazy atmosphere of the time, if it didn't get bigger, another company might acquire it. Saunders drew Bain deeply into the process, not only preparing a list of candidates and vetting them but, in the person of Roux, actually negotiating bids, working them up with investment bankers and lawyers and pitching their merits to bankers and the press. In its research, Bain did its usual, dizzyingly thorough job. Of its study of Arthur Bell & Sons, a scotch whiskey maker that Guinness would ultimately win in a takeover battle, Saunders would testify, "Bain had done an extremely detailed analysis on the scotch whiskey business as a whole and on Bells in particular. I would say that having subsequently looked at what information Bells had when [we] acquired it that, through the work done by Bain, we had far more information and knew far more about Bells than it did itself."

By 1986, profits at Guinness were up sixfold from what they had been when Saunders started work there, and the stock price had increased from the dollar equivalent of $0.81 in 1981 to $5.75 a share. It was in fact the stock price, or more precisely the need to prop it up, that would lead Saunders to ruin, and Bain & Company close to it.

In 1985, shortly after closing the deal for Bells, Saunders learned that the British supermarket chain Argyll was contemplating a bid for Distillers, a company that was much larger than Guinness. Owner of a panoply of strong brands, Distillers was a formidable potential competitor of Bells. With Bain's estimate in hand that Distillers was worth much more than the £2 billion that Argyll was offering, Guinness decided to launch a takeover fight, what promised to be the highest-priced such competition ever staged in the United Kingdom. Since Guinness proposed to pay for Distillers with a combination of cash and its own shares, it was imperative that the brewer maintain the level of its stock price.

And here Saunders went seriously wrong. With Roux as his intermediary, he approached Gerald Ronson, a British industrialist and a major investor in Guinness who had recently stopped buying its shares. Saunders and Roux offered Ronson a £5 million "success fee" if he were to resume his buying and if Guinness ultimately prevailed in the takeover fight. Guinness would also cover any losses Ronson might suffer from the purchase of its stock. Ronson agreed to the deal, the buying to be done through stock broker Anthony Parnes.

In April 1986, Guinness won the contest for Distillers, agreeing to pay £2.5 billion for the larger company. From his offices in Boston, Bill Bain extended congratulations to his London operatives. By that time, though, relations between Saunders and Roux had begun to disintegrate, in part because in the course of the takeover fight, the consultant had argued that Saunders was bidding too high. By December, when both learned that the British Department of Trade and Industry had begun to investigate the deal, focusing on the "success fees" paid, the gulf between the two men widened to a chasm, with Saunders falling in.

Roux refused to be represented by lawyers from Guinness, meeting instead with Bain & Company lawyers, who, it was quickly decided, would represent both him and the consulting firm. Within a month, working from the lawyers' offices, Roux had written a letter to the Guinness board. In it, he described the payments made to prop up the stock, said the scheme had been Saunders's idea, and claimed not to know there was anything illegal about it. (A stretch, but perhaps not as preposterous a claim as it sounds: British law in the area, like U.S. rules against insider trading, wasn't the clearest.) A judge summarizing the evidence in the subsequent case described Saunders's reaction to the letter: "He noticed his name incorporated in every third line and he felt livid. Mr. Roux had been involved in a classic buck-passing exercise. [Saunders] regarded the letter as pure poison." Just what you want from your consultant.

The poison acted fast. The Guinness board fired Saunders and then, a couple of months later, sued him. Quickly thereafter, charges were brought against him for theft, false accounting, and conspiracy. Ronson and Parnes were also charged, as well as Sir Jack Lyons, a merchant and philanthropist whom Bain had put on retainer as a front man and corporate door-opener when it opened its London office. Lyons had become enmeshed in the machinations at Guinness, along the way writing a crucial letter in support of the deal to his friend, Prime Minister Margaret Thatcher.

Probably the most damning witness against the four men was Olivier Roux, who had agreed to testify and been granted limited immunity. As the scandal had unfolded, Bain had acted quickly to end its relationship with Sir Jack and, within two months of his letter to the Guinness board, with Roux as well, though not before paying him compensation owed of more than $925,000. Roux was never charged with any offense, nor was Bain & Company, as Bill Bain is emphatic in pointing out. Indeed, he argues, the Department of Industry and Trade exonerated the consulting firm of any culpability in the matter.

For their role in what some historians describe as the biggest corporate scandal to afflict Britain in the 1980s, Ronson and Parnes each served several months in jail. Sir Jack Lyons, in his late seventies and poor health, avoided that unpleasantness but forfeited his knighthood and paid a £3 million fine. Ernest Saunders, his five-year sentence reduced on appeal to two and a half years, spent about ten months behind bars and then was let out early, after being diagnosed with a mental disorder alternatively described as presenile dementia or possibly Alzheimer's disease. Released from prison in June 1991 at the age of fifty-five, he promptly set up as a management consultant, which trade he practiced with relative success for several years thereafter.

Where's the Money?

After the fact, observers of the consulting industry would shake their heads in wonder at how little bad press Bain got for its part in the Guinness scandal, particularly on the American side of the Atlantic. One reason was that the role Roux and Bain & Company played only dribbled out as the judicial proceedings against Saunders and the other conspirators unfolded. Another reason was that there was excitement enough at home—KKR's takeover of RJR Nabisco, the toils of Michael Milken—to crowd the business pages. Bill Bain says his firm didn't lose a single existing client because of the Guinness affair. Where it did hurt, he allows, was in Bain & Company's ability to attract new clients, which began to fall short of what he and his partners had projected. He's confident that some of the trouble came from competitors showing around clips from the British press suggesting that this was what could happen when you let Bain consultants come in and take over your company.

By early 1987, while the results-driven firm was still riding fairly high in a milieu besotted with stock-market gains—the Dow Jones Industrial Average would peak in August of that year 44 percent higher than its close at the end of 1986—even the press was beginning to pick up on signs that Bain may have overdone its act in some instances. By way of a partial response, the traditionally secretive firm agreed to talk to *Fortune*'s Nancy Perry, showing her (as it did potential clients) a Price-Waterhouse-audited graph that demonstrated that the stock-market value of Bain's U.S. clients had soared 319 percent since 1980, compared with the Dow-Jones Industrial Average increase of 141 percent and a 67 percent gain for an index of industries in which Bain clients competed. The ensuing article noted that "chief executives at Baxter Travenol, Chrysler Motors, Dun & Bradstreet, Owens Illinois, and Sterling Drug rave about Bain's services." It also paid homage to the accomplishment at Guinness, quoting a London businessman, who said, "The turnaround at that terrible, awful company was the most beautiful thing I've ever seen . . . What Bain did for Saunders was extraordinary."

But the very title of the article, "A Consulting Firm Too Hot to Handle?" suggested a measure of skepticism. While it didn't rehearse all the details of the Guinness scandal, most of which were only then emerging, it raised the main allegations, limned the conflict-plagued position of Roux in it all, and recounted a 1984 conference call when all the Bain partners brainstormed ideas to help Saunders oust his deputy chairman, a rival for power. The article also looked more widely at the experience of Bain clients, which led it to the conclusion that the "real problem for Bain & Co., though, may be the firm's tendency to alienate and weaken lower-level managers at the companies where it works."

Monsanto had been Bain's biggest client in the early 1980s; when its CEO retired in 1984, the company dispensed with the firm's services. Similar problems, it was suggested, had led to Bain's ouster from Black & Decker and Texas Instruments. Probably the most memorable lines from the article came in a quote from the head of another consulting firm: "Their product is brilliant. It's the package that has been a problem. Five million Bainies saying, 'Stand aside, asshole. Here we come.'"

And if the firm didn't lose any clients because of the Guinness affair, big clients such as Baxter, Bridgestone/Firestone, Canadian Pacific, Chrysler, and Dun & Bradstreet nevertheless began cutting back on the amount of Bain consulting they required. Some pleaded worsening economic conditions and consequent belt-tightening. After a sharp recession in 1982 brought on by the Federal Reserve's inflation-busting draconianism, the economy had enjoyed a thumping expansion. But by 1986, the party was looking a little tired.

As only a small coterie around Bill Bain knew at the time, this contraction of the firm's prospects came at a damnably inconvenient moment. Among founders of strategy consulting firms, Bill Bain and his original compadres probably rank as the most entrepreneurial. The question he had learned to ask at Vanderbilt's development office—"Where's the money?"—extended to his personal financial situation. After putting money into the start-up of Bain & Company, he and his partners were constantly on the lookout for other profit-making ventures, at one point contemplating investment in a new exercise machine developed by a trainer at a health club they frequented, at another, in 1983, sending Mitt Romney off to start up Bain Capital.

One can make a decent living as a senior partner at a major consulting firm—these days, a productive type can earn upward of $3 million or $4 million a year—but as a few of the breed complain privately, it's no way to become seriously wealthy. The challenge is building equity, a problem that in the 1980s and 1990s, corporate executives increasingly overcame with stock options granted them by their employers, occasionally to the envy of their consultant-advisers. Most professional service firms aren't publicly held; what is there to invest in, after all, except the assets who go down in the elevator at the end of the day—or off to work for a competitor?

After much deliberation, by 1984 Bill Bain and the half dozen other partners who represented the business-getting core of the firm thought they had found the way to realize a sizable sum for themselves from Bain & Company's success. They discovered it in the form of an employee stock ownership plan. But unlike Bruce Henderson, who had engineered an ESOP at BCG in the late 1970s, Bill Bain put his in place largely in secret, concealing the plan's existence and details even from the junior partners on whom it was to confer a measure of ownership. In some respects, this simply reflected Bill Bain's traditional tight-handed control of his firm: from its founding until 1985, Bain & Company had been governed by a partnership agreement that, as a former partner put it, was not "a bill of rights, but the rights of Bill." Even after Bain & Company was incorporated in 1985, much of the mystery and centralization of power in the founder's hands persisted.

In interviews for this book, Bill Bain described in great detail the processes by which the Bain ESOPs—there were in fact two of them—were constructed over the course of 1985 and 1986: the impartial outside experts consulted, the independent valuations by bankers, how the plans were to be part of a management succession process that he had already begun to think about. Neither he nor the firm will confirm the financial details, though. After the plan came to light, newspapers reported that he and the small original partner group had sold a 30 percent interest in Bain & Company to the ESOPs for $200 million in cash and notes, the proceeds to be paid them with money from a loan that the firm would take out from a local bank. With the Bain & Company's annual revenues topping $200 million in 1988, the valuation implicit in the ESOPs and the repayment plan would have worked just fine, Bain says, provided that his firm had continued to grow at the rates it had been experiencing.

But it didn't. Beginning in 1987, existing clients began to cut back and potential new clients were scared off. In November of that year, a stock market crash helped trigger what for many felt like a recession and in 1990 actually became one. In 1988, the firm that had seen its revenues double from 1985 to 1987 conducted its first mass layoff of ninety professionals and administrative employees, about 10 percent of its workforce. Another followed in 1990, amounting to over two hundred employees.

In 1991, the partners at Bain outside the founding group learned, to their shock and horror, that the firm owed a $17 million payment on the loan taken out to pay for the ESOP, a payment it might not be able to make. Bankruptcy loomed as a real threat, not to mention crippling mass defections from the ranks of the firm's professionals. To try to save the enterprise, some concerned partners approached Mitt Romney, their former colleague and the head of Bain Capital, to negotiate a solution with the consultancy's leadership.

While Bain Capital was its own firm, independent of Bain & Company, Bill Bain and many of his partners had invested in every fund the private equity outfit had raised, reaping terrific returns. Bain himself maintained what he describes as a friendly informal-adviser relationship with Romney, almost bordering on the avuncular, to hear him tell it. "Mitt came to me and said he would conduct an election" among the partners to choose new leadership, Bain says, adding that he regarded the process as an "acceleration" of the management succession he had been planning.

Perhaps not quite as much in Bain's plan was the settlement Romney negotiated, presumably using skill honed in years of doing acquisition deals for Bain Capital. While Romney persuaded Bain & Company's lending bank to restructure the debt—Bill Bain had been smart, even his detractors say, in securing the loan from just one institution, which itself couldn't afford to let a big borrower go belly-up— he also secured giveback of a reported $100 million from Bill Bain and his partner group. As part of the arrangement, in 1991 Bill Bain resigned from the firm he had founded; he was fifty-four. All but one of the founding partners also made their way out the door.

Romney, by this time making far more money at Bain Capital than he could have at the consultancy, stayed on as interim head long enough to stage the election he had promised. In 1992, a vastly more democratic Bain & Company partnership elected two people from its rising generation to newly created leadership positions. Orit Gadiesh, a thoroughly engaging and—for a consultant—flamboyant Israeli American woman, became non-executive chairman; Tom Tierney, more of a hearty California matinee-idol type, worldwide managing director.

If one wanted to point a moral or adorn the tale of Bill Bain's rise and fall, one could probably do worse than a variant on ontogeny recapitulating phylogeny, the trajectory of the individual mirroring that of the larger phenomenon of which he was part, in our case, not strategy but one particular approach to strategy. Bill Bain founded a consulting firm based on a version of strategy that was holistic—from conception through implementation—aggressive, elitist, slightly paranoid, and, to use its own favorite descriptor, ravenously results-oriented. The firm was without equal in teaching its clients the principles of Greater Taylorism and its uses. With Bain's help, many of those clients achieved spectacular results, often reflected in the wealth they created for shareholders. And yet, the client relationship frequently didn't endure—Bain has some clients of many years standing, but not as many as does McKinsey or BCG—and in their wake, Bain consultants often left behind festering resentments, a sense that the company had been taken over by an alien force (which strategy can be).

By many measures, Bill Bain is himself a proud tower of worldly success. How many other people do you know who created not one but two global firms with hundreds of millions, billions in revenue, firms that will keep his name alive in corporate circles for decades to come? His personal wealth, I suspect, surpasses that of any of the other lords. But at the consulting firm he created, this same man—transformative, masterly and masterful, utterly results-oriented—left behind a legacy of bitterness that endured for years. It would be more than a decade after his departure before the partners would invite him back, and then only over objections from some, to speak to a meeting of Bain & Company.

13.

How Competencies
Came to Be Core

ROM THE 1980s ON, the imperatives of shareholder capitalism would hang over the strategy revolution. But the revolutionaries didn't always pay much attention. Blame the fact
that by then, an establishment of consultants and scholars had already
grown up to tend strategy's flame, and this far from the clamor of Wall
Street. Which helps explain an abiding irony: much work done under
the name of strategy has less than an ineluctable effect on a company's
stock price. At firms such as a BCG and McKinsey, consultants who
take improving that price as their primary concern come across as specialists, slightly outside the mainstream. As the rationalization goes,
many variables can get in the way between the strategy recommended
and what shows up on the Bloomberg, ranging from the company's
talent for execution to the updrafts and downdrafts of the market. Absolute and unforgiving insistence that strategy had to translate into improved asset value would await the rise of private equity firms.

If they weren't quite prepared to commit themselves to improving
the client's stock price in every assignment, what were leading thinkers
on strategy to devote themselves to as the 1980s became the 1990s? For
many, the answer lay in trying to integrate the human and the strategic,

this through a new focus on behavior. But given the discipline's long-standing veneration of the hard-edged and quantifiable, this couldn't be behavior as mushily (if aspirationally) described by the school of excellence. No, it had to be behavior more tightly packaged, made rigorous, in fact—to use a favorite word of 1960s student Marxists, if not of consultants—"reified," turned into a thing. That thing would variously be labeled "capabilities," "processes," or "competencies."

In a speech from late in the 1990s, George Stalk Jr., arguably BCG's leading thinker on strategy over the prior fifteen years—and certainly the firm's most prolific—neatly summed up the main themes of the era, in the process making clear how far his firm had traveled from original Hendersonianism: "In this new environment, the essence of strategy is not the structure of a company's position in products and markets, but the dynamics of its behaviors. The goal is to identify and develop the hard-to-imitate organizational capabilities that distinguish a company from its competitors. A capability is a set of business processes, strategically understood."

Partly in response to new pressures to create shareholder wealth, companies did indeed improve their capabilities, but over time, the effort would prove a fillip more for Greater Taylorism than for the cause of strategy. As the 1990s were to make clear, advantage based on capabilities could be competed away just as quickly as that based on position. By the middle of the decade, as Michael Porter would return to the discussion to announce, being state-of-the-art in your processes—what he called your "operational effectiveness"—merely constituted table stakes, the minimum required to keep you in the game. Strategy, he would argue, still finally came down to choosing.

Time as the Measure of All Things

Philip Evans is a senior partner at the Boston Consulting Group. His British-accented acuity and ability to see into the future sometimes tries the patience even of his partners. He offers a wonderfully condensed, I-was-there-at-a-critical moment explanation of the evolution of strategy in the 1980s, from the effect of *In Search of Excellence* through the evolution of BCG's signal concept of the decade, time-based competition, into the early 1990s succès fou, reengineering.

Evans sees *In Search of Excellence* as feeding "a swing around 1980 away from analytically derived, top-down strategies towards the idea that it really didn't matter what product, what market, what segment . . . What mattered was whether you were excellent, and excellence meant, Did you manage yourself in accordance with certain principles?" He doesn't think much of the rigor of the authors' analysis, but allows that "what Peters and Waterman had done was to throw down a challenge: 'You strategists have been assuming that competitive advantage is all about what we might call structural factors—product, market, position, scale. And you have been implicitly assuming everybody is the same in how they manage themselves. Logically, it's quite possible the reverse is true—that position, for example, doesn't matter,'" but how you manage yourself does.

At about this time, Evans had been working on a BCG consulting project for a major money-center bank. He concluded that in the case of this industry leader, "Peters and Waterman were right: what mattered was not how big the bank's global network was, or how many people it had per branch. All the stuff we'd normally look at was irrelevant. What mattered was, 'Do you make the right credit decisions? Do you control country risk appropriately? Do you control asset-liability exposure appropriately?'" ("Parenthetically," Evans adds, "the bank lost a half billion dollars" by not doing the last of the three particularly well.) "These are skill issues, systems issues, control issues, but they're not structural issues by any regular definition of the term." Having observed this, Evans allows he didn't do much with it at the time.

Meanwhile his colleague, George Stalk, was arriving at similar insights, though from a very different set of client experiences. Trained as an engineer but also a Harvard MBA, Stalk had begun studying

Japanese manufacturing in 1979, at first in service to client John Deere, which had asked BCG to help it come up with a strategy for Asia. Stalk's research took him first to Deere's Japanese affiliate, Yanmar, and later to Hitachi. What Stalk discovered startled him: as he summarized it in the preface to his 1990 book, *Competing Against Time*, the factories of Deere's Japanese affiliate had "substantially higher productivity, better quality, significantly less inventory, less space, and much faster throughput times." Stalk also recorded Bruce Henderson's comment on learning all this: "Until the causes of these differences can be explained much of the conceptual underpinnings of corporate strategy are suspect."

In the early 1980s, while both Stalk and Evans were still wrestling to make sense of what they had seen, the two found themselves together at a conference on Cape Cod. They went for a walk, along a cliff, Evans recalls, describing their discussion as "one of the most wonderful, most memorable of my entire professional career." Stalk was "full of stuff," Evans says, "typically George, unbelievable nerdy stuff about forgings and castings. But embedded in it, with all the complexity, was a little idea that you could compete by being faster. I said to him, 'Scrub everything else, just talk about that.' The bell was ringing in my head that this was the same thing as the bank's being good at controlling risk; it's embedded in behavior."

It was what Stalk added to the basic insight that was to make time-based competition BCG's most successful concept-cum-product of the 1980s. "The thing that George did," Evans says, "which I hadn't done and Peters and Waterman hadn't done was measure the damn thing. He had an engineering-friendly, and therefore, of course, BCG-culture-friendly approach, because he had [fastened on] a capability, speed, you could measure. He defined an analytical method you could use with clients. You could map it, measure it, understand it, bottle it." Evans argues that this was the beginning of what came to be known as reengineering, or at least that it paralleled what Michael Hammer, the father of that movement, was doing. Both Stalk and Hammer "were taking the agenda defined by Peters and Waterman but casting it in quantifiable and analytical terms such that you could then make it a real consulting product."

The empirical launch point for the concept of time-based competition was Stalk's observation of flexible manufacturing in Japan. The classical view, thoroughly in keeping with the experience curve, held that manufacturers faced an inevitable trade-off between scale, cost, and variety. They could turn out long runs of the same item and, over time, drive down the cost of making it, or they could offer a wider variety, with smaller production runs, but at higher cost. What Stalk saw in Japan was that companies such as Toyota had devised production systems that blew up, or blew past, the traditional trade-offs. Through a combination of production design, technology, and unstinting effort to learn and improve, a flexible manufacturer could turn out a wider variety of products than a traditional player could, and at lower total cost. This was what so shocked Henderson.

Stalk's greater intellectual accomplishment, and what set him apart from other boffins inveighing, "You gotta adopt this nifty Japanese production system," lay in first tracing out the implications of flexible manufacturing for the rest of what a company did. Then—with a nudge from Evans—he focused on one dimension, time, as a proxy for gauging the overall efficiencies that could be realized. What finally made all this strategic, Stalk argues, is that with the whole complex of processes knit together properly, a company could connect to customers in ways that offered a decided and enduring competitive advantage.

Stalk's work culminated first in a 1988 *Harvard Business Review* article, "Time: The Next Source of Competitive Advantage," and then two years later, in *Competing Against Time*—the latter coauthored with another BCG intellectual notable, Thomas Hout, who was John Deere's longtime consultant. They argued for essentially taking the Porterian value chain of activities and speeding up not just the portion devoted to manufacturing, but the whole caboodle, to wring the maximum benefit from what flexible manufacturing enabled you to do. Indeed, that's the hidden magic of time-based competition, and also the encompassing challenge in implementing it ("a great theory," a consultant at another firm asserts, "and a disaster in practice for clients"): if you want to go from offering the customer a choice of one of three models to be delivered in six weeks to a pick of twenty with next-day delivery, you're going to have to revamp not just what goes on in your factories but also every process going into and coming out of them.

That includes planning, order taking, distribution, and delivery. Nor can you rest content with revolution just at the operational level. Operational reforms need to be buttressed with increasingly speedy innovation, particularly product innovation. In his *HBR* piece, Stalk noted that Toyota could already come up with a new-model car in half the time, and with half the people, required by its competitors in the United States or Germany.

The choice of time—or as translated into action, speed—as the übermetric was inspired. The general rubric encompassed more specific temporal measures particular to different activities along the value chain: how long it took you to respond to a customer inquiry, for your top management to make a decision, to produce an item in the factory, to get an idea from the lightbulb-going-off-stage to a reality being sold in the market. The time spent on each activity could be readily gauged, whereas, for instance, the cost of keeping a customer waiting could not. Then they all added up to determine just how quick a competitor you were. Time was a measure, too, that could be readily understood by all, not just by engineers but also by financial types, shop-floor workers, even human-resources executives, in contrast to, say, standard deviations from the mean.

And what could have better fit than the ever-more-spirited zeitgeist, the perception that the winds of change were blowing faster and increasingly from quarters difficult to predict? In 1993, Stalk wrote another *HBR* article on time-based competition with coauthor Alan

Webber, a former editorial director of the journal. Even as the piece went to press, Webber was working to start up a magazine that would become for many the essential guidebook to what was coming to be known as the "new economy." (Stalk was an investor in the venture, as was Tom Peters.) Its name: *Fast Company*.

The Imperative to Innovate, the Wisdom to Hold Fast

The cartoonishly oversimplified version of what happened to processes and their place in the history of strategy can be envisioned as a caravan of experts splitting up with subsets heading in different directions. Some made for the uplands, the winds of aspiration at their backs, eventually to command applause and renown from crowds below. These would be C. K. Prahalad and Gary Hamel, with their notions first of strategic intent and then of core competencies.

Another few would hack their way through the jungles of process, discovering treasures therein—much consulting business—before eventually losing their way. Their mission was business process reengineering, their leaders Michael Hammer and Jim Champy, and their course such that they rather lost sight of strategy.

The third group covered more familiar ground, though its leaders—George Stalk and Philip Evans of BCG—would argue that their concept of competing on capabilities was both more rigorous and more encompassing than core competencies. Mostly, this expedition went nowhere, at least in terms of its reception in the market, as its heads would later admit. To understand where all three took off from requires two quick side trips on our part, the first into the subject of innovation, the second to, of all places, the groves of academe.

In the mid-1980s, some of the same minds that had concerned themselves with strategy began to focus on innovation, this partly in response to the dawning sense that successive waves of new technology were coming along faster, spaced closer together, hitting the beach harder. This became intertwined with the contention—loud in time-based competition, positively screaming in business-process reengineering—that reforming your existing processes was a strategic necessity. Innovation would be tied in with processes more directly than it ever was with the first of the three Ps of strategy, positioning.

Academics had been studying innovation for years. In the early 1960s, a Midwestern professor, Everett Rogers, had surfaced a graphic construct, the S curve, to describe how new technologies catch on. When a new whizbang is introduced, only a few people try it out, their experiments proceeding with grinding slowness. Then, with apparent suddenness, it catches on, people rush to use it, and before long, it has become so common that further gains are eked out only by winning over the few remaining laggards.

In the mid-1980s, McKinsey's Dick Foster turned his attention to innovation. His research culminated in a 1986 book, *Innovation: The Attacker's Advantage*, featuring his own version of the S curve to plot the trajectory by which a technology improves (figure 13-1).

On the vertical axis, he charted a measure of performance—the thinness of men's pocket watches, for example—and on the horizontal, effort, perhaps measured by funds invested in developing the new wonder. In the first stage, the technology crawls along the horizontal axis (watches get only slightly thinner over the eighteenth century). Then, in the "explosion" phase, performance improves markedly and quickly (the 1850 model looks about a sixth as thick as the 1812 model), culminating in the "gradual maturation" phase (watches can't get much thinner; let's compete instead on reliability or price).

A charming construct, you might conclude, but what does it have to do with strategy, attack, or advantage? The call to arms came in Foster's further observations: S curves almost always come in at least pairs, he argued, with the successor technology experiencing its own slow start but beginning from higher on the performance axis. The evidence also suggested that a company that was master of one technology and S

FIGURE 13-1

The S curve

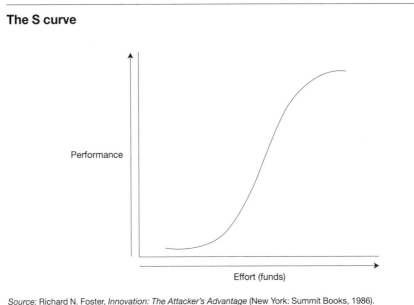

Source: Richard N. Foster, *Innovation: The Attacker's Advantage* (New York: Summit Books, 1986).

curve almost never succeeded in jumping successfully to the next one. Here, the killer graphic was a chart showing that a list of the top three makers of vacuum tubes in 1955 bore no relation to the list of three leading transistor manufacturers that same year, which in turn bore no relation to the list of the top producers of semiconductors ten years later. Approximately the same terrifying point would be made again ten years later in a best-selling book, *The Innovator's Dilemma*, by BCG consultant turned HBS professor Clay Christensen.

Foster argued that what he called technological discontinuities would arrive with increasing frequency in the years to come and that the competitive battles they fostered would usually go to whoever was riding the fresh beast, the attacker, in other words. The capacity to innovate would be the key to competitive and strategic success.

If Foster and Stalk were focused on change and speed, back in the academy what was to become the dominant school of thought about strategy in those precincts was fastening instead on what abideth. In

1984, Birger Wernerfelt, a young professor at the University of Michigan, published a paper titled "A Resource-Based View of the Firm." Although almost no one talked about or cited the piece for five years, Wernerfelt had given the name to an approach to strategy, the resource-based view (sometimes abbreviated RBV), which was to be at the center of most academic research on the subject for the following two decades.

Another professor far from the banks of the Charles, Jay Barney—he has taught at Ohio State since 1994—did more than anyone else to flesh out the resource-based view. The title of one of his papers, "Looking Inside for Competitive Advantage," sums up the difference between his approach and the consultants'. Both Wernerfelt and Barney trace their work back to, of all things, the thinking of Ken Andrews and in particular to the SWOT framework (strengths, weaknesses, opportunities, and threats) he enunciated. Barney argued that lots of progress had been made by Porter and his ilk on the opportunities and threats part, or what he called "environmental analysis." But that was only half the story, Barney maintained. To really get at what made for competitive advantage, you had to analyze a company's "internal strengths and weaknesses" as well.

To some extent we're back in Peters and Waterman land here, and in at least one of his articles, Barney extensively cited their writing. Precisely what constituted a resource remained invitingly open-ended. In certain lights, it might even look like an element plucked from the seven-S construct—staff, perhaps, or system. This wide-open definitional door partly accounts for the size of the academic herd who rushed in to embrace the resource-based view. To make a contribution to it, you didn't need to be trained in economics, à la Michael Porter. Even scholars with a background in so-called organizational science were admitted.

To their credit, the founding fathers of the resource-based view did try to establish criteria for judging resources on their potential for contributing to strategic advantage.[1] They settled on four criteria, whose first letters gave birth to still another acronym, VRIN. A resource must be *valuable*, in the sense of adding value by enabling the company to better exploit opportunities or reduce threats. It must be *rare*—if it's available to anyone in the industry, it won't confer much advantage. It must be *inimitable*; if your advantage is to be sustainable, the resource can't be something competitors can easily duplicate. Finally, the resource must be *nonsubstitutable*: barrels of whale oil won't do you much good when competitors are already filling your customers' lamps with kerosene.

Not exactly hard-edged, is it? Or something that a consultant could sink his or her sharp-edged, little quantifying teeth into. Even other academics criticized Barney and his fellow pioneers, arguing that the resource-based view didn't pay enough attention to the markets—oh, that outside world—or offer much guidance on what a company was supposed to do with its resources. Perhaps most cruelly, detractors charged that the resource-based view was "tautological": value-creating resources are valuable, and so on down a hall of mirrors. This led to scholarly debate on issues such as the "parameterization of imitability," from which we may, without great loss, tiptoe away as rapidly as possible.

Where Core Competencies Come From

I have never heard an actual businessperson mention the resource-based view. But I've heard legions talk about "core competencies." For this we can thank Coimbatore Krishnarao (understandably, everyone calls him "C. K.") Prahalad and Gary Hamel. Even Wernerfelt gives them the credit in a 1995 paper: "I believe these authors were single-handedly responsible for [the] diffusion of the resource-based view into practice."

Hamel and Prahalad met in 1977 at the University of Michigan, where Prahalad was a professor and Hamel a doctoral student in international business. Each had made his way to Ann Arbor by a path that would subtly inflect his subsequent career, bringing to their work a certain edginess that one frequently associates with an outsider. Prahalad was born in 1941, one of nine children of a Madras judge and scholar. Early in his life, from age nineteen to twenty-three, he helped manage a Union Carbide battery plant near his home—this more than twenty years before the Bhopal disaster of 1984. His experience at the plant helped charge the young man, up until then mostly a physics whiz, with a zeal for management.

He went on to study at the Indian Institute of Management–Ahmedabad, the country's leading business school, and then, sparked partly by their families' opposition to his marrying a student from a nearby university, went off with his bride to the United States, where he earned a DBA from the Harvard Business School in 1975. He returned to teach at IIM, but not finding much interest there in his specialty (the management of multinational companies), he soon decamped to join the faculty at the University of Michigan's business school.

Hamel, thirteen years younger, had arrived in the same halls after getting both his undergraduate degree and an MBA from Andrews University in Michigan. Andrews, in various incarnations around since 1874, describes itself as the "flagship" educational institution of the Adventist Church, a denomination still familiar to most people as the Seventh-Day Adventists. That church's worldwide missionary fervor gave Andrews a look-beyond-U.S.-shores inclination uncommon among American universities. Hamel clearly picked up an eye for the international, and also perhaps a bit of the fervor.

Hamel is a mesmerizing presence at the podium, currently ranked by one magazine as "the world's most influential business speaker"—as his Web site will tell you. When you watch him or read his writings, you can detect an occasional note that seems almost millenarian: that the triumphant (including the competitively triumphant corporation) will be utterly triumphant, that an upsetting of all things is probably not such a bad idea (c.f. his 1996 *HBR* article "Strategy as Revolution"), and that the sheep will damn well be separated from the goats (and if you have any trouble distinguishing the two, just ask Gary).

Prahalad and Hamel first made big noise with their 1989 *Harvard Business Review* article, "Strategic Intent," the McKinsey Award winner for that year. The piece inveighed that most Western companies were losing out to competitors from abroad (read "Japan")—Caterpillar to Komatsu, Xerox to Canon—in substantial measure because the Westerners were following wrongheaded, constraining notions of strategy. Indeed, the authors maintained, "as 'strategy' has blossomed"— referring to most of the concepts discussed so far in this book—"the competitiveness of Western companies has withered. This may be a coincidence, but we think not." They can't resist hammering away at the point, poking fun at the petty constructs of little minds: "It's not very comforting to think that the essence of Western strategic thought can be reduced to eight rules for excellence, seven S's, five competitive forces, four product life-cycle stages, three generic strategies, and innumerable two-by-two matrices"—sparing only the partridge in a pear tree. Reliance on such ideas isn't merely unimaginative; it can have "toxic side effects," reducing "the number of strategic options management is willing to consider."

What you want instead, learning from the Asian masters—and yes, Prahalad and Hamel invoke Sun Tzu—is an encompassing "strategic intent," something like establishing global leadership in a particular market or industry. Just seeking to increase shareholder wealth, the piddling measure by which most American CEOs gauge their success, hardly qualifies and won't get the troops excited. (But then, one wants to ask, do all those Japanese CEOs, embedded in *keiretsus* and backed by the Ministry of Trade, feel quite the same pressure from the stock market?) True strategic intent envisions the dominance to be achieved, as in Komatsu's stated goal to "encircle Caterpillar" or Canon's to "beat Xerox," along with criteria for judging progress to that goal.

While the "Strategic Intent" article is longer on exhortation than on specific advice, the authors manage to etch out a little practical guidance to distinguish their approach from the positioning school. The aim of strategy should be to "create tomorrow's competitive advantages faster than competitors mimic the ones you possess today." The secret to doing this lies in the corporation's skills and its ability to acquire new ones—"learning," in other words—which the authors describe as "the most defensible competitive advantage of all."

Pretty much buried in the 1989 article is their term for the most critical type of these skills: "core competencies." Cottoning to a potential winner of an idea, and in the process returning closer to the resource-based view, the following year Prahalad and Hamel published an even more celebrated *HBR* article, "The Core Competence of the Corporation." Another grand phrase had entered the vocabulary of management, albeit one that would eventually muzzy up more corporate conversations about strategy than it would clarify.[2]

The piece maintained that smart companies, again almost all Asian, view themselves not as portfolios of businesses but rather as portfolios of competencies. Just what constitutes a core competence remains a little slithery throughout, though. "The real sources of competitive advantage," Prahalad and Hamel argued, "are to be found in management's ability to consolidate corporatewide technologies and production skills into competencies that empower individual businesses to adapt quickly to changing opportunities." Such competencies are the "collective learning in the organization"; they're "about harmonizing streams of technology" and "the organization of work and the delivery of value." A core competence is "communication, involvement, and a deep commitment to working across organizational boundaries."

The author's efforts to be a tad more specific take us right back to the resource-based view, in particular to a couple aspects of the VRIN framework. A core competence "provides potential access to a wide variety of markets," Prahalad and Hamel argued, and "should make a significant contribution to the perceived customer's benefits of the end product," which sounds a lot like *valuable*. It should be "difficult for competitor's to imitate," in other words, *inimitable*. Real-world examples of core competences seem surprisingly few in the article. Canon has them in precision mechanics, fine optics, and microelectronics; NEC in computing, communications, and components.

In the years following the publication of "The Core Competence of the Corporation," BCG and McKinsey would each offer their own versions of the idea that capabilities were central to strategy, but in both cases without achieving anything like the name-on-everyone's-lips success of Prahalad and Hamel's concept. Stalk, Evans, and BCG colleagues such as Larry Shulman would join the chorus to the effect that advantage based on positioning was being competed away faster than ever. What you needed now were enduring "strategic capabilities" that allowed you to innovate and revolutionize markets. Managing such capabilities entailed working across business units, sometimes banging their little heads together, and hence necessarily was the responsibility of the CEO.

The BCG thinkers would also argue that the concept of core competence was too narrowly focused, in their view, emphasizing "technological and production expertise at specific points along the value chain." In contrast, their entry, "capabilities," were "more broadly based, encompassing the entire value chain," in keeping with the sweeping purview of time-based competition. Picking up on another term then becoming electric in the managerial air, they argued that the "building blocks of corporate strategy are not products and markets but business processes," and that competitive success depended on a company's transforming its key processes into "strategic capabilities."

McKinsey's John Stuckey has argued that the Firm had, almost from its beginnings, believed that special capabilities were the key to strategic success, but that this very emphasis had left McKinsey whacking vulnerable to attacks from those who instead concentrated on industry structure, the devils at BCG with their experience curve, or Michael Porter with his popularization—Stuckey's term—of the structure-conduct-performance model. By the time he wrote his "Perspectives on Strategy" in 2005, Stuckey and his partners had reached the

Solomonic view that "*both* special capabilities and industry structure are important." But this broad-church understanding didn't keep McKinsey from making some observations about capabilities that crisped up the definition of the subject.

Stuckey, too, maintained that by the 1990s, capabilities were becoming more important strategically than advantages based on structure, citing (without attribution) an estimate that "75% of the *Fortune* 100's total market capitalization is represented by special capabilities such as brands and licenses." Nodding to the problem that clients kept misleading themselves about which of their capabilities were truly special (as they would mislead themselves about which of their competences were core), he sensibly maintained that to qualify as special, a capability had to result in either significantly lower costs or better products. McKinsey's work suggested that two types of capabilities usually came up to that standard, "tradable privileged assets"—everything from brands like Coke's, to patents, to physical assets such as low-cost mines—and "distinctive competences," mushier but including such skills as the ability to "attract and retain talent," "continuously innovate," and the capacity to "build and sustain corporate reputation."

Reengineering Flashes and Crashes

Capabilities never lived up to the hopes that consultants entertained for them as a product, for reasons we'll touch on below. By way of contrast, consider the brief, flashy life of a concept that did take off into the heaven of popular renown, business process reengineering, only to crash back to earth almost as quickly. It bears looking at not just for the content of the idea but also for its demonstration of how robust, deeply specialized, crafty, and lucrative the market for management ideas had become since the days of the first BCG *Perspectives*.

Participants in that market were sharpening their calculations all the time. In the late 1990s, during my service with Harvard Business

Publishing, authors of *HBR* articles would occasionally confide in me about the value of being published there. Gushed a solo-practitioner consultant then charging $20,000 a day and up, "You can get a year's worth of business, maybe two, on the strength of one article." Another, a partner at a strategy firm and the author of both articles and best-selling books based on them, had even more detailed calculations: "You get nothing for the article." (The *Review* then paid a $100 hono-rarium per article while retaining all rights to reprint and resell it.) "You might get a little money for the book advance." (Figures like $15,000 were common.) "If the book takes off, you may begin to see some money worth paying attention to from speaking fees." (He was then doing about a hundred appearances a year, typically for $25,000 an outing.) "Of course, where you make the real money is from the consulting projects you land from the article."

Over the ten years after the 1982 publication of *In Search of Excel-lence,* individual experts and the organizations behind them woke up to the opportunities presented by an ever-growing market for busi-ness wisdom. As a genre, business books boomed, their total sales sub-sequently doubling over the course of the 1990s, according to some estimates. By the end of the decade, just before the Internet and stock market bust of 2000, business was the second-best-selling category of books at retailers Amazon.com (after technology) and Barnes & Noble. Business conferences and corporate speaking engagements had grown apace (before falling off their own cliff that year).

Not surprisingly, by the early 1990s, a small literary-industrial complex had emerged to take advantage of these trends. It was cen-tered in Boston, home to the *Harvard Business Review* and the *Sloan Management Review,* book publishers such as Addison-Wesley, and too many management consulting firms. Potential authors might be rep-resented by literary agent Helen Rees, who made a specialty of busi-ness books. (So tenacious was she that one client said of her, "The difference between Helen Rees and a Rottweiler is that eventually a Rottweiler will let go.")

To become an author, one didn't even necessarily need to know how to write. For a person with the right credentials and an intriguing idea to push, editorial help was readily available. Alan Webber, the leading staff editor at *HBR* during this period, later described how the process worked: "The dirty little secret of the *Harvard Business Review* is that most of the great articles that we published when I was the editor weren't exactly written by people whose names were on the byline. And that's not to say they weren't the author. But they didn't write them. If you go talk to the professors at the Harvard Business School and you ask them to write an article, you very quickly discover they can't write a lick. In order to get a very advanced degree, you have to be taught how not to write very, very well. Now, what they can do is talk. And so, what we would do would be to sit down with these really smart professors and put a tape recorder in front of them. And they would talk. And we would transcribe the tape. And then we'd clean it up and we'd give it back to them. And they'd say, 'But of course, that's what I said. That's what I wrote.'"

Or you could pay someone to provide you so-called editorial services, probably Donna Sammons Carpenter's firm, Wordworks, Inc. By its own account, this enterprise "produced" over seventy trade books, five million copies of which are in print, and which collectively occupied "more than 500 weeks" on the *New York Times* and *BusinessWeek* bestseller lists. The roll call of authors and titles it assisted is a revelation—it includes Tom Peters, Richard Pascale, various Harvard professors, and Senator John Kerry—particularly if one clung to images of an author toiling away in a lonely garret. Wordworks' services extended well beyond mere ghostwriting to what is better described by the not-particularly-beautiful term *book packaging*. For fees that could easily run to tens of thousands of dollars, Carpenter and her team could turn a proposal of a few pages and subsequent conversations with the would-be author into a thoroughly marketable management tome.

Probably the chief beneficiaries of these ministrations were authors associated with the Index Group consulting firm, later CSC Index, who also happened to be the leading proponents of business-process reengineering. Index had been founded in 1969 by an MIT graduate and doctoral student, Tom Gerrity—later in life, he was dean of the Wharton School for nearly ten years—and three of his friends from that institution, one of them Jim Champy. From its modest beginnings and through the subsequent modest fifteen years until it sold itself to Computer Sciences Corporation and became CSC Index, the firm explored the application of information technology to improving management. By the mid-1980s, in part inspired by BCG's work on time-based competition, it was looking at business processes and what might be done with them. The firm's research director was a young Harvard PhD (in sociology) named Tom Davenport.

Much of the firm's inquiry was being conducted through what came to be known as a *multiclient research program* that CSC Index put on in conjunction with Michael Hammer, another former MIT professor—he'd left to start up his own firm—with whom CSC Index had an ongoing, if somewhat loose affiliation. Multiclient research programs would enroll companies as paying participants—the annual tab was typically somewhere in the middle five figures—with which the consultants or commissioned academics would do research on a particular topic. The results were then played back at periodic meetings during the year, some held in swell places like Pebble Beach.

Partly from the results of the multiclient research, Davenport and a coauthor published "The New Industrial Engineering: Information Technology and Business Process Redesign" in the summer 1990 issue of the *Sloan Management Review*. Mere weeks later, Hammer published his take on the subject in *Harvard Business Review* in an article bearing the somewhat punchier title "Reengineering Work: Don't Automate, Obliterate." You can guess which piece became a runaway best-seller.

The gravamen of Hammer's argument was that companies were stuck with business processes—how they took orders, or managed payables, or made their products—that were outdated and hopelessly inefficient in a computerized age. Rather than trying to reform these relic millstones, you should just blow them up, Hammer counseled. He proposed starting with a blank sheet of paper and redesigning successor processes that incorporated the latest information technology. In so doing, you should knock down traditional bureaucratic partitions in how you arranged work, keeping always in mind the ultimate beneficiary, usually your customer.

Recall the economic context in which reengineering appeared. After the stock market shock of 1987, the U.S. economy had sputtered and then recovered slightly, but by the summer of 1990, it was in recession. The Four Horsemen of the Corporate Apocalypse continued their depredations, and Japanese competitors appeared ever more threatening (this just before that country's economy would slip into a decade-long malaise). CEOs still felt the tremors from the great merger-and-takeover wave of the 1980s and knew they had to do something, perhaps even something slightly desperate, to make their companies competitive in the new world aborning.

Reengineering seemed a wonderful solution. It not only addressed the call to change but also smacked of the strategic—processes, competences, capabilities: the little differences between them didn't seem to matter much if you took the big view—enabled by the magically transformative power of new technology. (George Stalk and others would subsequently claim, though, that reengineering in fact had little to do with strategy, in that it didn't help you figure out which processes were critical to your competitive success.) Not only did management consultants leap on the bandwagon, but so did vendors of hardware and software, looking for a cause under which to install multimillion-dollar computer systems. Greater Taylorism had found its enabling technology.

CSC Index and Hammer led the parade. Companies and corporate audiences paid thousands to hear Hammer, no slouch as a barn burner, inveigh that if your old organization didn't work anymore, then "Nuke it." "To succeed at reengineering," he'd happily declare, "you have to be a visionary, a motivator, and a leg breaker." Meanwhile,

CSC Index honed its model of conference as marketing tool, reaching beyond research program participants. Prospective clients of the CEO stratum would pay twenty-five hundred dollars or more to come hear the greatest names in management wisdom, not just the firm's consultants but also Michael Porter, Warren Bennis, or Peter Drucker (who would declare, "Reengineering is new, and must be done"). In the afternoon, there would be golf, with guests frequently in foursomes with hosts from CSC Index. Occasionally, one presumes, some consulting might be sold.

Building on the original *HBR* article and with lots of editorial help from Wordworks, Hammer and CSC Index's Jim Champy published their 1993 book, *Reengineering the Corporation: A Manifesto for Business Revolution*. It would go on to sell more than three million copies and spend over a year on the *New York Times* best-seller list.

Success has many fathers, they say, or claimants to that role, and CSC Index's with reengineering rather confirms the maxim. There are Hammer and Champy, of course, along with their writing helpers. Tom Davenport, who went on to a distinguished career as a professor, consultant, and guru in his own right, clearly counts as one of reengineering's intellectual fathers *avant la lettre*. Tom Waite, CSC Index's senior vice president for innovation and marketing during this period, today notes on his Web site that he "conceived the idea of writing and publishing a series of business books and led the promotion" of the firm's best-sellers.

Ron P. Christman, a PhD in nuclear science and, more than anyone else, the man behind CSC Index's research-program and conference model, on his Web site attaches numbers that give weight to his claim to paternity: "His [Christman's] creation of CSC Index's Research and Advisory Services (of which he was president) is widely acclaimed as the driving factor behind the growth of CSC Index from a $10 million I/T consulting firm to a $225 million consulting organization over a ten year period." He also notes that his team "invented and branded the concept of 'business reengineering.'" Christman would subsequently take the multiclient-research-program model and the accompanying pleasant conferences with him to his next venture, the Concours Group—which still puts on events built around experts such as Jim Collins, Tom Davenport, and Gary Hamel.

Except for Davenport, none of the intellectual fathers have quite as much to say about reengineering's collapse, which was even more rapid than its ascent. The one-sentence explanation is that in the eyes of the corporate world, reengineering came to be seen as synonymous with downsizing, and underlings as resistant to its introduction. Champy, Davenport, and Hammer each have argued that layoffs never were the principal point of the exercise, but somehow, in the face of pronouncements like "Carry the wounded, but shoot the stragglers," that nuance had been lost.

In a 1995 *Fast Company* article, Davenport marshaled evidence of the movement's failure, citing CSC Index's "State of Reengineering Report" from the prior year: "50% of the companies that participated in the study reported that the most difficult part of reengineering is dealing with fear and anxiety in their organizations; 73% of the companies said they were using reengineering to eliminate, on average, 21% of the jobs; and, of 99 completed reengineering initiatives, 67% were judged as producing mediocre, marginal, or failed results." Devilishly, Davenport even detailed what subsequently happened at some of the corporate examples in Champy and Hammer's book. The Direct Response Group's parent had thrown out its management and "dismantled the process-oriented organization," Mutual Benefit Life was "basically out of business," and Hallmark still took a year to develop a new greeting card.

In 1996, Champy, the chairman and CEO of the CSC Index, left the listing ship, to resurface as chairman of Perot System's consulting practice. In 1999, CSC Index's parent, CSC, essentially liquidated what remained of the firm, which had once numbered over six hundred people in fourteen offices, absorbing a few staff members into its other operations but firing most of the rest.

The Eclipse of Capabilities

If the advent of strategy as based on core competencies or capabilities was announced in the pages of *Harvard Business Review*, so was its eclipse. Among the first discouraging words were those of Stalk and coauthor Alan Webber in their 1993 article, "Japan's Dark Side of Time." The authors depicted a hellish world typified by the Akihabara district of Tokyo, where 10 percent of Japan's sales of electronic goods took place and in which all players had learned to compete on the basis of time.

The result was something out of the Disney cartoon "The Sorcerer's Apprentice," but with the robotic, ever-faster efforts of several apprentices all colliding at once. Japanese manufacturers were piling into the same product categories—portable music players, coffee makers, refrigerators—offering an ever-greater variety of models, of which each arrived more quickly than the last. And almost no one was making money. The problem was not in the concept of time-based competition, Stalk and Webber maintained, but rather in everyone's rush to embrace it, damn it. The pesky Japanese, with their "penchant for excess" and conformity, had taken "a strategy tool designed to create differentiation through increased variety" and instead "reduced everything to a commodity."

An even louder blast at the notion that you could compete solely on the basis of capabilities was sounded three years later by Michael Porter in his *Harvard Business Review* article "What Is Strategy?" A bit like another student of aeronautical engineering, Ludwig Wittgenstein, who decided he had solved most of the problems of philosophy by age thirty and went off to think about something else for the next ten years, Porter had, after the 1985 publication of *Competitive Advantage*, largely absented himself from the conversation around strategy. Not that he had been idle. In 1990, he had published an 850-page volume, *The Competitiveness of Nations*, which had helped make him a valued adviser not just to companies, but to whole governments. (Giving his consulting firm,

Monitor Company, a nice line of business in that area, too.) He had served on a presidential commission, written and talked about what competitiveness could bring to environmentalism and the inner city, and lectured and consulted tirelessly.

But he hadn't necessarily gotten along that well with the rising generation of faculty teaching strategy at Harvard Business School, despite having launched many of them himself. Some critics spoke of a "Banyan tree effect," after the variety of fig whose ever-spreading vines strangle its host tree. (The more apt arboreal comparison may have been to some great, rooted blossomer in whose shade the saplings have trouble gaining much height.) Other critics suggested that Porter hadn't done as much to build a cohesive team in the competitiveness and strategy area as other faculty heads had in theirs. Porter allows that he seems to have trouble with the "half generations" of faculty who proceeded and followed him. He got along fine with Roland Christensen and Ken Andrews, he says; it was the succeeding half generation that voted not to promote him. And he works splendidly with the generation of strategy faculty just reaching scholarly maturity now, if less happily with their immediate predecessors.

By 1996, though, whatever academic tiffs may have existed were overborne by Porter's sense that strategy, his real baby, was in trouble. Part of this he took to be an attack on his own work. "People were being tricked and misled by other ideas," he later told *Fast Company*. Indeed, heretical tendencies had even grown to the point of arguing that in a world of ever-faster change, you didn't need a strategy and might even be held back by one when you should be reinventing yourself. Porter's answer was his "What Is Strategy?" article.

At the outset of the piece, Porter rejected what he called the "new dogma" that in a world of more dynamic markets and changing technologies, "rivals can quickly copy any market position, and competitive advantage is, at best, temporary." People who fell for this canard did so, he maintained, because they failed to distinguish between "operational effectiveness" and "strategy." With a grand sweep and no little intellectual sleight of hand, he consigned to operational effectiveness a jumble of management tools that had, he claimed, "taken the place of strategy," including "total quality management, benchmarking, time-based competition, outsourcing, partnering, reengineering [and] change management."

The point of operational effectiveness is to outdo your rivals on all the activities that result in greater value for customers, which enables you to deliver a superior product for which you can charge more or to offer them what they can get elsewhere but at a cheaper price. Operational effectiveness thus boiled down, for Porter, to pretty much performing the same activities as your competitors, but more efficiently than they do. In contrast—drumroll here—"Strategic positioning means performing *different* activities from rivals' or performing similar activities in *different ways*."

Porter acknowledged that over the preceding decade (about 1985 to about 1995), managers at U.S. companies had become "preoccupied with improving managerial effectiveness," in part because they were responding to the Japanese, who were so much better at it. (As if by way of compensation, his accompanying sidebar, "Japanese Companies Rarely Have Strategies," must have been a comfort to readers still cowering before the Godzillas invoked by Hamel, Prahalad, and Stalk.) Two fatal flaws attached to competing on operational effectiveness, Porter argued. First, competitors quickly copy one another's techniques and technologies, pushing what he called the industry's "productivity frontier" ever outward, "raising the bar for everyone." Soon you're engaged in a never-ending race to stay up at the frontier as the price of remaining in the game, even if no one is making much money at it. Second, because everyone is benchmarking one another and often outsourcing activities to the same superefficient suppliers, the strategies of competitors converge and become "a series of races down identical paths that no one can win."

The answer, of course, and the essence of strategy, is to be different. To this end, Porter offered three alternative "bases for positioning" that, he claimed, take to a new level of specificity the generic strategies—cost leadership, differentiation, and focus—that he originally offered in *Competitive Strategy*. You can go for "variety-based positioning": rather than focus on a particular customer segment, you concentrate on a particular product or service as, for instance, the Vanguard Group did on index mutual funds. Or "needs-based positioning": zero in on the needs of a particular group, as Bessemer Trust's private-banking operation does on families with a minimum of five million dollars in investible assets. Or "access-based positioning": even though your customers' needs may not be that distinctive, the ways of reaching them are. Carmike Cinemas, for example, only operates movie theaters in cities and towns of less than 200,000 people.

While you have to choose—the point Porter kept battering away on—just choosing a positioning isn't enough. You have to go on choosing, recognizing that there are trade-offs entailed in going down one path rather than the other. Your goal here is to align all your activities in such a way as to achieve Porter's other desideratum, which goes by the not-exactly-lyrical name of "fit." Porter's lead example of fit done right—indeed, in this era, seemingly everyone's favorite example of fit or what others called focus—was Southwest Airlines. In pursuit of its fly-cheap strategy, it had confronted the trade-offs, made the choices, and achieved the fit: only short flights, no meal service or link-ups with other airlines, only one type of aircraft for shorter turnarounds and more time in the air. While the value of fit was one of the oldest ideas in strategy, Porter claimed, people had lost sight of it in their bewitchment with core competencies or key success factors.

In his peroration, like a good evangelist, Porter offered both a glimpse of heaven and warnings of the snares that imperil an executive attempting to follow the rightful path. A company that achieves his "third-level fit," its activities reinforcing one another, the overall effort optimized, can expect to enjoy a strategic position that has a "horizon" of a decade or more; Porter didn't say exactly that your advantage will last that long, but the hint was there. To achieve that bliss, though, a company's leaders must avoid "a macho sense that [to make trade-offs] is a sign of weakness," the sense that they can compete on all dimensions simultaneously. They must also resist the siren call of operational effectiveness, which is "seductive because it is concrete and actionable," capable of delivering "tangible, measurable performance improvements," though without necessarily improving profitability. Most of all, the leaders have to fight the temptation to grow the business, which too often leads to "extending product lines, adding new features, imitating competitors' popular services, matching products, and even making acquisitions." No, if you're forced to grow, then you should deepen your position, "making your company's activities more distinctive, strengthening fit, and communicating the strategy better to those customers who should value it."

We're wafting off here toward what might be called the high platonic view of strategy, a world of immutable truths transcending and not particularly in touch with the grimy realities of day-to-day. Many of his readers may have felt left behind. In the face of Porter's ever-more-vociferous "You have to choose," they're still stuck with the classic question from the strategy-as-learning school, "But how much choice do most companies really have with respect to their position?" Don't they more often inherit one rather than being given the chance to start anew as, for instance, Southwest did? And what if the industry doesn't seem to offer any ready openings to doing something different?

With all that had gone with strategy over the prior ten years, it's also striking that Porter never mentioned shareholders or the increasingly desperate imperative to create wealth for them, which probably had something to do with the temptation to grow the business. He did allow that "managers have been under increasing pressure" to deliver those "tangible, measurable performance improvements." But this hardly addresses the near panic in some quarters, with companies downsizing, right-sizing, wrenching, pulling apart, and seeking new combination under the wheels of Greater Taylorism and a stock market's seemingly insatiable desire for more and better. Partly as a result, much of the thinking embodied in what Porter described as his first article really about strategy seems familiar, even tired, a throwback to an earlier time when competition seemed not so ferocious and the possibility of making a fresh choice readier to hand.

Maybe at some level Porter sensed this himself. He quickly received a contract to publish a book expounding and further developing the ideas in "What Is Strategy?" Thirteen years after the article appeared, that book remains unpublished. A mystery, perhaps, but not as intriguing as the question of why this man, whose work has had more effect on how companies chart their future than any other living scholar's, has yet to receive the Nobel Memorial Prize in economics.

Even before Porter's pronouncements or the collapse of reengineering, companies struggled to get much practical value from their understanding of core competencies and capabilities. Strategy consultants repeatedly observed that clients had difficulty defining their competencies precisely, these slippery creatures typically being a lot less quantifiable than, say, market share or even activities that made up one's value chain. Out of the confusion, a tendency emerged to claim a long list of competencies along with an unwillingness to concentrate on just a few, as the consultants and original authors on the subject all advised. As the trend toward downsizing gained strength, chief executives who took seriously the mandate to manage capabilities across traditional business boundaries found themselves increasingly confronted with unit managers digging in to protect their silos.

The still bigger problem may have been the perennial one, taking us back into strategy's Jungian shadow. I asked George Stalk about why capabilities, as a product, never did nearly as well for BCG as, say, the experience curve or the growth-share matrix. Normally a feisty man, he almost sighed. Putting capabilities to work involved changing behavior, he allowed. That was a lot more difficult than just "buying a concept off the shelf."

14.

The Revolution
Conquers the World

T HE WANING YEARS OF the twentieth century brought a
steady barrage of new questions for strategy. Will the Internet destroy my business model? We've retrenched for
years; now how do we grow? Those bastards from abroad are killing
us; we give up; how do we become a global competitor ourselves? Predictably, consultants and professors would try to supply companies
with fresh answers.

But while the ideas hawked as new at the turn of the twenty-first
century—"deconstructing" strategy to take into account the blowing to
bits of traditional value chains, growing from the core, strategy as a
portfolio of initiatives—did manage to move the ball down the field a
few yards, they hardly invented a new game. In 2005, McKinsey's
John Stuckey summed up this point: "Thinking on strategy has advanced steadily within and outside the Firm over the past forty years,
although not much progress has occurred in the past decade or so."
While another McKinsey partner would observe that former practice
heads always said that sort of thing years after stepping down, most

consultants and academics seem to agree with Stuckey. If you run into someone who doesn't, give said person the following challenge: name one strategy guru on the order of a Porter or Hamel who established his or her reputation after 1995, or the title of a best-selling book on the topic published since then. How many out there snap to at the names of W. Chan Kim and Renée Mauborgne?

Where partisans of the strategy revolution should find excitement in this era is in the spread of the paradigm around the globe, to wherever there were companies of sufficient size and sophistication to enlist the help of a McKinsey or Boston Consulting Group. And, increasingly, that was everywhere: Russia, China, India, anywhere opening itself up to the transformative power of free markets and the apparent triumph of American-style capitalism. As early as the 1970s, the firm that Bruce Henderson had started in 1963 derived nearly half its profits from outside the United States. Pound for pound, the best market in the world for high-level consulting today is Germany—McKinsey and BCG each have seven offices there—as it has been for two or three decades. As of this writing, McKinsey, with 94 locations in 52 countries, is headed by the Canadian-born Dominic Barton; BCG, 66 offices in 38 countries, by a German, Hans-Paul Bürkner.

The widening international reach of the strategy consulting firms provides a clear demonstration of how strategy itself was seeping into every corner of the world economy. But even more central to its triumph may be how it and related concepts had come to permeate managerial consciousness by the end of the twentieth century, the intellectualization of business on the march. The evidence for this is necessarily more subtle and indirect, mostly to be found in the astonishing increase in the number of MBA degrees granted not just in the United States but around the world. And in the ever-growing proportion of executives who have MBA degrees, including the swelling ranks of CEOs with not just an MBA but experience at a strategy consulting firm as well. These new business intellectuals were no longer just whomping up ideas. Increasingly, they were running the show.

McKinsey Exceeds Fred Gluck's Expectations

In 1988, his first year as managing director, Fred Gluck addressed McKinsey's partner conference and looked forward to the year 2000. By then, he predicted, the Firm would be operating in thirty countries—it was then in twenty-one—from seventy-five locations. He also outlined what he thought were the three major tasks that lay ahead. The first two were laced with globalism: accelerating "the development of our global consultants and [increasing] the effectiveness of our global networks" and continuing to "grow in countries where we are already well established" while at the same time expanding "our global network." The emphasis on the word *network* was not misplaced. Networking, with the word used in its modern sense as a verb, would play a crucial role in how McKinsey was to build its global business.

McKinsey had been international in a sense since it opened its first office abroad in 1959, in London. Its business abroad had grown quickly, mostly in the form of installing the M-form, or divisionalized structure from Alfred Chandler's work in companies such as Royal Dutch/Shell and Geigy, the Swiss manufacturer of chemicals and pharmaceuticals. The M-form was virtually unheard-of in Germany in 1950; twenty years later, according to one estimate, fifty out of the largest one hundred companies there had installed it, many with McKinsey's help.

Concepts weren't at the heart of McKinsey's approach to new clients, though; relationships were. In keeping with his belief that a company's original gene pool largely ordains its corporate destiny, Tom Peters observes that the essential strand of the Firm's genetic endowment reads "Advisor to CEOs." Creating that role for itself in new countries and new industries, if necessary working its way up the hierarchy from planners and divisional heads to get to the CEO, was the animating impulse behind much of its expansion.

257

A lot of this activity simply took the form of referrals. For example, Royal Dutch/Shell heard about McKinsey first from the chairman of Texaco. But in its early years abroad, the Firm was not averse to actively recruiting distinguished personages to help the process along. In 1966, with the London office already going strong, it had brought in Sir Alcon Copisarow as a director, or partner, the first from outside the United States, this despite the fact he had no prior consulting experience. What Sir Alcon did have were friends in the highest reaches of government, and they were soon bringing in McKinsey to consult on key projects.

The Firm's ability to insinuate itself into local elites drives its competitors slightly berserk with envy. In their eyes, McKinsey partners seeking to open a new office arrive in town bearing letters of introduction to the local corporate gentry from their counterparts elsewhere, satisfied clients typically. Somehow, given their backgrounds and polish, the partners are soon invited to join the most exclusive clubs. They play golf in such environs. They begin holding small dinners, perhaps at the club, perhaps in their swank homes—just a few congenial people like yourself, to kick around some issues we may have in common. They become active in local not-for-profits, almost certainly at the board level. And mysteriously, the son or daughter of a local corporate chieftain, attending business school far away, may find his or her interest in joining the Firm as a junior consultant heartily reciprocated.[1]

McKinsey partners don't deny that they're socially active, but they also note that it's been a longer, tougher slog to achieve acceptance as a peer to CEOs than their detractors might realize. Over a course of a thirty-year career, Herb Henzler built and led the Firm's German practice, became one of the three or four most powerful figures within McKinsey, and ceaselessly pushed the idea of building long-term relationships with clients. "I was driven by one experience," he says. As a young associate, he had two goals: working only on the client's biggest problems and dealing with client executives as an equal, not as a flunky adviser. This ambition was seared into his consciousness in the mid-1970s, when he attended a Bonn conference on co-determination, new laws that mandated a role for workers in management. "It was the first time I'd see the top hundred business leaders and the leading politicians, and I figured, we're here for the whole day and at the coffee breaks they'll come to us and say, 'You McKinsey folks, you must know how to deal with co-determination.' You know, nobody ever talked to us the whole day. Can you imagine what that does to you when you're twenty-eight years old and full of ideas—and of yourself? I said to myself afterward, 'Either you change this, or you leave.'"

He did the first. The effort consisted partly of what today we'd call coaching of executives whom he came to know: "I helped clients on their personal development, on how they positioned themselves vis à vis headquarters. I would help them prepare presentations they had to deliver." As the objects of his attention ascended through the ranks, McKinsey's ties with them and their companies became deeper and ever more enduring. By the time he retired from McKinsey in 2001, Henzler had consulted to Siemens without interruption for twenty-seven years, he calculates, and for nearly two decades to both Daimler and Bertelsmann.

As we've seen, strategy was an ideal product for a consultant aiming to work at the highest corporate levels, not just in Germany—Henzler credits McKinsey's nine-box matrix with getting the Firm in the door at Siemens in 1974—but also around the world. It offered the chief executive or division chief a framework with which to sort the unruly collection of businesses clamoring for attention and corporate investment. It also armed the corner office with analytic tools to justify any decisions about those businesses, reinforcing the power of the corporate center (power some of which may have been given away back when McKinsey had helped reorganize the company into strong product divisions).

By the early 1980s, after Gluck and Dick Foster had run most of the partners through strategy training sessions in Vevey, the Firm counted itself the leading purveyor of strategy consulting in the world. In

1980, upstart BCG's annual revenues had climbed to the point where they amounted to almost 35 percent of McKinsey's. By 1985, the Firm had beaten back the threat; BCG's total for the year amounted to 17 percent of McKinsey's $315 million (figure 14-1).[2]

In the language of the trade, McKinsey had taken share largely by growing the market. After merely doubling its revenues between 1975

FIGURE 14-1

Revenues of the "Big Three" strategy firms

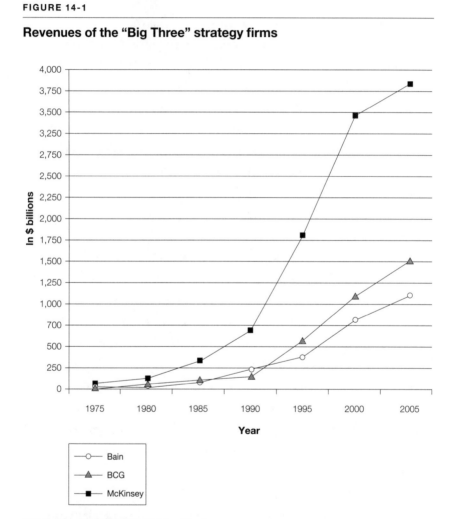

Source: Data compiled by Kennedy Information, Inc.

THE REVOLUTION CONQUERS THE WORLD

and 1980, it nearly tripled them in the five years thereafter. While the increase didn't all come from strategy work, much did, a more precise figure probably incalculable, given that the definition of what constituted a strategy study was becoming blurred to include almost any top-level assignment. What was clear was where the Firm was placing its bets geographically: between 1979 and 1988, when Gluck succeeded Ron Daniel as managing director, it opened twelve new offices. Three were in the United States, nine in Europe, and one in Hong Kong. Strategy was following the McKinsey flag, and that flag was being planted in Brussels, Lisbon, Geneva, and Helsinki.

Tellingly, in his 1988 maiden speech to his partners as managing director, Gluck barely mentioned strategy, secure as he and his colleagues were in their sense that the Firm had regained its place as "the preferred strategy consultant" to its clientele. But what just about everyone present also realized was that strategy by itself wouldn't be enough to sustain the kind of enduring relationships that McKinsey was seeking with giant corporations. (Gluck bragged to his partners that in the prior five years, the Firm had "served 76 of the top 100 companies in the *Fortune* 500, 21 of the top U.S. banks, 19 of the top insurance companies, 19 of the top diversified financial companies, and 23 of the top utility companies.") Yes, the challenges faced by these behemoths were steadily becoming more complex, but still, you couldn't and shouldn't expect them to overhaul their strategies entirely every year or two.

Partly in response to this concern, as an element in his campaign to make McKinsey's culture a "knowledge-based" one, Gluck had from the early 1980s been plumping for the creation of *centers of competence*, working groups that would build the Firm's expertise on rather grandly defined topics such as change management, integrated logistics, and corporate leadership. Perhaps more significantly for its subsequent history, he had also put energy behind the Firm's continued development of what it grandly called "clientele sectors" and what everyone else calls "industry practices"—automotive, banking, energy,

steel. This, despite the horror McKinsey partners traditionally registered at being thought specialists.

By 1983, McKinsey had eleven clientele sectors. While some of the
change may be attributed to Gluck's calls "to let 1,000 flowers bloom"—
Mao trumping Sun Tzu—more derived from the Firm's realization that
if it were to keep doubling or tripling in size, it would have to follow
the trajectory of its clients' needs for ever-more-specialized and technical knowledge. Industry practices were rooted in an easily identifiable
and repeatable set of clients.

Both of its principal competitors would eventually end up following
McKinsey's lead into industry practices and greater specialization, BCG
beginning with banking and health care in the late 1980s, Bain only after
it had escaped its ructions of the early 1990s. Today, each of the three
still proudly wraps itself in the appellation *strategy firm*. McKinsey, if
asked how much of its business comes under that heading, will usually
shrug gracefully and say "Perhaps thirty percent." Slightly keener-eyed
estimates from insiders put the figure for each of three firms at between fifteen and twenty percent. None of the three resemble what a
security analyst might call a pure-play strategy consultant. That beast
no longer exists, or if it does, it is the size of an insect and can escape
our notice.

Two other organizational changes after Gluck's election to managing director signaled a broadening and softening of the original push
to build a knowledge-based culture in favor of greater worship at the
altar of client service. Gluck handed off the role he had played in
championing practice development to a new committee headed by
Ted Hall. The "let 1,000 flowers bloom" approach had been so fecund
that by Hall's calculation, the original sectors and centers had spread
to become some "72 islands of activity," many the fiercely guarded pre-
serves of a single expert or two. As Hall explained to Harvard Business School professor Chris Bartlett, "By the early 1990s, too many
people were seeing practice development as the creation of experts
and the generation of documents in order to build our reputation. But

knowledge is only valuable when it is between the ears of consultants and applied to clients' problems. [W]e shifted our focus from developing knowledge to building individual and team capability."

Gluck himself had begun to thump the tub of "client impact," the notion that the Firm had to more deliberately ensure that its insights were actually making a difference for clients. In the best McKinsey tradition, a committee was organized to study just that. Perhaps the most important of its successful recommendations was for a change in what Bartlett calls the firm's "key consulting unit," away from the "engagement team" toward the client service team. Instead of focusing on discrete projects of three or four months—"engagements," in McKinsey-speak—teams would be formed with a core group, usually partners, drawn from different engagement teams and tying these teams together to serve a particular client for longer periods, preferably forever. The client service team would thus incorporate some of the virtues of Bill Bain's original consulting model, but without the unpleasantness of confining oneself to just one competitor in an industry. Ted Hall's committee told the new leaders of industry practices and capability groups that henceforth, their units would be judged on how well they supported client service teams.

In 1994, with Gluck barred by his age from running for another three-year term, McKinsey's partners elected Rajat Gupta as their new managing director, the first maximum leader born outside the United States. Equipped with an undergraduate degree in mechanical engineering from the Indian Institute of Technology and an MBA from Harvard, Gupta had headed the Firm's offices first in Scandinavia, then in Chicago. Certain parts of Gluck's legacy, most notably the push for growth and global expansion, he clearly embraced. When Gluck left office, McKinsey had 58 offices in 24 countries, with 3,300 consultants, among them 425 partners, generating annual revenues of $1.5 billion. By 2001, with Gupta in his third term, the world's preeminent strategy firm—as it thought of itself—had 81 offices in 44 countries, 7,700 consultants, 891 partners, and revenues of $3.4 billion.

The emphasis on building long-term relationships with clients also continued unabated, indeed intensified. In 2002, John Byrne would report in *BusinessWeek* that the Firm had more than four hundred active clients whom it had been serving for fifteen years or longer. The days of the one-off engagement were largely over, taking with them, perhaps, some of the avidity for short, sharp, empirically based insights that might unsettle the client.

Each new generation of organizational leadership typically wants to overthrow aspects of what it inherited. In the case of McKinsey under Gupta, among the discards were some of the means by which Gluck had sought to build McKinsey's knowledge culture. Speaking for the record, most who have held senior positions at the Firm since the Gluck era resolutely deny that McKinsey has yarded back on its efforts to discover new concepts. Quite to the contrary, they argue, pointing to a series of sallies mounted under Gupta: an institute formed in the late 1990s to study manufacturing, following the example of the McKinsey Global Institute, which enlisted scholars from outside to study issues of worldwide import; seven "special initiatives" launched on topics of high interest to clients (e.g., the Internet and its impact, globalization); a beefing-up of the industry groups, which came to number sixteen. In 1996, two years into his first term, Gupta would tell Harvard's Bartlett, "We have easily doubled our investment in knowledge over these past couple of years."

But at the same time, production of McKinsey staff papers, once the sword points of the Gluckian revolution, virtually ceased, a casualty of the perception that they were too much a part of "the creation of experts and the generation of documents in order to build our reputation." A qualification for partner advancement that Gluck had tried to install, requiring each candidate to demonstrate expertise in an area, perhaps by authoring a significant research paper on a subject, was abandoned. So-called administrative partners who had designed and proselytized for the systems by which McKinsey internally shared its insights left the Firm. Looked at another way, perhaps the point is that

Fred Gluck's efforts to build a new culture, like the strategy revolution itself, had succeeded, were institutionalized, and now could be happily subsumed in the pursuit of other ideals—client service, work and learning as teams, continuing global expansion, more technical competence in particular industries or functions.

The collapse of the technology boom and the stock market at century's end would land many of the Firm's clients in trouble—most famously Enron, headed by former McKinsey partner Jeffrey Skilling and a consistent generator of around $10 million a year in billings, but also Global Crossing, Kmart, and Swissair, all of which declared bankruptcy. McKinsey's growth leveled off in 2001, for the first time in memory, and partners were called on to inject capital back into the Firm. As senior consultants who have been through such experiences at McKinsey or other firms attest, when business falls off, partner interest in breaking new intellectual ground largely evaporates; the rallying cry becomes client development, maintaining current relationships, and hunting for fresh ones.

You can find voices among McKinsey alumni arguing that the effects of the 2001 shocks still linger, even though the Firm soon began to grow its revenues again, albeit more slowly than in the golden years, the 1980s and 1990s. Strains born of the 2008 global financial collapse, while seemingly milder in their effect, may have heightened the discipline around client focus. "They're just not as interested in developing ideas anymore" goes the refrain from a half dozen former partners. Surveying the intellectual landscape around strategy at least, it's sadly difficult to find evidence to prove them wrong.

What BCG Learned in Europe

The Boston Consulting Group's successful penetration of continental Europe is a tale of two cities, Munich and Paris. It's also the tale of Dr. Hermann Grabherr of Siemens, who almost singlehandedly sparked the founding of the first German offices of both BCG and Bain, while also helping to underwrite the research of Tom Peters and Bob Waterman at McKinsey. For Grabherr, the story did not lead to a happy end.

Founded in 1847 and with a long history of making equipment to generate electricity, Siemens had by the late 1960s rebuilt itself from the rubble of World War II. It employed over 270,000 people worldwide, had annual revenues of around $2.5 billion, and had recently reorganized itself into six large operating groups, with a few central departments to guarantee consistency in at least some corporate policies. Grabherr was a corporate planner and a hound for the latest concepts that might be of use to his employer.

As the story goes, Grabherr first encountered Bruce Henderson and his ideas when the consultant spoke, some say, to an executive course the German was attending at Harvard Business School; others say it was at a BCG strategy conference. In the ensuing discussion, Grabherr asked a question, which, ever the diplomat, Henderson brusquely dismissed. But Grabherr persisted, approaching Henderson afterward to begin a series of increasingly intense discussions about BCG's ideas. Finally, in 1975, Grabherr invited BCG to open an office in Munich, where Siemens had its headquarters, intimating that his company would provide enough work to justify the start-up. Henderson dispatched John Clarkeson, he of the first experience-curve studies and by now an alumnus of both the London and Milan offices, to establish the beachhead.

In temperament, Clarkeson, who in 1985 would succeed Alan Zakon as chief executive of BCG, seems almost the opposite of his predecessors in the role. Quiet, self-effacing, a declared believer in the power of empathy and of listening instead of talking, he would head the firm until 1998, as much as anyone "heads" a band of fiercely independent types like BCG partners. More than any other individual he's responsible for pulling the firm up out of the tough period of the early 1980s and setting it on a growth trajectory that would increase its revenues tenfold over the next decade.

Like other veterans of BCG's early days, Clarkeson fervently espouses the distinction between strategy and strategic planning; he says
he doesn't think the firm ever wrote a strategic plan for a client. But at
Siemens he found himself supplying a set of concepts and frameworks—not just the experience curve and growth-share matrix, but
also the industry-attractiveness grid—that Grabherr pushed out to
business units in the hope of eventually standardizing their use across
divisions. There were competing frameworks on the premises in the
person of Henzler with McKinsey's nine-box matrix; indeed, Grabherr's boss seemed more inclined in the Firm's direction. But BCG's
conceptual apparatus won out and was broadly installed, in part,
Clarkeson thinks, because his firm's approach was seen as more rooted
in empiricism. The BCG monopoly didn't last long, only until about
1980, but by that time, close to half of the firm's profits came from its
German operations.

And not just from Siemens. BCG had also deployed in Germany the
key weapons it had used in establishing the retail market for business
concepts in the United States. It had mailed out *Perspectives* translated
into German. In 1976, it introduced a conference on strategy for senior executives at Kronberg, in Hesse, at a luxury hotel that had once
been the residence of Germany's last dowager empress. Even though
BCG largely gave up holding conferences in the United States by the
late 1980s—too many events, including CSC Index's, competing for
too little executive time—the Kronberg Conference continues to this
day. The BCG pioneers soon found, though, that clients weren't interested in just their ideas. German companies pulled them in new directions, toward helping more with implementation and getting down
into the trenches, for reasons that reflect why that country proved
such a wonderful market for strategy consulting.

Some of the commonly cited reasons flirt with stereotypes. For instance, there's the contention that German executives actually like theory, in sharp contrast to their counterparts from the United States. (In
Europe, one is more likely to encounter companies where everyone in

senior management possesses a doctorate. Or maybe they just use the title more. How often do you hear references to Dr. Andy Grove and Dr. Jack Welch, both holders of the degree?) There's also the impression that Germans were more inclined toward precision and deep analysis, while being not uninterested in domination and control. (Von Clausewitz, anyone?)

Other reasons for the consultant's success have more of a substratum of fact. While Germany virtually invented the modern research university in the nineteenth century and has a distinguished history in technology and science, it has had no business schools or systematic education in management until very recently, well after the strategy consultants arrived there. (This, coupled with the lack of investment banks to compete with for recruits, enabled the likes of BCG to bring on board some of the brightest young minds in the country who had an interest in business.) A majority of top managers in German companies had backgrounds in engineering, with the valence that brought with it concepts like the experience curve.

The backbone of the country's economy, and still its largest employer, is the so-called *mittelstand* companies, medium-sized—annual revenues in the tens of millions of dollars, perhaps hundreds of millions, but not billions—often family owned and built around manufacturing a single type of highly engineered product for sale at home and abroad. But partly because the triumphant Allies after World War II had worked so hard to break up German conglomerates, even giant recombinants such as Siemens lacked bench strength in disciplines such as finance and marketing, which a McKinsey or BCG could supply as part of a strategy package.

As the consultants pushed into Germany with their ideas, they soon found their clients pushing back a bit. "The Europeans were much stronger on 'How do we execute it?' says Bolko von Oetinger, formerly a senior partner in BCG's Munich office, longtime director of the Kronberg Conference, and founder in 1998 of the firm's Strategy Institute. "Clients forced us; we had to change if we wanted to grow our market share." Siemens, for example, had insisted that project teams include its managers as well as BCG consultants, a requirement that became common among German clients. "The clients said, 'We paid not only for solutions but also for training for our best people,' and not just planners, but lots of line executives. And line people, of course, say, 'Yeah, it's a fascinating idea, but tell me how to make it work, tell me how to do this.'"

Von Oetinger sums up what BCG was hearing from German management: "Let's go down to the shop floor and change things there. That will be the source of our competitive advantage." It was, he notes, the Germans teaching their consultants to look for a strategic edge in capabilities, and this long before George Stalk and others had begun to proclaim the importance of same.

Not that the BCG consultants wrote up their findings. An intriguing pattern had begun to emerge, not just at BCG but at McKinsey as well, intriguing at least to students of how ideas gain circulation in a globally integrated economy. While most of the critical ideas on corporate strategy would originate with Americans, or native speakers of English, it was often in countries outside the United States that the strategy consulting firms were learning to work most effectively with clients and in the most lasting ways. Combing through the library of BCG *Perspectives*, McKinsey staff papers, or the books that emanated from either firm, one has difficulty finding any literature from Europe or Asia, with the conspicuous exceptions of the work of George Stalk and Tom Hout from Japan for BCG and Ken Ohmae's from that country for McKinsey. And yet it was from outside the United States that the firms increasingly derived the bulk of their revenue and found ways to work with clients, seemingly in perpetuity. The consultants were clearly supplying to distant lands something that companies there couldn't find in their own backyard.

With the imprimatur of their work at Siemens and fresh clients coming in after each conference, BCG steadily expanded its practice in Germany, opening new offices across the country to better enable its consultants to maintain a fairly constant presence at client headquarters. Beginning in the 1980s, as David Hall ramped up the firm's financial-services practice, a young colleague, Hans-Paul Bürkner, began knocking on the doors of Germany's large banks, many of them already McKinsey clients. He won enough of a welcome to steadily build BCG's share of the business as even Germany's banking sector gradually registered the effects of deregulation and globalization. His standing within the firm rose accordingly, even as the financial-services practice worldwide, which he headed, came to represent nearly a third of BCG's total revenues. In 2003, his partners elected him chief executive of BCG, the first one to have never written a *Perspectives* piece (although he had coauthored articles on finance for the firm).

Grabherr didn't fare as well, though not for want of energy in his quest for the best ideas. In the acknowledgments pages of *In Search of Excellence*, Peters and Waterman single him and another Siemens executive out for special thanks for their support of the research project and for the "relentless and always thoughtful questioning [that] was often critical to the honing of our ideas." Bill Bain tells of how at about the same time Grabherr approached him, telling him that while McKinsey was Siemens's principal consultant, some said the company didn't get sufficient input from other quarters. Would Bain & Company like to work on a substantial project, one of sufficient magnitude to justify creating a Munich outpost? Bain did, opening its first office in Germany in 1982. (The office ended up lasting only as long as the project, some two years. Bain & Company would go back into Germany later, but then its international expansion was always more opportunistic and less systematic than that of its principal competitors.) Van Oetinger sums up Grabherr's attitude: "If I use all of them, I'll get the best from all and I won't have missed anything."

What he did miss out on was advancement within his organization. Consultants who worked with him tell of his failure to move up to the second level of management, never mind the first. Some attributed it to his tendency to hoard the concepts he was bringing in, not sharing them widely with colleagues and instead earning their dislike. Whatever the causes of his bitterness and unhappiness, in 1986, Grabherr committed suicide, a sad fate for the man who had done much to introduce the strategy revolution to his native land.

How BCG came to work for most of the largest companies in France represents still another instance of adaptive localism, but Gallic in its details just as the German success was Teutonic. René Abate, a young engineer and graduate of one of the *grandes écoles*, earned an MBA degree from Harvard and then joined the Boston Consulting Group in 1974, a year after it had opened an office in Paris. The operation was tiny, some six people compared with ten times that many in McKinsey's Paris office. BCG's nascent French operation mounted the standard campaign, sending out *Perspectives* in translation, putting on conferences. The firm's concepts began to generate interest, including at the senior-most levels. "We brought to CEOs power they had lost, levers they were missing to exercise their power," Abate says, giving them frameworks to justify their allocation of resources across different divisions and businesses, just as strategy had in the United States. "And the quantitative dimension of our work, the rational, was very much congenial to their frame of mind. BCG was the most Cartesian U.S. consulting firm."

As in the United States, the Boston Consulting Group's image in France, its intellectual presence, grew faster than its book of business did. After the battering that American companies had suffered in the 1970s, followed by recession there in the early 1980s, the United States came to seem less a beacon of managerial wisdom. For a few years after the election of Socialist President François Mitterrand and the nationalization of the largest French companies, the Paris office merely puttered along.

Something had to change, and in 1985, it did. With Clarkeson now chief executive back in Boston, encouraging more globalism and experimentation, the French operation decided to effectively relaunch itself, focusing on large and promising companies and vowing, as Abate puts it, "that a client was a client forever." It began tracking the length of its service to clients, with the ideal of providing billable help every single month, possibly excepting August, when everyone was out. Abate, who by now headed the office, also abandoned the traditional BCG focus on measuring its consultants according to the hours they billed. No, he told his colleagues, take time your time and get to know the client's organization, its people, where they went to school.

It helped that in 1986, France, with a newly elected conservative prime minister "cohabiting" with Mitterrand, began reversing the nationalization of companies that Mitterrand had launched on coming into power earlier in the decade. Giants such as Saint-Gobain (in glass and plastics), Rhône-Poulenc (chemicals and pharmaceuticals), and Thomson (electronics and media) found themselves liberated to recast themselves, an imperative given the opportunities and dangers of globalization pressing upon them. And BCG could help. "In the last twenty years, French companies have done more reshaping of their portfolios than companies in the U.S." Abate argues, "or in Germany." He also boasts that "in the eighties and nineties, we did more strategy work"—real, transform-the-corporation strategy work—"than any other BCG office in the world." Its clients became far more focused, he says, on businesses where they had, or could build, a competitive advantage.

Today, with three hundred consultants, BCG's Paris office is fully the equal of McKinsey's, Abate observes, if not larger. It now serves two-thirds of the forty largest French companies, including a number of the big banks, on a continuing basis. Certain topics did not sell as well among them as they did in the United States—Abate says that their interest in shareholder value developed only recently. But with Greater Taylorism following in strategy's wake—though in France, perhaps better to label it *Cartesianism*—that, too, may eventually follow.

The Golden Horde

Today, when the terms *hotshot* and *MBA* are not infrequently used together, it may be difficult to recall that there was a time in living memory when both the degree and its holders were rather looked down upon. In the late 1960s, at some allegedly elite colleges in the United States, if you were judged brilliant in your studies it was expected you'd go on to take a PhD in your field and perhaps go from there to the faculty ranks that were steadily expanding to greet the incoming baby-boomer wave. For those an intellectual peg lower, medical school and law were perfectly respectable alternatives. And then for those whose gifts ran more to athleticism, hearty interpersonal skills, and a dazzling smile, there was always business school.

This began to change materially in the 1970s, and the strategy consulting firms had a role in driving the change. So did economics, at both the individual and the institutional level. The MBA degree was already becoming more in demand. In 1948, slightly more than 3,000 master's degrees in business were granted in the United States. By the late 1960s, the number exceeded 20,000 a year. As Rakesh Khurana recounts in *From Higher Aims to Hired Hands*, in 1972 some 32,000 MBAs graduated from about four hundred schools or programs, almost twice as many programs as were around in 1964. By 1980, degrees granted exceeded 57,000, and programs numbered more than six hundred. (And the throng would continue to grow over the rest of our history: in 2006, 146,406 MBA degrees were granted in the United States.)

Institutional supply propelled some of the trend. Schools found they could make money teaching business. Candidates were prepared to make the investment, particularly after the economy turned tough in the early 1970s, because they increasingly saw the degree as almost guaranteeing a job, and one with a healthy salary and assured prospects.

The rise of the MBA degree may not be a perfect proxy for the spread of strategy first in the United States, then around the world, but there are strong threads tying the two together. We've already noted how with the rise of Michael Porter, strategy came to displace traditional business policy courses in the Harvard Business School curriculum.[3] With the massive sales of Porter's books, faculty at HBS and elsewhere woke up to the centrality of the subject and the opportunity it presented. While they couldn't always agree on how it should be taught, or by whom—at Stanford, for example, the subject seems sometimes the province of economists; at other times, the property of the organizational-studies types—strategy gradually became a fixture in the MBA curricula.

In 2008, Peter Navarro published the results of an online survey he had conducted on what was taught at the top fifty business schools in the United States, as ranked by *BusinessWeek*, the *Financial Times*, and *US News & World Report*. Corporate strategy, he found, was part of the core curriculum, the courses required of all students, at 92 percent of the institutions. Only marketing, finance, accounting, and operations had higher percentages, and those disciplines had been around for six or seven decades at least, strategy for a mere three.

No comparable survey exists for the curricula of business schools outside the United States—or none that I can find—but this shouldn't distract us from the larger point, one with great import for the further global spread of strategy: management education is on a tear worldwide, booming, effulgent. The *Financial Times* recently reported that "around 500,000 students will graduate with MBAs globally this year"; that number seems high, but not beyond the realm of possibility. There are over one thousand degree-granting programs in India, producing north of eighty thousand graduates a year, all educated in English. China, which had virtually no business-school education ten years ago, now graduates around thirty thousand students a year, according to the *FT*.

To be sure, most of these programs are not spending a lot of time on high-level Porterian analysis; they concentrate instead on basic business skills such as accounting and rudimentary finance. We can, however, expect such efforts to move up the intellectual food chain, including into the empyrean of strategy. This in keeping with an overall global trend toward greater and more sophisticated learning.[4]

We can also be reasonably confident that the strategy consulting firms will continue to have their pick of the best graduates of the best programs. Coincident with the rise of strategy and a driving force behind it, an ever-greater share of MBAs from elite institutions has been hired by consulting outfits. Khurana notes that in 1965, only 4 percent of Harvard's MBA class went into consulting. By 1975, the proportion was up to 12 percent, by 1985 to 22 percent. It has bounced around since then, depending on how consulting stacked up in a particular year against, say, investment banking, but always from a high base, up to 30.5 percent in 1993, down to 22 percent in 2007, when the siren call of Wall Street was particularly strong.

And among consultants recruiting at Harvard and other schools like it, the three strategy firms were preeminent, both in the prestige conferred and in the money offered. As we've seen, from their founding, BCG and Bain set out to hire the smartest people they could find at Harvard Business School and its ilk, driving up the price for McKinsey, which had pioneered MBA recruiting in the 1950s. Their policy of continuing to offer graduates a premium compared with other potential employers continues to this day. Of the eight "functions"—approximately "types of job"—that HBS tracked its 2007 graduates as going into, consulting had the highest median base salary, at $120,000. Add in a typical signing bonus of $20,000 to get closer to the true first year's pay.

As MBA compensation plumped up from the 1970s on, so did the quality of the people seeking the degree. Khurana nicely sums up the progress made, suggesting in the process another force making for the intellectualization of business: "By the late 1970s, the intellectual gap (as measured by standardized test scores) between students entering an elite business school and those matriculating at an elite law school or a doctoral program—a gap that had persisted more than eight decades—was rapidly closing. The typical student in the elite MBA programs in the 1970s was much more academically oriented than earlier business school students had been, owing not just to increased competition for slots in these programs, but also to qualitatively differ-ent admissions standards reflecting the new analytical orientation of the curriculum"—think Michael Porter—"and the values of research-oriented faculty."

As the MBA talent available to consulting firms grew ever more lus-trous and the share of the talent they scooped up ever larger, it became a commonplace to decry the woeful diversion of the brightest young business minds from the real work of management into the ranks of parasitic consulting. I wrote an article or two along these lines myself. This, I now realize, was a monumentally stupid argument—though some continue to make it—for at least two reasons. First, it is premised on the assumption that the fresh-caught MBA will remain a consultant the rest of his or her life. The odds are dauntingly against this. The up-or-out policies of the consulting firms, a reflection of their struc-ture—the income of the seniors being dependent on the firm's ability to bill out teams of lesser-paid juniors—dictate that no more than one out of eight or ten who start will survive the progressive weeding process and eventually make partner. While 25 percent of Harvard's MBAs may go into consulting in any given year, only 11 percent of HBS alumni say they continue to work in the industry. It's probably more accurate to view a two- or three-year initial stint in consulting as akin to the postdoctoral program a newly minted PhD scientist might embark on, as an opportunity to develop and hone analytical skills originally acquired in school.

Second, for all they may complain about not being able to hire the best MBAs, it isn't at all evident that most traditional companies, in-cluding industrial giants, have entry-level positions that fully put to use the education, particularly in analytics, that a new, hotshot gradu-ate comes equipped with. Among the reasons why large companies hire strategy consulting firms is that the companies don't continuously

THE REVOLUTION CONQUERS THE WORLD

need, and can't support economically or organizationally, the concentrations of high-octane brain power that the consulting firms can assign to a project.[5] Which is not to say there isn't a place for such MBAs in the management of a company. More and more of them are finding such a place. The question is, by what route? Tom Tierney, Bain & Company's managing director for much of the 1990s, tells the story of two men he knew, both of whom graduated from the same business school the same year. One went to work at a large industrial company, working his way upward slowly through various line jobs. The other joined a strategy consulting firm and after a few years was recruited by the same company. But the former consultant took a position two or three levels above that occupied by his classmate, and at a superior salary level, comparable to the pay he got as a consultant.

Taking Share of the Chief Executive Brain

Evidence for the percolation of strategy into the consciousness of CEOs ranges from the hit-you-in-the-face obvious to the more indirect, if possibly more interesting. In the first category, one can simply call the roll of executives who are alumni of the modern strategy consulting firms and who have gone on to become CEOs of major corporations.[6] Viewed from a greater height, most of these individuals can be taken as a subset of a larger phenomenon, the ascent of MBAs—their ranks growing, their quality improving—into ever more of the senior management positions at large companies. As of this writing, for example, General Electric, Procter & Gamble, and J.P. Morgan Chase & Co. are each headed by a modern-era Harvard MBA. GE's Jeff Immelt held a summer internship at BCG; P&G's A. G. Lafley entertained an offer from McKinsey before deciding to go to work at the consumer-products giant.

Throughout much of the postwar period, business schools such as Harvard's had swollen their coffers and broadened their influence with so-called executive education, courses to which companies sent rising executives for a few weeks or months of schooling, preparatory to higher office. Two of the most prestigious were Harvard's Program for Management Development for "high-potential middle managers" and its Advanced Management Program, for senior executives about to be promoted into the very highest corporate ranks. The not-so-secret rationale for both these programs, which granted certificates, not degrees, was to equip their students with many of the technical and analytic skills they would have acquired by getting an MBA. By the 1990s, Harvard was having trouble filling these two programs with sufficient applicants from the United States, partly because few Americans felt they could take two or three months off for the experience, but, even more significantly, because more of the natural candidates *already had* MBAs.

Once they found themselves in the CEO's chair, the highest responsibility of this, the best-educated generation of managers, was to make strategy, of course. Indeed, it was about this time that the consulting firms began to complain that clients were becoming more demanding, often because the advice-givers now found themselves dealing with MBAs at least or, even more exacting, with former strategy consultants.

For an example of how a consultant becomes a CEO, consider a famous blazer of that particular trail, Louis V. Gerstner Jr. Born in 1942 to a close-knit Catholic family on Long Island, he went to Dartmouth on a scholarship, taking a degree in engineering science—what else?—and then proceeding on to Harvard for an MBA. On graduation, he joined McKinsey & Company, where by his early thirties, he became a senior partner in charge of three big clients. After twelve years at the Firm, he left to join one of them, American Express, as the head of its Travel Related Services Groups.

Even though his departure from McKinsey in 1977 slightly preceded the Gluckian revolution, by his own account, Gerstner picked up on its antecedents. In his best-selling 2002 memoir, *Who Says*

Elephants Can't Dance? Gerstner reports that the most important thing he learned at the Firm "was the detailed process of understanding the underpinnings of a company. McKinsey was obsessive about deep analysis of the company's marketplace, its competitive position, and its strategic direction."

In his twelve years at American Express, Gerstner would expand the charge-card business mightily, develop what he called "a sense of the strategic value of information," and be disappointed to find that the free flow of ideas that had obtained at McKinsey didn't course quite so freely up and down the hierarchy of a more traditional company. A bit frustrated, too, by his inability to advance to the top of that hierarchy, in 1979, he won the "beauty contest of the decade" and was selected to become chief executive of RJR Nabisco, which had just been the prize of a leveraged buyout by Kohlberg Kravis Roberts. All of Gerstner's strategic smarts didn't keep him from leaping atop the wrong horse at just the wrong time, however. Soon after his arrival, the leveraged-buyout bubble burst, and Gerstner found himself scrambling to refinance the company, selling off $11 billion of assets—that would be businesses and people—in his first year on the job. The experience left him with "a profound appreciation of the importance of cash in corporate performance," he says.

For the purposes of our example, what all this led up to was Gerstner's being recruited in 1993 to take the CEO position at IBM, a fabled paragon of American enterprise that had seemingly lost its way. In a press conference in July of that year, announcing cost-cutting initiatives and layoffs—a departure from Big Blue's traditional norms—Gerstner spontaneously offered up what he admits was "the most quotable" remark he ever made: "There's been a lot of speculation as to when I'm going to deliver a vision of IBM, and what I'd like to say to all of you is that the last thing IBM needs right now is a vision." He was promptly pilloried in the press for his shortsightedness.

What doesn't get quoted, and more accurately reflects the spirit of the times, is what he went on to say: "What IBM needs right now is a series of very tough-minded, market-driven, highly effective strategies for each of its businesses—strategies that deliver performance in the marketplace and shareholder value. And that's what we're working on." While organs like the *Economist* would ask, "But does cost-cutting amount to a strategy for survival?" in other quarters there were cheers. Michael Hammer would tell the *New York Times*, "This is the most important kind of change that can come from the top."

Gerstner's subsequent successes at IBM are outside the purview of this history, though not the observation that most were rooted in his focus on the three Cs of strategy, or as he puts it, the "customers' needs" of a company, "its competitive environment, and its economic realities." In 2002, Gerstner retired, generally credited as having worked a turnaround. Later—completing the perfect trajectory for our narrative—he joined a private equity firm.

Gerstner's example also points us to a hypothesis, not proven or even provable, about one of strategy's effects on the sociology of corporations: namely, that the emergence of the paradigm both helped accelerate the trend toward greater mobility of CEOs between companies and, even harder to nail down, increased the distance between the top and those who worked in the ranks below them. These days, when each morning's newspaper seems to carry a story of a fresh chief executive hired in to save a troubled enterprise, it's easy to forget what a relatively recent phenomenon this is. Up until a decade or two ago, companies of any reputation prided themselves on promoting from within, carefully grooming the new leader by years of rotation through ever-more-challenging assignments.

In his 2002 book, *Searching for a Corporate Savior: The Irrational Quest for Charismatic CEOs*, Harvard's Khurana charts how the "dismissal rates" for CEOs have increased dramatically, with the chief of a large company appointed in the first half of the 1990s being three times as likely to be fired for the same level of performance as a CEO appointed in 1980. Khurana attributes much of the change to more active corporate boards, themselves pressured by institutional investors hungering after greater shareholder returns. Egged on by an executive-search industry that had more interest in moving talent from one company to another than in seeing enterprises grow their own, boards increasingly turned to a "charismatic" outsider, one holding out the promise of working change, in part because such a candidate is unencumbered by ties to the people or managerial ways of the company he or she is recruited to lead.

I'd question whether directors weren't as often concerned with the candidate's ability as a strategist as they were with the individual's charisma. Had he or she demonstrated an ability to devise a winning formula and execute it? After all, by what other construct but strategy could an executive structure an understanding of the enterprise he or she was to head and communicate that understanding to both employees and the board? To be sure, boards wanted "a good operating executive," someone able to "get the job done." But for the top post, for the maximum leader, surely more must be required. Vision, charisma, seem a little, well, soft—how do you attach dollars and cents to them? Ah, but a strategy laying out a nice, clear path to increased shareholder value, with the stock price as a readily available measure of how the new honcho is doing—that's the ticket. Khurana notes that what boards were looking for at bottom was the ability to work change, and as we've seen, in the modern corporate era, bringing in a new strategy was *the* way to beget change.

And what possibly could be lost thereby, in bringing someone, say, from Motorola to Kodak (George Fisher), or from GE, that preeminent modern academy for CEOs, to The Home Depot (Robert Nardelli)? What threat could that pose to the fabric of a corporation? One possibility suggests itself from one of the best studies ever conducted of how executives actually succeed in getting anything done: John Kotter's 1986 book, *The General Managers*.

Kotter, a professor at HBS, shadowed thirteen general managers—a technical use of the term, we'd call almost all of them senior executives—who were judged by their companies to be high performers. What he found tracking their daily rounds was that they moved the world forward not by issuing orders or making speeches, but rather by a seemingly endless series of small interactions—a question here, a brief comment there—with scores or even hundreds of people they knew, networks within the company and the industry that they had built up over years. The new CEO from outside, gifted as she may be in decision-making and the interpersonal arts, what can she lean on in the absence of such a network? Often some people, known to her from a prior job, whom she'll bring with her. But also the dream, the confidence, the clarity, the hope embodied in a strategy.

15.

Three Versions of Strategy as People

AS THE U.S. ECONOMY of the 1990s bubbled its way toward the twenty-first century, the appeal of strategy as process began to give way to the greater urgencies of fiercening capitalism. Corporate attention paid to the three Cs intensified. "Reengineering kind of overwhelmed time-based competition," laments Mark Blaxill, until recently a partner at BCG. Even after the vogue for that particular construct collapsed, the pressure for continual, relentless cost cutting went on unabated.

As if finally listening to voices like those of Tom Peters, companies began paying greater heed to customers, or at least heed in new, more analytic forms befitting the march of Greater Taylorism. In 1996, Bain's Fred Reichheld published *The Loyalty Effect*, beautifully titled to capture the eye of managers who felt loyalty leaching away from every corner of corporate life. The book taught legions to calculate the lifetime value of a customer, not just what you made on the last transaction with him or her. Software makers pushed into the market with so-called customer-relationship management packages, enabling companies to track each jot and tittle of business they did with buyers. The

Internet was celebrated as providing broad new avenues into the customer's mind and wallet.

Where the picture seemed more confusing and getting blurrier all the time was in the small matter of figuring out just who your competitors were and where they came from. Consultants spoke of "industry boundaries becoming more porous," while laypeople were riveted with stories of traditional players driven to the wall by competition from unexpected quarters—encyclopedia publishers brought to their knees by Microsoft, the music business upended by Apple and the iPod.

Michael Porter may have inveighed that you had to choose what would make you different. But where were you to look for that difference, and even if you found it, how long was it likely to last? It was all enough to make one doubt whether there was such a thing as a sustainable competitive advantage.

Today, sentences like the following have become mandatory in the literature of management: From Gary Hamel's latest book, "Recent research by L. G. Thomas and Richard D'Aveni"—as yet unpublished but apparently an update on D'Aveni's 1994 book *Hypercompetition*—"suggests that industry leadership is changing hands more frequently, and competitive advantage is eroding more rapidly, than ever before." Or this from the 2008 tome that concluded a trilogy on strategy from Bain's Chris Zook: "In our 2004 Growth Survey of 259 executives worldwide, 60 percent reported that their primary source of competitive advantage in their core business was eroding rapidly; 65 percent said that they would need to fundamentally restructure the commercial model they used to serve their core customers; and 72 percent believed that their primary competitor in five years would not be the company that was currently their primary competitor." To borrow a wonderful line from *The Communist Manifesto* on the effect of capitalism, all that is solid melts into air, including, apparently, competitive advantage.

In the face of such gasification, where was a company to seek an edge enduring enough to build a strategy around? One possibility, seemingly more valuable all the time, was McKinsey's "tradable privileged assets"—brands, patents, trademarks—that could be sold or, more importantly, bought. Some observers widened the discussion to argue that "intellectual capital" constituted the "new wealth of organizations," as posited by the subtitle of the best book on the subject, Tom Stewart's *Intellectual Capital*. But unlike the financial variety, intellectual capital beyond the tradable was damnably difficult to measure, anatomize, or capture, no easier than core competencies.

If your existing advantage was always evaporating, might not the only practicable course be to create a new competitive advantage— invent the product that will make the other alternatives obsolete, create a market where none existed before? Besides, innovation and entrepreneurialism seemed so much more exciting than, say, knowledge management—the quotidian work of tending your intellectual capital. Glamorous, too. In the eyes of the public, the heroes of business were becoming not the "captains of industry"—when was the last time you heard that phrase?—such as the CEOs of a DuPont or a General Motors. Rather, they were the entrepreneurs behind an Apple Computers (founded in 1976), a Microsoft (1978), an Amazon.com (1994), an eBay (1995), or a Google (1998).

Fastening on people as the critical resource for innovation and growth is the first of three ways of conceiving of strategy as centered on people we'll look at in this chapter. Consider each approach a new, young branch on what was becoming quite a thick, in places tangled bush. The second version of strategy as people consists of attempts to use the concept of the network to analyze ways in which individuals relate to one another, this as a stepping-stone to competitive advantage.

The third version may seem the most surprising: private equity, and what private equity firms do with the businesses they acquire, as a kind of apotheosis of strategy. The argument here is that private equity outfits typically employ tactics straight out of the classic strategy playbook. Moreover, their MO represents a form of transformation likely to become increasingly common in the years ahead, particularly for long-established companies with less-than-clear prospects. It's no accident that private equity (PE) firms have become among the biggest clients of the strategy consulting giants. Also no accident that private equity has become the destination of choice for partners leaving the strategy consulting business, at least until the recent global financial collapse slowed the outflow in that direction. If you want to know what it would look like for a strategy consultant to actually run a company, gaze no further than the properties held in the portfolios of many a PE firm; that is precisely what's going on there.

Our discussion of the third P of strategy's history will be incomplete, to be sure, and may take us down a limb that will eventually end up going nowhere. This is history still raw, inchoate, unfolding. When asked, many contemporary lords will readily assent to the proposition that people will be central to strategy's next phase. "I absolutely agree that the intellectual and social capital represented by the people in an organization will be the key to its competitive advantage in the future," runs a typical comment, this from a senior partner of a consulting firm. But beyond such attestation, no one can much agree as yet on what "strategy as people" actually means.

But cracking that particular case will be critical to our subject's future. In the next stage of its evolution, if the paradigm is to evolve, strategy will finally have to come to terms with its Jungian shadow. This is never an easy undertaking, psychologists who believe in such things tell us, but it's usually the only way to move forward into growth and wholeness.

The Lure of the Entrepreneurial

In the waning years of the twentieth century, the Harvard Business School finally figured out what it wanted to teach its MBA students by way of required training in general management. After Michael Porter had blown up the old model of Business Policy I and II, no one had succeeded in devising a workable, pull-it-all-together capstone course to take the place of Business Policy II. At the doorstep of the new century, the dean and a majority of the faculty decided that the answer lay in entrepreneurship, or more specifically, in a course titled "The Entrepreneurial Manager," instituted as a required element of the MBA curriculum in 2000.

The change amounted to a triumph for the dozen or so faculty members who taught entrepreneurial studies. It was also the culmination of a twenty-year effort that mirrored what was going on in the U.S. economy as a whole. While the business school had flirted with the subject at times since the school's founding, by the 1970s, it had largely given up trying. But prodded by John McArthur in the 1980s, Howard Stevenson and Bill Sahlman built a program on entrepreneurship that attracted ever-larger numbers of students.

Their call to battle echoed arguments heard from the likes of *Inc.* magazine and later *Fast Company*, proponents of the notion that a "new economy" was emerging to displace the old. Forget *Fortune* 500 companies, went the cry; they are mostly engaged in restructuring, reengineering, and laying people off. When it came to creating jobs and wealth, the action lay instead with new businesses being started up, a historically astonishing 1.5 million of them in the United States over the 1980s. While most of these nascent enterprises remained small, a few had grown to sufficient size to disrupt whole industries: companies such as Amgen, Federal Express, MCI, Nucor, Oracle, and Staples, to cite a few of Stevenson's favorite examples.

Stevenson and his colleagues took pains to distinguish their take on the subject from the more traditional, psychologically based view that regarded the entrepreneur as a distinctive type, approximately a crank who hated authority and insisted on doing everything his or her own way. No, Stevenson argued, the entrepreneurial mode represented instead a "way of managing" distinctive from that employed in established companies, or "administrative organizations," as he described them. (No loading the dice here.) Defining entrepreneurship as "the pursuit of opportunity beyond the resources currently controlled," he maintained that it differed from conventional management along at least six dimensions. These included *strategic orientation*—entrepreneurial outfits that "are driven by the perception of opportunity, whereas administrative organizations are driven by the resources currently controlled"—and *strategic experimentation*, the upstarts being willing to make "revolutionary, short-duration commitments to opportunity," while the old corporate bags plodded along with evolutionary, longer-duration bets.

In sum, entrepreneurial management was a subject that could be taught and learned. The required MBA course would cover behaviors that seemed to cross functional boundaries, just as had the outmoded ideal of general management: identifying opportunities (as marketers did); obtaining resources (like finance); managing the entrepreneurial organization (shades of applied organizational behavior); and creating and harvesting value to stakeholders (maybe through a "liquidity event" such as an initial public offering, every entrepreneur's dream).

Some denizens of the Harvard strategy faculty would dismiss the whole supposed discipline as little more than an exercise in managing cash cycles—how to raise it, how to use it, how to cash out. But such a view may just reflect strategy's classic blind spot, for at its heart, entrepreneurial studies was and is about people, not just individuals but also the networks, teams, and alliances they formed. It was often through these networks that you would find the critical opportunity, locate the financing and other necessary resources, and identify the team to manage the start-up. In 1997, Bill Sahlman would author a widely read *HBR* article, "How to Write a Great Business Plan," reflecting his experience of having read thousands of them. Don't belabor the financial sections, he advised—all plans say the company will achieve $50 million in sales by year three. Do what experienced venture capitalists do, he wrote, and skip immediately to the section outlining "the team": who was going to be involved, what their track record was.

By the mid-1990s, companies many decades past their entrepreneurial beginnings were starting to feel pressure to act more like start-ups, specifically, to grow. In response, a small wave of management books rose up bearing titles such as *Customer-Centered Growth, Go for Growth!* and *Grow to Be Great.* Their common theme was that cost cutting and reengineering were by themselves no way to build value for shareholders. To do that, you had to simultaneously increase both your top and your bottom lines. Statistics on how bad most companies were at this became a routine feature of the genre: for example, from 1983 to 1993, only about 30 percent of *Fortune* 1000 companies managed to grow revenues 10 percent a year. Later calculations of the percentage of established companies demonstrating sustained growth, like those of Dick Foster and Chris Zook, would be even more demoralizing.

The advice offered in these tomes was nothing that would surprise a student of the strategy revolution: carefully sort through your customers. You're likely to find that 20 percent account for 60 percent, even 80 percent, of your profits. Focus on that segment, learn more about their wants and needs, then see how much more and different you can sell to them. Or establish control of a market, as Microsoft did with its DOS operating system for personal computers, and grow as the market grew. Or rethink how you get your product to customers, as Dell did selling PCs over the phone, then online. As usage of the Internet exploded—by some estimates, in 1995 and 1996 it grew 1,000 percent a year, before falling back to a measly 100 percent per annum thereafter—the call to traditional companies to explore new online sales channels became a semihysterical scream. Consultancies—start-ups and established outfits, including the strategy firms—stood willing to help clients figure out how to make sense of it all. By the end of the decade, some BCG offices derived nearly half their business from projects related to new technology.

The best books on growth didn't just tout examples of successful entrepreneurial ventures; they also wrestled with the question of where established companies would find the springboards for their resurgence. In a trilogy of books beginning in 2001 with *Profit from the Core*, Chris Zook made the case that a company's "core businesses" often had great untapped potential and that exploiting this potential almost always worked better than trying to buy an unrelated business. Criteria for judging what constituted a core business were precisely what you'd expect from someone who led Bain & Company's strategy practice: such a business had a competitive advantage, loyal customers, and superior profitability rooted in "unique skills" (read "capabilities"). Among the evidence Zook adduced for his argument was the experience of private equity firms, in particular, Bain Capital, in buying neglected, noncore businesses from overdiversified bloatfests and then, by making them lords and core of their own freestanding enterprises, seeing their results soar.

Others were more forthright in identifying people as the source for innovation, growth, and corporate renewal. This had long been a theme of Tom Peters and Bob Waterman, if anything growing more explicit in the books each wrote after *In Search of Excellence*. The inaugural issue of *Fast Company*, in November 1995, blazoned forth on its cover the rallying cry "Work Is Personal, Computing Is Social, Knowledge Is Power, Break the Rules." Inside, in a manifesto called "Handbook of the Business Revolution," the founding editors proclaimed that "smart people working in smart companies have the ability to create their own futures . . . The possibilities are unlimited." They promised to "identify the values of the revolution and the people who are building companies that embody them: a commitment to merge economic growth with social justice, democratic participation with tough-minded execution, explosive technological innovation with old-fashioned individual commitment."

Soon even established strategy gurus were clambering aboard the corporate equivalent of the train to the Finland Station. In 1996, beating Porter's "What Is Strategy?" into print by a couple of months, Gary Hamel published an *HBR* article, "Strategy as Revolution." The piece would rehearse some of Hamel's old saws—strategic planning as practiced at most companies was "ritualistic, reductionist, extrapolative, elitist, easy" and about "positioning." But he would also raise the volume on his slightly millenarian calls for companies to break with their pasts and subvert the traditional beliefs constraining their industries and strategies.

Hamel offered nine "routes to industry revolution," gambits such as "radically improving the value equation," "compressing the supply chain," and "driving convergence." But the main thrust of the article and the ensuing book was that strategy-making must be made democratic. Companies should seek out revolutionaries from among their twenty-five-year olds, from people serving on the corporate periphery far from headquarters, and from newcomers "who have not yet been co-opted by an industry's dogmas . . . What senior executives must not do is ask a small, elite group or the 'substitute brains' of a traditional strategy-consulting firm to go away and plot the company's future." Indeed, in the heaven he painted, every company would constitute a democracy of ideas (as McKinsey in its best moments aspired to be).

Hamel would continue to sound the tocsin in his book *Leading the Revolution*, published in 2000. While he was prescient in warning against being caught up in dot-com mania, the book's message was slightly undercut in the months after publication when its principal example of corporate self-transformation, Enron, proved to have been carried a bit too far by its transgressive energies. (Forget the fact that the company had been using the "substitute brains" from McKinsey at a $10 million-a-year clip.)

Undaunted (and with the Enron example replaced by UPS in subsequent editions), Hamel repeated many of the same arguments in a 2008 book, *The Future of Management*, though with slight shadings in emphasis. This time, it was management itself as practiced by traditional hierarchical organizations that had to be put through the cleansing fires of innovation. Down with denial, "allocational rigidities," old mental models, and "creative apartheid" that limited to only a select few the right to express their revolutionary potential. Up with freedom, democracy, and the creation of "communities of purpose."

Who would want to argue against such inspiring ideals, particularly who among legions of aging baby boomers who had set out to change the world just that way before they got slotted into corporate jobs? The question, as it had been for all those long-established companies looking to become excellent, or to go from good to great, or to move into a distinctive Porterian position, was, Just how capable were they of making the journey? Critics of *The Future of Management* pointed out that each of three main corporate examples—Whole Foods, W.L. Gore, and Google—had been created with self-consciously revolutionary values. How much of the route to Hamel's democratic paradise could be learned from angels born there?

Networks and the Need for New Ontology

At the Boston Consulting Group, changes wrought by the Internet sent at least a few of the brainies into, of all things, an exploration of the philosophical underpinnings for strategy. They were fascinated by the example of Linux, the largely self-organized online collaborative that without much economic incentive had constructed software by many measures as good as Microsoft's. Spurred by its example, Philip Evans, coauthor of the 1999 best-seller *Blown to Bits*, a treatise on how the Internet was "deconstructing" existing industries and strategies, found himself trekking through new realms—self-organizing networks, social-network analysis in general, transaction costs, economics of property, wikis, blogs, Napster, Friendster, and other social-networking sites.

Evans is the only thinker I've encountered who talks about the ontology of strategy (the philosophy of being it's premised on) and its epistemology (its theory of the nature of knowledge, in this instance, the knowledge of how to achieve competitive advantage). "Porter took a lens from structuralist economics, but he applied it to, quote unquote, an industry," Evans argues. "What's an industry? A small number of largely similar organizations, internally collaborative, externally competitive, that connect to each other through the mechanism of a competitive market, and connect upstream to suppliers, downstream to customers. If structural advantage was the epistemology, the ontology was that picture of who the players are," namely, companies. "Both Bruce Henderson and Porter subscribed to that set of premises."

But strategy evolved. "When capabilities came along," Evans argues, "that changed the epistemology—it said, 'No, competitive advantage is not identification of structural differences; it's the identification of capabilities.' But the ontology stayed exactly the same—companies competing with one another in an industry." Perhaps not forever, though. "The deconstruction logic challenges the ontology," argues Evans. "It says, 'Wait a second. Who says there's this thing called "*the* business," or "*the* company," or "*the* industry"?'" He then cites a soon-to-be former industry in which he did a lot of consulting: "What's the media industry, anymore? Blogs? Who are the customers, who are the suppliers? If customers start talking to one another, who's supplying whom?"

Evans is building toward his larger point: "Once you start from the idea that the unit of competitive advantage is not necessarily the corporation, as conventionally defined . . . it's like in biology, going from thinking of competition among animals to thinking of competition among genes. The generation of strategic thinking we're now entering challenges the earlier ontological assumptions. It says that the only irreducible unit in this picture is the person—the customer, worker, or executive. It says that people engage in transactions, broadly defined, that may be competitive, or may be cooperative, but what emerges is a network. As technology drives down the costs of transactions, breaking the constraints of distance or of institutions, those networks become more fluid."

In this emerging world, according to Evans, "the key way to think about competitive advantage is to think about how to design ecology in such a way to achieve goals you're trying to pursue. To say that we're trying to design an ecology means I'm trying to shape my behavior, the behavior of people who are co-employed with me, the behavior of people who are not co-employed with me but with whom I'm collaborating, and with people who are not employed with me and with whom I'm competing."

As you might imagine, it has proven somewhat difficult to create a consulting product out of such thinking. Evans allows as much, suggesting that most of his partners now regard him as even further gone into the intellectual ozone than usual. But a few other enterprising souls within the firm also tried to parse the implications of networks for strategy making, though not necessarily taking off from the full height of the Evans platform, or rather from the depths of its subcorporate granularity. They are members of a small but growing posse of academics, practitioners, and consultants attempting to explore how theories of network analysis can be applied to business.

Mark Blaxill, until recently a partner in the Boston office, was charged with leading an early twenty-first-century BCG effort to identify the Next Big Thing in strategy. He, too, decided that understanding open-source software as exemplified by Linux was probably key, in the way that understanding Japanese manufacturing had been key to the process revolution. Parting ways with his onetime collaborator Evans, Blaxill focused more on the implications of networks for competition, good old-fashioned "What makes Linux a threat to Microsoft?" (Part of the answer: the former can move faster than the latter in making changes and adapting its system to new realities.)

He concluded that intellectual-property issues were everywhere in this realm ("in India, China, piracy, Napster"), were essential to an understanding of what was going on, and were often capable of being used as a means of attack or defense. (The importance of intellectual property was one of the subjects on which he and Evans fell out.)

Managing intellectual property had to become part of the strategic agenda, in Blaxill's view. Examining Linux more closely, going online and examining the social networks of the developers and how they functioned, he also found that "there are patterns—it's not this commune or free-for-all. There's a hierarchy and a formal organization structure, though it's not written down." Blaxill wanted to push on to the issue of motivation, of why people worked on Linux for free, even into issues of creativity, but couldn't find time or support within the firm for exploring those dimensions. "The antibodies resisted that," he says. In 2006, Blaxill left BCG to set up his own firm, 3LP Advisors, to concentrate on the intersection of strategy, intellectual property, and innovation.

As of his departure, Blaxill was the only BCG partner ever to have sold a network-based project to a client. While that has changed, for now most of BCG's efforts with network analysis consist of developing tools for use in its practice areas—one to help clients "extract, construct, and analyze networks of medical research and publication," as the product brochure reads, or another that "visualizes and analyzes patent data as networks of relationships." The firm's practice in intellectual property is increasingly rooted in such analysis. But as Blaxill and Evans admit, this remains a far piece from fully unlocking Linux's import for strategy, much less finding a new framework to integrate the human and the strategic.

Wealth Creation on Steroids

For a near perfect if slightly specialized example of the strategy revolution in action before the global financial collapse, where the revolution had brought us, and where it is still likely to take us, we could hardly do better than to look at the operations of private equity firms. This, too, is a version of strategy as people, but as a very small and determined set of people—the partners of the private equity firm, the few executives whom the partners hire to run the businesses acquired, and the PE firm's consultants, if any.

Private equity as an industry is essentially the old leveraged-buyout business brought up to date, given slightly more dignity, and leaving much bigger footprints across the world's economy, particularly in the years just prior to 2008. Some of the players are the same as in the 1970s, most notably, Kohlberg Kravis Roberts. Private equity firms raise pools of capital from investors, mostly institutions—pension funds, university endowments—but also from so-called substantial individuals. This capital, chunked into successive funds, each typically with a five- to seven-year duration, is then used to buy businesses—whole companies or "carve-outs" from larger enterprises.

The aim of the exercise is to increase the value of these portfolio businesses such that they can be taken public or sold again to another buyer, this within the life of the fund and for a high enough price to provide everyone, particularly the PE firm, a healthy return. It typically charges investors an annual fee amounting to 2 percent of the money under management plus 20 percent of any gains realized on the investment. Think of it as the creation of, if not exactly shareholder wealth—investors usually don't receive shares—then owner wealth, but on steroids.

As of the summer of 2009, private equity is on the downward side of the third cycle in the industry's history, experiencing a steep fall just as it did in past contractions. (In the first two, the dollar volume of LBO deals done by U.S. firms declined about 80 percent from 1989 to 1991, and about 35 percent from 1999 to 2001.) But each cycle, especially the latest, has lifted the industry to a loftier high-water mark. According to the best estimates, nearly $700 billion was invested in 2007 by PE firms worldwide; the business is thoroughly established in Europe and on its way there in Asia and the Middle East. The biggest players—KKR, for example, or the Blackstone Group—have proved they can raise over $10 billion for a single fund. A Credit Suisse First Boston analysis in 2007 suggested it was within the reach of the PE industry as a whole to buy one out of every five companies in the United States and Europe with market capitalizations of under $30 billion.

While PE firms keep to themselves with a vengeance (consulting firms are garrulous by comparison), the size of some acquisitions during the so-called mega-buyout boom from 2005 to 2007 called attention to just how significant a force the industry was becoming in resculpting swaths of the corporate landscape. TXU, with huge holdings in Texas energy companies, was taken private for $44 billion; the Hospital Corporation of America, for $33 billion; and gambling-casino operator Harrah's Entertainment, for $18 billion.

The role that strategy consultants play in the business hasn't received much attention, but represents a remarkable convergence of mind-sets, analytical inclinations, and shared profit motivations. Through the first twenty years of its history and still today to a lesser extent, PE was largely run by financial types, men—and they were almost all men—whose passion was for financial engineering and doing deals. But gradually, former consultants began to infiltrate their ranks. We've seen how Bill Bain dispatched Mitt Romney to start up Bain Capital in 1983. For years, the PE offshoot would use Bain & Company as its primary source of talent, recruiting those who had proven themselves among the hottest of the hotshots. Don Gogel, formerly a partner at McKinsey, is now CEO of Clayton Dubilier; one of his senior partners there who helps run portfolio companies is Chuck Ames, long a powerhouse at the Firm. And the trend reaches across the great waters: Sir Ronald Cohen helped found Apax Partners & Co., the second largest PE firm in London, but only after years of service at McKinsey. At least until the recent crisis hit Wall Street, the estimate was that one out of three McKinsey alums worked in PE or other branches of financial services (such as hedge funds).

Private equity's attraction to consultants, beyond the chance of amassing riches unavailable to them in the advisory business, is in part the opportunity to actually run something. What consultants bring to jobs in private equity, at least to hear them tell it, is experience in improving the performance of companies—experience based on years of analyzing and advising. This is also what the strategy consulting giants offer PE firms that retain their services. The argument the consultants make, and some clients echo, is that as the PE industry has grown and new players piled in, any competitive edge that your deal-structuring ability might once have provided has long since disappeared into a sink of commoditization. "Any MBA can figure out the finances of what we do in a couple of days," runs the typical comment from PE veterans, this specifically from Jim Coulter, cofounder of TPG (formerly the Texas Pacific Group). In the game of generating big returns, what will increasingly distinguish the winners from the losers—and there are lots of these; by Bain & Company's calculations in 2007, 75 percent of PE firms fail to earn more than their risk-adjusted cost of capital, a figure undoubtedly made worse by the recent disruptions— will be the ability to ratchet up the performance of their portfolio companies and, with it, their eventual sales price.

While all three of the great strategy houses have practices consulting to PE firms, the market leader has been Bain, and for reasons that go deeper than its historical relationship to Bain Capital. The practice was started up only after the firm's near-death experience in the early 1990s, and then in the face of skepticism from many of the suddenly conservative survivors. But it proved a wonderful fit with Bain's longstanding, semimaniacal focus on "results" and its preeminent skills at Greater Taylorism. "Quite frankly, it's the purest type of Bain work there is," says Dan Haas, one of the founders of the practice, "because it's all about creating value, you've got a motivated management team, and the stakes are incredibly high for everyone. For a firm of impact junkies, it doesn't get any better than that." Consulting to PE operators and their portfolio companies represented about 25 percent of Bain's revenues at private equity's peak in 2007, Haas reports, and Bain Capital is not always its largest client in the sector, and hasn't been for some time. He also estimates that 80 percent of the largest PE firms now use Bain or one of the other strategy houses. For Bain partners, commitment to the business isn't merely institutional. "As a partner group, we've invested over four hundred million dollars of our after-tax income in the last six or seven years in those deals and those funds we've worked on," Haas says. "It's a set of economics that forces us to eat our own cooking."

Bain's help to its PE clients comes in two forms. Before the decision to buy a particular business, it will perform what it calls "strategic due diligence," surveying the industry and players across the potential property's value chain, from its suppliers to its customers. The point here is to develop what Haas described in a 2002 *Harvard Business Review* article as "an investment thesis": how we are going to make this business more valuable within three to five years, including what parts of it we will want to sell off. After the purchase has been consummated, Bain then works with its client to develop a performance improvement plan, particularly for the first one or two years: targets to be achieved, including financial goals, often plotted down to the month, with the steps to be taken to get there.

The result is a design for what I would term a strategy workout, and it isn't just Bain clients who put the businesses they acquire through such a drill. Looking at the practice of most big PE firms, we can identify several common elements of their regimen, all of which will be familiar to students of strategy's intellectual history. The PE firms use debt aggressively to leverage up the acquired assets, part of what Haas calls "working the balance sheet." They concentrate on just a few metrics, chief among them usually cash flow, abandoning the dizzying panoply of measures the acquired business may have layered on over its history. They reduce costs relentlessly.

At every step, the PE firm will typically be thinking about who would be the best owner for the business—as in, should we sell it now, and if so, to whom?—and ponder how long it, as owner, should hold on to the property (seldom "forever"). In his article, to make his point that PE firms "maintain a willingness to swiftly sell or shut down a company if its performance falls too far behind plan or if the right opportunity knocks," Haas quotes TPG's Coulter: "Every day you don't sell a portfolio company, you've made an implicit buy decision." And in furtherance of its investment thesis, the PE firm will usually build a strategy around the line of business in which the acquisition dominates its competitors, and then often sell off its other businesses.

The beneficent effects on the performance of properties put through such a workout can last even after they're sold again. A much-cited 2006 study by Josh Lerner of Harvard Business School and Jerry Cao of Boston College's Carroll School of Management indicated that businesses that have been taken public after being owned by a PE firm long enough to be put through a workout—at least one year—typically outperform both other IPOs and the overall stock market over the next three to five years.

Not that everyone gets to enjoy the fruits. While PE operators like to cite examples of retaining the leaders of the businesses they acquire, heaping the longtime executives with financial incentives to work the required transformation, there are just as many stories of incumbent managers chucked out on completion of the acquisition. After all, who else is to be held responsible for the business's prior failure to maximize the value of its assets?

The issue of what happens to overall employment at businesses acquired by PE firms was controversial even before the recent economic crisis. Private equity buckos are inclined to the view that certain functions, like human resources, can often be outsourced. But in the face of charges that they're no more than asset strippers and perpetrators of mass firings, the PE industry cites studies suggesting that employment at companies they own actually has been growing faster than the overall rate for all public companies, at least in Britain. Academic experts aren't sure the news is that good, but no one has yet produced proof that being acquired by a PE outfit consistently results in downsizing any more ruthless than what has become the general corporate norm.

At the crest of the industry's latest wave of success in 2007, private equity's most vociferous advocates hailed it as a new version of capitalism that would find ever-wider currency—management by the most economically rational of owners. At the very least, some in the trade saw their MO as arguably establishing a new benchmark for corporate chieftains and their handling of assets. As TPG's Coulter told me, "In every period, there's one organization or type of organization that leads the way, sets the pace. In the early 1990s, that might have been GE under Jack Welch. Now it may well be us."

Perhaps with a slight seen-it-all-before weariness, students of strategy's history will recall that Michael Jensen said much the same thing in 1989, just as the first wave of LBO mania was peaking. Of late, such brave talk has fallen away with the global financial crisis, along with the number of PE-backed acquisitions, the eagerness of investors to commit to new funds, and—most critically—the willingness of banks to lend money for deals. ("You have to understand," the senior partner of a PE firm told me in 2007 with surprising modesty for a supposed master of the universe, "it's the banks that drive our business," supplying the leverage for LBOs.)

Many strategy consultants of a certain vintage, say, from the discipline's first three decades, register little sadness over private equity's current troubles. They point with a degree of relish to overleveraged portfolio companies teetering on the edge of bankruptcy or already plunged into it, viewing this as just comeuppance. They deride the rapacity of PE operators, especially those who took bags of cash out of acquired businesses rather than putting them on a sound footing. These guys were only interested in making big money fast, the consultants argue, whatever the consequences for the underlying business. Such an approach is almost the opposite of strategy, the traditionalists' protest goes, which is about building for the long term around a competitive advantage.

For their part, the princes of PE allow that their world currently faces fierce challenges—not merely a lack of financing for new deals but the necessity to refinance billions of dollars of existing loans over the next few years; the imperative to navigate the businesses they own, most still heavily freighted with debt, through still choppy economic seas; even, some concede, the requirement to operate in an industry grown mature, with huge firms competing for the next deal and no one likely to see the consistently extraordinary returns of yore.

But don't count the PE model out, its proponents hasten to add. It's clearly not applicable for every stage of a business's life, usually only for companies that have reached a certain maturity. (For start-ups, the comparable force is venture capitalists, another breed of ul-trarational investor.) But then it can work wonders, particularly if the existing management has run out of steam. A world of fiercening capitalism is also a tiring one. The lords of private equity, biding their time even as they shore up their finances, foresee no lack of opportunity ahead.

16.

And Where Was Strategy When the Global Financial System Collapsed?

THE PRECEPTS OF STRATEGY have helped make companies more competitive, alert to their circumstances, and resilient. Why, then, toward the close of 2008 did many enterprises thoroughly dosed in the discipline become enmeshed in a worldwide financial crisis, with some accused of precipitating it? Were the ideas behind the revolution at fault? Did strategy consultants lead astray the management of the great banks and financial service firms? Looked at from a certain distance, perhaps through eyes inflamed with rage or disappointment, the evidence suggests a fairly decent case for the prosecution.

Begin with the element of propinquity. The consultants were clearly there in the alley when the lights were turned off on the global financial system. At the crest of the system's success in 2007, banks (mostly) and other financial service firms—insurance companies, for example—represented the largest single client sector for BCG, accounting for around 30 percent of its revenues. McKinsey's practice among such institutions was even larger, measured by its revenues; in 2002, the Firm had attested to the press that it served 80 of the world's 120 top financial service firms. If you lump private equity firms in with other financial operators—and you should—the proportion of Bain's revenues from the sector reaches a level comparable to BCG's.

Nor were the three strategy giants the only consultants vying for the business. Oliver Wyman, a firm set up in 1984 specifically to minister to the financial services industry, was doing so well by 2003—over $300 million in annual revenues—that it was acquired by Marsh & McLennan. Four years later, Marsh rolled up all its consulting units, some with long histories in strategy, under the Wyman brand name and its president. The combined entity, still leading with its expertise in financial services and risk management, was judged the fastest-growing major consultancy by industry watchers.

The consultants' boats were rising on a spring tide of profitability coursing through the financial sector. While few voiced concern about the matter before the crash, the share of corporate profits in the United States sopped up by banks, investment banks, insurance companies, and other purveyors of financial services had swelled generously in the first years of the twenty-first century. In the early 1980s, the profits they earned accounted for a mere 15 percent of total U.S. corporate profits. In the 1990s, as good times prevailed in the economy, the sector occasionally garnered a 30 percent share of the rising profit pie. By 2007, at the pinnacle of the financial-service firms' success, their share of U.S. corporate profits amounted to 41 percent of the whole.

Spreading the Obloquy Around

Looking at the profits pile up in the financial-services sector in the early years of our century, a student of strategy's history might well have concluded that many of the principal corporate beneficiaries seemed to be acting according to the tenets of the discipline and benefiting thereby. This impression would only have been strengthened by the knowledge that major industry presences such as AIG, Bank of America, and Merrill Lynch had been longtime clients of the strategy consulting firms.

The banks and other financial-service outfits were coming off a long period coping with just the kinds of external shocks—including the Four Horsemen—that impelled companies to embrace strategic thinking. Lines of business that had made the industry a relatively stable one from the 1930s until the 1980s crumbled as, for instance, big depositors increasingly turned to money market mutual funds and as large corporate borrowers moved to the commercial paper market. Securitization, the process of bundling assets, repackaging them in convenient lots, and then selling them to investors—whether of mortgages, car loans, or credit card receivables—drained billions of dollars of business from the banks. New technologies, including computers and, later, the Internet made for economies of scale that gave regional or national competitors a cost advantage over local institutions.

The result, cheered on by the strategy consultants and in many cases actively charted out by them, was massive consolidation of the banking industry, what Bruce Henderson might have described as building scale to gain share. For example, over the course of seventeen years, the following institutions, which in 1990 had market capitalizations totaling $19 billion, were rolled up into a single huge enterprise, JP Morgan Chase, with a market capitalization in 2009 of $172 billion: Chemical Bank, Manufacturers Hanover, Chase Manhattan Bank, J.P. Morgan, Bank One, First Chicago, and National Bank of Detroit. A similar combinatory mania went into the making of the current Bank of America and, to a lesser extent, Citigroup.

From the 1980s on, leading thinkers on strategy had ever more loudly proclaimed that innovation was increasingly the key to competitive advantage. Financial institutions appeared to take this message to heart as well. They invented new products, as Merrill Lynch did with wrap accounts ("Let us help you invest in a dizzying variety of funds, all for a small annual fee"), or expanded the use of older offerings beyond recognition, as Citibank did with credit cards. Much of the effort went into using technology to give customers new ways to be in touch with their money, whether through computerized phone systems or the ultimately ubiquitous automated teller machine.

The other form of innovation that would come into question after the global financial collapse was organizational. Marching under matching banners that read "Free markets know best" and "Down with restrictive regulation," financial firms and their lobbyists steadily chipped away at laws restricting interstate banking or setting limits on what kinds of businesses a bank holding company might be in. Increasingly, Brobdingnagian giants such as Citigroup or Bank of America would end up offering their clients not just banking services but also mutual funds, brokerage, and insurance, all this with an eye toward plumping the institution's "share of wallet." Later, after the cataclysm, when voices would be raised wondering, "Who let all these institutions into businesses they didn't necessarily know how to run?" students of strategy arcana would recall that among the list of special capabilities McKinsey's John Stuckey had listed as growing in importance was "capture ability to influence regulator," a subtle foreshadowing of the phenomenon subsequently to gain notoriety as "regulatory capture."

To hear strategy consultants tell the story, though, it wasn't expansion or the more conventional forms of innovation that were the proximate cause of the financial system's collapse. Like many commentators, BCG's Philip Evans traces the origins of the crisis back to "global imbalances," mostly the U.S. trade deficits that resulted in a vast pool of dollars sloshing around—think of all those Asian countries that, after their own financial crisis in 1997, insisted on holding their reserves in U.S. Treasury securities. After the bursting of the dot-com balloon in 2000, housing became one of the few industries holding out the allure of big money to be made fast, and the Federal Reserve helped the party along. Wanting to spur the recovery, it lowered interest rates from the 6.5 percent that prevailed in May 2000 down to 1.75 percent in December 2001. Housing boomed: prices of existing homes rose, construction abounded, and owners borrowed against their rising asset values and spent the cash.

Meanwhile, the deregulation of financial markets, and especially the 1999 repeal of the Glass-Steagall Act, permitted a wave of mergers whereby banks, investment banks, and insurance companies piled into each other's traditional markets. The question of which agency was going to regulate which business became less clear—why not shop around for the most agreeable overseer, or just yard back the regulation and let the free market work its magic? All of which made it easier for the great financial minds devising products to sell to investors eager for higher returns than the pitiable rates available from, say, plain old bonds in the low-interest rate milieu. How about a nice mortgage-backed security, maybe repackaged into a collateralized debt obligation? Or a credit default swap? By 2007, there had grown up a shadow banking system, mostly beyond the regulatory sunshine illuminating the traditional system, with about $60 trillion in assets—at least on paper—some four times the size of the U.S. gross domestic product.

Liberal amounts of gasoline were poured on this conflagration waiting for a match by the combination of ultimately dysfunctional incentives and what Evans labels the "stupidity of bankers" (though surely not any of BCG's banker clients). Since the mortgages the lenders originated were to be promptly sold off and securitized, the friendly folks at your local mortgage-lending company had every incentive to make as many loans as possible and almost none to worry about whether those loans would eventually be paid back. The financial geniuses on Wall Street and in London inventing derivatives of ever greater complexity were paid their enormous bonuses according to contributions to this year's profits, not on how what they were selling inured to the long-term benefit—or detriment—of their employer.

In September 2008, the wheels began to fall off the juggernaut: the abysmal quality of many subprime mortgages became manifest. The housing market, already in decline, tanked. Firms holding securities based on the mortgages failed (Lehman Brothers) or had to be rescued by the government. Stock markets crashed around the world. The enormity of the counterparty risk entailed in AIG's credit-default business came to light, along with AIG's inability to pay off on its obligations. Credit markets seized up; even worthy borrowers were unable to get loans. The economies of major nations plunged into recession, or deeper into recessions already under way.

Most consultants have a deep-dyed respect for the power of free markets—that's what they spend their time helping clients contend with—and a complementary skepticism about the power of government to do much good. And in their account of the financial crisis, government action or inaction is often the culprit. They blame politicians for rolling back regulations that might have stabilized the banking sector, the Fed for setting interest rates too low, the SEC for letting investment banks increase their leverage to 30 or 40 to 1, and quasi-governmental Fannie Mae and Freddie Mac for encouraging subprime borrowing right up until 2006. In perhaps their grandest accusation, some tar the federal government for its bailout plans to try to rescue banks and other financial institutions in the wake of the crisis. The bankers got all the upside when times were good, the consultants argue; now the taxpayer is being forced to pick up the tab for all the downside.

While there's clearly obloquy enough to go around in assessing the causes of the financial crisis, lots of it attaching to governmental actors, the consultants' case seems one-sided, riddled with contradiction, and afflicted with short-term memory loss. They fault some agencies for acting too aggressively (Fannie and Freddie, the Fed in its rate-setting function) and others for not acting aggressively enough (the SEC, the congeries that let derivatives fall between the regulatory stools, the Fed in its oversight function). A cursory review of the consulting literature on the financial sector prior to the debacle turns up very little banging the drum for greater regulation. And where, other than in references to the stupid bankers and lax mortgage originators, is the place of the great corporate actors in the drama, the companies that were lending consumers too much money, ginning up bewildering new securities, taking on too much debt themselves, and in general assuming levels of risk their historical models didn't adequately account for? For that matter, where were their consultants? And the consultants' ideas?

Familiar concepts were clearly at work in certain critical instances. In a *New Yorker* article, Connie Bruck describes how the management of Countrywide Financial Corp. became obsessed with market share. The CEO of the mortgage lender, Angelo Mozilo, and his team were convinced that the stock market wasn't setting a high enough value on their enterprise. In strategic planning sessions in 2002, their consultant advised them that if Countrywide's market share was higher, so would be their stock price. The consultant, Eric Flamholtz, a professor at UCLA's Anderson School of Management, told how most industries evolved such that one competitor had more than a 40 percent share, the next more than 20 percent, a third competitor 10 percent, and the rest mere boutique status. (One can almost see Bruce Henderson nodding from the great beyond.) This, at a point when Countrywide's share was about 10 percent and the market share leader's was no more than 13 percent.

Mozilo and his colleagues thereupon decided that Countrywide would shoot to achieve a market share of 30 percent in five years. In 2003, the irrepressible CEO upset his colleagues by making the goal public, along with their ambition to be the "No. 1 player" in the industry by 2008.

As Bruck recounts, with abundant quotations from people present as the drama unfolded, the effect of the goal on Countrywide's lending practices was almost immediate and ultimately pernicious. Just about any loan was to be made, provided that the price exacted from borrowers was high enough. Whatever kinds of loans competitors were offering, Countrywide would offer, too. Loan-credit standards, including those for people taking out subprime loans, declined almost to nothingness.

While Countrywide never achieved its market-share goal—by 2005, it had only about a 14 percent share and admitted that seizing 30 percent would take a few years longer than originally anticipated—its portfolio grew so large that it finally outran the company's ability to continue financing it. Interest rates had begun to rise in 2005, sales and new construction of homes had slowed, and more and more subprime loans were defaulting. In the summer of 2007, investors largely stopped buying mortgage-backed securities, and the overall market for mortgages fell apart.

Faced with bankruptcy as an alternative, in January 2008, Countrywide sold itself to Bank of America—those bank acquisitions, they just keep rolling along—for stock worth one-sixth of Countrywide's market capitalization at its peak. (True to the predictions, its share price had gone from around $10 a share in 2002, when it adopted its market-share goal, to a peak of $45 in 2007. Mozilo's annual compensation midway through the ride, in 2005, had been valued at more than $140 million, but then think of all the value he was creating for shareholders.) It proved to be not a bad investment: By the summer of 2009, despite early warnings by some analysts that losses from the acquired operation would end up costing Bank of America tens of billions of dollars, mortgages became one of the healthier lines of business in the reviving bank's portfolio.

A More Embarrassing Picture

For students of strategy surveying the wreckage of the financial system, examples of strategic precepts leading the players astray won't necessarily come as a surprise. (Think back to all those companies that claimed to have been ruined trying to apply the growth-share matrix to themselves.) What may be more of a shock is how seldom strategy or the consultants who pushed it creep up in accounts of the misadventures that led to the crisis. This is not just because of the consultants' traditional determination to keep their work confidential.

Scrape through the record and talk to consulting-industry stalwarts, and a picture emerges that rather lets strategy's partisans off the hook for major crimes, but in ways leaves them more embarrassed: at most of the financial-service firms at the center of the tornado, by the time the winds really began to gust, the consultants' voices had fallen silent. The champions of strategy no longer had the CEO's ear, the client work their firms did for the financial powerhouses was typically way down in the trenches, and the sources of the most exciting new innovation was another breed entirely, the "quants," specialists in quantitative analysis and masters of financial engineering.

The sharper-elbowed of the Wall Street houses had never had much use for strategy consultants, peopled as the former are with "deal guys" and the transaction-minded. In *House of Cards*, his account of the fall of Bear Stearns, William D. Cohan tells of how as the new century dawned, that firm overcame its usual animus against using consultants to bring in McKinsey for a "Project Excel," this with the twin goals of "invigorate growth and cut costs." Cohan quotes a Bear Stearns executive on the result: "They come in and all they do is cut costs . . . and we did almost nothing on the revenue side." Hundreds of millions of dollars were eliminated from the bank's information-technology budget and legions of clerks laid off, but the executive-compensation structure remained untouched. "We did nothing to the way we run the place," the executive concluded, despite the project's $50 million price tag. "I view it as the lost two years of my life."

Many of the bank holding companies and brokerages that became too big to fail had drawn heavily on the consultants' strategic advice as they grew over the 1980s and 1990s. But by the time of the great run-up to the crash, a new generation of leaders had been installed in their top ranks and, perhaps from a desire to break with their predecessors' ways, had largely "thrown out" the consultants, as some of the thrown-out describe their departure. Bank of America and its organizational forebears reaching back to North Carolina National Bank had been a major McKinsey client under the relentless-consolidator-cum-CEO Hugh McColl. Kenneth Lewis, who succeeded McColl in 2001, didn't feel a need for the Firm's strategic advice. A similar pattern unfolded at Merrill Lynch. The management team under David Komansky had availed itself of the consultants' high-level counsel. When Stanley O'Neal pushed out Komansky, an undertaking that began in 2001, he also dispensed with the advice-givers.

Sanford "Sandy" Weill, who became undisputed chief of Citigroup in 2000, seemed almost to have an antipathy to consultants, unlike the co-head and longtime bank leader he forced out, John Reed. Jamie Dimon, Weill's onetime protégé and now head of J.P. Morgan Chase, shares the disinclination. Philip Purcell, chairman and chief executive of Morgan Stanley from 1997 until 2005, was a former McKinsey partner—indeed, he had become the youngest office head in the Firm's history. As supreme leader of the investment bank, he drew on the consultants' wisdom, for all the good it did him in his generally unhappy tenure there. Not so his successor.

An eager believer in the power of strategy might suggest that per-haps the consultants weren't needed anymore because the core princi-ples had been so successfully embedded in the large financial institutions by the year 2000. Alas, no, say the outside experts who strived to help with the embedding. "I don't think we succeeded in in-stalling strategy at the banks," admits a senior partner in one firm, his voice colored with regret after working for nearly twenty years on just that project. "I was drawing supply curves and demand curves for banks back in the early 1980s," he recalls. "I haven't seen it done much since. Do you think anyone in the credit default swap business was doing that kind of analysis, that the traders were drawing supply or demand curves?"

So what were the bulge-bracket consultants doing for their banking clients? As the Bear Stearns example suggests, much of their effort went to helping with Greater Taylorism in its most reductive, cost-cutting form. Often this work came under the rubric "sourcing." In the 1980s, the consultants had demonstrated that what was pulling the banking industry's profitability down was not the expense of the interest it paid out on deposits but rather the cost of new branches and technology, those ATM machines and computer systems.

A consultant who did millions of dollars' worth of projects on this front tells how the process worked: "We'd go through the list of all the bank's payables and tag them according to the vendors—this division was paying IBM so much for desktop computers, another paying another part of IBM a lot for mainframes. We'd ask the bank's chief technology officer if he was sure he was getting the best possible deal, and he'd say 'Absolutely; IBM guaranteed us we were getting the lowest price available.' But when you aggregated all that the bank was spending with IBM, it turns out the figure was huge, and armed with that information the bank could negotiate much better prices." Haven't we heard this song before, the client not knowing its own costs as well as it needs to, say, from the dawn of the revolution?

A Still Newer Breed of Business Intellectuals

The consultants helped their clients save millions, but the originators of the most exciting, complex, and ultimately destructive sources of new wealth for the banking powerhouses were another variety of wizards, the quants. As the first decade of the new century made ever clearer, two disciplines—or "conversations," in the largest sense—had come to dominate thinking about business. One was strategy; the other finance. (Recall Rakesh Khurana's account of how the two fields had achieved shared primacy in the curriculum of business schools, beginning in the 1980s.) While both were rooted in economics, they grew up along distinct branches—applied microeconomics and the study of competition in one case, and analysis of how to finance a firm and related securities in the other. By the go-go early 2000s, finance seemed in the ascendant.

While practitioners of the two arts sometimes share similar backgrounds—both frequently come from MBA feedstock—in their fully evolved form, they make up "entirely different communities," says Dick Foster, who knows each well. (Leave aside the complication that there are at least thirty distinct varieties of quants, according to the former McKinsey partner, each with a different focus or approach.) The ideal candidate for a job at a strategy consulting firm will necessarily have quantitative skills, to be sure, but also a certain well-rounded-MBA quality. The exemplary quant, on the other hand, might have a higher degree in mathematics or even physics, a degree of quirkiness, perhaps at the expense of the interpersonal, and a first-class berth in the research-and-development facilities of a Goldman Sachs or J.P. Morgan Chase.

There are certainly executives of a certain age who understand credit default swaps and other wonders invented by the quants. Some strategy consultants who saw him work—"He remembered every transaction he ever encountered"—believe that if eighty-year-old Maurice "Hank" Greenberg had not been forced out as head of AIG in 2005, the company's Financial Products unit would never have been allowed to plunge as disastrously into the swaps business. But in general, the art of the quants is a younger generation's game, incorporating as it does—or is alleged to do—advances in financial theory that have only been achieved over the last twenty years or so.

This puts the executives making strategy for financial-service outfits—usually its senior management, and usually of a more senior age cohort—at a disadvantage, particularly in judging the risk that all the newfangled financial instruments in their portfolios may carry. Foster estimates that perhaps fifty executives, no more, have both the strategic experience to help direct a great financial institution and an effective working understanding of the most esoteric of the new securities. In gauging the risk these instruments posed, the strategy consultants were not much help to their clients.

Strategists had been incorporating risk into their calculations as far back as Alan Zakon's work for Weyerhaeuser, when he showed that because the timber company had relatively low operating risk, it could take on more of the financial variety—that is, borrow more. But with the passage of time, the advisers' concern with risk had been subordinated to other themes or consigned to particular projects, say, the decision about whether a mining or oil company should make a colossal investment to try to discover new reserves. Here there were relatively clear decision trees that could be followed down to weigh choices, and the possibility of applying options theory. But elsewhere, even as Y2K fears and then the September 11 attacks piqued corporate interest in risk management, the consultants had mostly left the subject to others, often to the client's "chief risk officer," himself or herself usually a subordinate of the CFO and not typically a member of the client's inner councils on strategy.

Asked to name sins of omission or commission they may have committed in connection with the global financial crisis, most consultants will allow that in their advice they failed to make sufficient provision for risk, particularly systemic risk. Their analytics, like those of the quants, had done such a wonderful job of chopping the world into small, measurable pieces that they could not foresee how the bits, with the risk inherent in each supposedly mitigated by distribution across a wide population of owners and operators, could suddenly seize up together into a nonworking, credit-frozen-up, risk-all-concentrated-in-the-same-damn-spots whole. "We didn't see the danger of systemic risk," admits one senior consultant, "but then, nobody did"—only a slight exaggeration.

Part of the reason was because the new financial products that eventually triggered the crisis followed a very different start-up trajectory than the ones strategists were used to. For example, a paper company or cereal maker that wanted to launch a new line had to either retool existing facilities, build new factories, or buy up the operations of some entrepreneurial outfit—each of which took time. The rollout of the new whiz-bang could take months, including testing customer response in Muncie or Modesto before ramping up for nationwide distribution.

By contrast, new financial products—subprime mortgages, credit default swaps—could be ginned up as fast as Wall Street rocket scientists could create them, and the businesses selling them billowed out to global proportions almost overnight. Recall the *whoosh* as European banks rushed to buy packages of American mortgages. All of which helps explain how the financial sector became such a big part of the economy as quickly as it did. Moreover, if your company was going to get in on the latest bonanza, you'd have to jump in fast, before somebody else could build a dominant position—supposedly another lesson of the strategy revolution. (Poor Merrill Lynch almost missed the collateralized-mortgage-obligation train, only managing to clamber aboard as it was moving down the track.) This didn't leave a lot of time to analyze potential risks. Besides, you had computer models devised by your quants to do that for you. Why wait for the real world to actually test the thing?

While a few academic and journalistic voices raised questions about the hastiness of the innovation in the financial sector, there is little evidence of any strategy consultants throwing their bodies across the tracks in an attempt to slow down the process.

By this point, the fair-minded observer might reasonably conclude that while strategy and its champions may not have been a main causal factor in bringing on the global financial crisis, they did not do much to avert it either. Looking more widely across the burned-over economic landscape of 2008 and 2009, a disappointed student of the revolution could even be tempted to entertain notions along the lines of, "What good was strategy, anyway? A plague on the original lords, their successors in consulting and management, and all that they have wrought."

Consider the Alternative

Not so fast, please. In registering the pain from the biggest financial crisis since the Great Depression and one whopper of a recession, let us not point fingers too quickly or forget contributions made over the longer pull of history. For example, while consultants may have abetted the process, they weren't the ones who elevated shareholder value (a.k.a. the stock price) to its place as god above all others. That was Wall Street, egged on by swinish types like you and me, who came to expect our investment portfolios and 401(k) plans to increase in value by 10 percent a year. The larger story of what happened in the economy is complicated, with few unadulterated villains. Even the private-equity sharpies, whom critics deride as utter greedheads, can point out that most of their investors are players like your child's college or the pension fund that pays out your parents' retirement benefits. Don't you want *them* to be earning a superior return?

Yes, strategy and strategy consultants did help companies possessed of the requisite intelligence to become more efficient and competitive. Leaner and, yes, occasionally meaner. But as the world grew steadily more capitalist, with Chinese, Indians, and other entrepreneurial populations piling into the capitalist fray, isn't that what you'd hope your favorite companies would be doing?

Consider the alternative, as represented by the Big Three American auto companies. General Motors, Ford, and Chrysler have each availed themselves of the services of the strategy firms, but I've never known a consultant who did work for them who didn't come away cursing and muttering. Like the BCG partner who demonstrated to Ford that it could make more money financing cars than it could building them: "I told them the advantage wouldn't last, that even GM, dumb as it was, would eventually wise up to the game. Which it did, though it took a couple of years."

317

THE LORDS OF STRATEGY

So arrogant, silo-ridden, and inert were the Detroit giants that they never bothered to get their minds around the three Cs of the strategy revolution, despite much advice to do just that. (When it came to the auto companies' core operations, "We never laid a glove on them" ruefully admits the former head of one of the great strategy consultancies, speaking of both his own firm and that of his competitors.) Customers? Who are you talking about? Laws in every state prohibit automakers from selling a car directly to you or me; the sale has to go through a dealer, which the car companies came to regard as their *real* customer, with predictable, dismal effects. Costs? Easier to buy a few more years of peace with the United Auto Workers—kick the can down the road a little farther—even if it means that it costs us a few thousand more to make each vehicle than it does those devils from abroad. Competitors? Per the quotation from Henry Ford II in the preface, what do foreigners with their little "shitboxes"—his term— know about making *real* cars?

Without strategy and strategy consultants, we could have broad swaths of the U.S. industry that look like the automakers—that is, uncompetitive on a global basis (as are, for instance, many sectors of the Japanese economy once you get beyond automobiles and consumer electronics). The fiercening of capitalism isn't going away; if anything, it looks likely to grow more intense. In response, strategists will have to heighten and broaden their sensitivity to potential dangers, shedding any remnants of the profit-fueled complacency that, for example, allowed them to remain oblivious to systemic risk. To update Dr. Grove's maxim, in this new world, only the really, really paranoid may survive. Add to this William Burroughs's observation that sometimes, paranoia is just having all the facts. Strategy and its handmaiden Greater Taylorism will have to do a better job on that front as well. All this will probably entail a rewiring of certain circuits in the corporate brain, but as strategy contemplates its future, there are signs that the effort may already be under way.

Coda: The Future of Strategy

T ABOUT THE SAME TIME that the global financial system was freezing up, the Boston Consulting Group canvassed nearly twenty global companies—corporate titans from India and Japan as well as Europe and the United States—on the giants' latest thinking about strategy. More than one replied with a version of, "We don't *do* strategy."

Attentive students of the subject's history won't be shocked by this. They will recall Michael Porter's concern in the early 1990s that companies had largely abandoned strategy in favor of more faddish pursuits. Or the backlash in the early 1980s, when corporate disappointment over the failure of strategic planning to deliver on its early promises led to widespread cutbacks in internal staffs devoted to the discipline.

Indeed, when the consultants probed for the reasons behind the companies' response, much of what they turned up was dissatisfaction you might have heard two or three decades ago. With the world changing so fast, how can we make forecasts about the future? The old concepts and frameworks don't seem to make sense of the river of data pouring in on us. What good are a bunch of plans that just end up in binders sitting on the shelf? Isn't execution, after all, what really gives you a competitive edge?

Of more interest were the trends the BCG consultants identified in parsing the economic data, most of these trends reflecting the continued fiercening of capitalism along lines our narrative has already traced. Yes indeed, the length of time a company might expect its competitive advantage to last had steadily declined since the 1960s, reflected in a surge upward in what the consultants not-so-charmingly called "the positional volatility of leaders." Even while a few corporations were growing to a size larger than many governments, in most businesses, being the biggest was less and less likely to make you the most profitable. With a value-chain analysis in hand, companies were increasingly eager to outsource some of their activities, not just information technology and human resources but also procurement and logistics. And in a particular irony, just as many companies were realizing that people were the key to their future strategic success, they were also discovering that shareholder-value-driven pressures to work longer hours coupled with heightened job insecurity were making employees more likely to feel unmotivated and disenfranchised.

How is strategy likely to change to meet this, the latest round of challenges? Put that question to consultants from BCG, Bain, McKinsey, and other firms, and you will find the same word coming up in the answers from each: strategy will necessarily become more *adaptive*. But then, as we have witnessed, hasn't strategy always been adaptive, a set of conceptual responses to the most vexing problems companies were facing at the time? What's new here?

Over its history, strategy has usually been smart, if not always wise. It has seldom been humble. Part of what the consultants are pointing toward would seem to be a discipline that is less sure of itself, less certain that its concepts apply to every situation, particularly if that certainty gets in the way of accurately sizing up business circumstances that are radically new or rapidly changing.

Martin Reeves and his colleagues at BCG's Strategy Institute, the firm's in-house think tank on the subject, have ideas about what adaptive strategy might look like in corporate practice. Instead of headquarters dictating a strategy based on "analysis, prediction, and deduction," the goal would be to set "optimal conditions for the continuous emergence of superior strategies through an adaptive—or evolutionary—process." In concrete terms, this would mean giving more responsibility for strategy to the people on the corporate "periphery," the troops in daily contact with customers, competition, and changing market conditions. They would be encouraged to probe and experiment, even if this meant the occasional failure, with their findings being continuously fed back to the corporate center for incorporation into its strategic consciousness. As the consultants note in their as yet unpublished white paper, adaptive strategy would require distinct competences on the part of a company, and one übercompetence in particular: what they italicize as "*learning how to learn* across industries."

The call for companies to become learning organizations may seem familiar. It has been sounded from other quarters since the days of Peters and Waterman, perhaps most notably in Peter Senge's 1990 book, *The Fifth Discipline*. What makes the summons mildly notable in this case is the fact that it comes from the Boston Consulting Group, through most of strategy's history not exactly a font of interest in the human dimensions of the discipline. But BCG isn't alone in its appreciation of the heightened, ever-more-critical importance of making your people and your strategy as one. While Bain's Chris Zook won't go as far in conceding power to the periphery—the troops' entrepreneurial undertakings need to be bounded by clear strategy guidelines laid down by the corporate center, he argues—he freely concedes that there is a "higher synthesis" of organization and strategy under way. "I don't know whether organization is the new strategy," he admits, "or strategy the new organization, but it's something like that."

Corporations will be under mounting pressure to sort the matter out, as will the practitioners, consultants, and scholars who will create strategy's future. Our history suggests four issues in particular that will press on the strategic consciousness of companies, whether that consciousness is centralized or more widely distributed: risk, boundaries, corporate purpose, and, as the apostles of the new adaptiveness suggest, figuring out for the twenty-first century how to power a company's strategy with the maximum energy and imagination available from its people.

Since strategy's beginnings, the experts have wrestled with how to build contingency into their calculations. (Again, recall Alan Zakon's work for Weyerhaeuser.) Frequently, this has translated into prescriptions for the use of debt, usually more debt. As the recent turmoil in the world's financial markets brings home, calculations of risk need to be constantly reexamined as the global economy evolves, and disturbing new possibilities somehow taken into account. And not just financial risk. Economic collapse in countries far away, Internet bubbles that pop, terrorist threats to ever-tighter, leaned-down supply chains—how can the people in charge make provision for these in the corporate strategies they devise?

At the heart of many consulting projects nowadays is "building the model," that is, using software to plot the variables in a situation, chart how they affect one another, and run iterations of how it all might play out. It's a process that 1960s consultants with their slide rules could only dream of. But what if the models, with all their comforting quantified precision, prove wrong? As they have of late for the bankers, hedge-fund managers, inventors of derivatives, quants in general, and most of the other wizards of finance? In some ways, the challenge to strategy here is another one related to integrating the human element, namely, finding a place in strategy's deliberations for judgment, even intuition, that can hold its own with the numbers.

Throughout its first fifty years, strategy has tussled with boundary questions. What's the right way to define our market or to segment it?

Which activities should be included in this business unit? How broad a scope must we consider for our value chain?

As the trend toward outsourcing and the necessity to think in terms of business networks forewarn us, such questions are only going to get knottier, or woollier, and of greater import. The analytics born of Greater Taylorism make it possible now to bore down to "markets of one," that single consumer about whom you can learn volumes. In the other direction, the melting winds of globalization have dissolved the difference Americans traditionally saw between business and international business. Why not the entire world as market for your product?

Experts on strategic alliances estimate that currently, perhaps 20 percent of the revenues of large corporations derive from joint ventures. Where do *they* fit in your portfolio of businesses? Or if, like Procter & Gamble, you aim to increasingly "outsource" your product development, letting a small company invent the new wonder and then buying the innovation from its creator, how does that affect your lineup of core competencies?

The tightly bounded company so long at the core of strategy's deliberations increasingly seems a limiting assumption. The twenty-first-century version of the discipline will have to offer more help if, or when, the dominant verb for corporate behavior becomes not *compete*, but something like *co-create*.

As we've seen, strategy was an abettor of shareholder capitalism, not a propulsive force behind it. For too much of its history, the discipline has had little to say about the interrelated issues of shareholder primacy, the rights conferred by ownership, and corporate purpose. But that failure to think the matter through has begun to chafe, and in unlikely quarters. When Michael Hammer died in the fall of 2008, the *New York Times* ended his obituary with a surprising quotation, coming from one of the fathers of reengineering: "I'm saddened and offended by the idea that companies exist to enrich their owners. That is the very least of their roles; they are far more worthy, more honorable, and more important than that."

The global financial crisis only added to the ranks of those questioning the maximization of shareholder wealth as the be-all and end-all of corporate activity. In March 2009, Jack Welch—of all people—told the *Financial Times* that "on the face of it, shareholder value is the dumbest idea in the world." The man once viewed as the poster CEO for value creation went on to explain: "Shareholder value is a result, not a strategy," and, more surprisingly, "Your main constituencies are your employees, your customers, and your products."

Other onetime champions of the shareholder are prepared to go further. Dick Foster, quoted earlier placing the shareholder at the absolute top of the capitalist food chain, has changed his mind in the wake of the financial meltdown. He now believes that the crisis has completely discredited the efficient-market hypothesis, the theoretical underpinning for the idea that the stock market knows best about the value of an enterprise. The turmoil also confirmed his belief, first enunciated in his book *Creative Destruction*, that management's actions can affect no more than 20 or 30 percent of what determines a company's stock price. So, if the yardstick of shareholder value is to be abandoned as the principal measure of strategic success, what should a company be managed for? "Stability and growth," Foster says, an answer Ken Andrews would have thoroughly approved.

Foster is radical in his apostasy. The consensus emerging among strategy consultants, and seemingly what Jack Welch was getting at, is that the recent paroxysms should remind us that shareholder value is not something to be tracked quarter by quarter, much less trading day to trading day. It is, rather, an edifice that takes years to construct, four or five at a minimum. And hasn't that always been one of the messages of strategy, veterans of the discipline add, that you have to look to and build for the long term?

Most strategists would probably like to leave the question of corporate purpose right there. They sense that they walk a path on the edge of much larger questions, some of which the recent financial crisis threatened to open to the size of yawning chasms. Principal among these is how to parcel out fairly the wealth created by companies as well as the pain their activities can sometimes generate.

For the last two decades, corporate profitability has increased steadily—strategy at work—as has the size of the slice of the overall economic pie that profits represent. That has made for higher stock prices, which helped satisfy all those greedy shareholders (like you or me or anyone else who invested in the market). Higher profits have also entailed relentlessly pushing costs down—strategy abetted by Greater Taylorism—and the largest line item for most companies is still its people. Strategy had already helped shred the old social compact between employer and employee. (At some companies, you could almost hear the light bulb clicking on in the heads of senior executives back in the early 1990s: "Now that we know what our costs are and understand how they stack up against our competitors', how can we possibly afford so large a payroll or such a generous deal for our people? Besides, if we can't shape the business up, we'll just sell it off to somebody who will.")

Over the last ten years, the additional pressure from globalization on these trends has led to an increasingly lopsided distribution of incomes—the CEOs, deal-doers, and strategy-makers getting a larger share of the wealth generated; and a squeeze on what used to be known as the middle classes. Unlike the 1950s and 1960s, when increased corporate prosperity meant general prosperity and an ever-larger population of well-off consumers, now the only way most folks can maintain the levels of consumption they've come to expect for themselves is by taking on greater debt—run up those credit cards, take out a home-equity loan—to the point where household indebtedness has reached record levels. In some ways, it was an eerie echo of a lesson that strategy taught most companies: you ought to be borrowing more.

Are we now, as a society—or a number of societies all inhabiting a capitalist world—ready to rethink our reliance on market mechanisms to produce the larger good? Are we prepared to sacrifice a degree of corporate profitability if that were to bring with it lessened extremes of wealth and poverty? What would be the right way to think about the goals of a corporation if the superordinate goal were not to maximize the wealth of its owners, the shareholders? And would an accounting that somehow, finally, accurately reflected all the ways employees contribute to corporate success make for organizations less inclined to chew up people? These are questions with enormous implications for strategy, but not ones that strategists have shown much willingness to engage.

They have lots of company. Even in the aftermath of the global financial crisis, there seems little prospect that the fiercening of capitalism will abate anytime soon. Too many people across the planet have opened their lives to the power of free markets, clambering to make those lives richer, but at the same time speeding up the gears of competition. While many a strategy consultant—Philip Evans is one—warn of years of slower growth ahead, as of the summer of 2009, the world economy had avoided total, Depression-type collapse. Voices calling for a root-and-branch rethinking of our economic arrangements have quieted, their place taken by others calling our attention to the "green shoots" of recovery.

With respect to its fourth—and perpetual—challenge, demographic trends will only add urgency to the necessity that strategy finally come to terms with its Jungian shadow. Populations in Europe and Japan are aging, the baby boom in the United States gradually disengaging. Yes, you can outsource even high-level functions to India or China and open your nation's labor markets to immigrants. But here and there, the decline in the number of available workers may outstrip the ability of companies to rationalize and do with fewer people.

Companies nevertheless continue to push mightily in that direction. Every day, Greater Taylorism applies its analytic engines to more aspects of what workers are doing, slicing the data ever finer—IBM modeling individual employees, retailers using so-called human-capital management systems to time even the smallest task and to schedule people accordingly. This is another form of the intellectualization of business, of course, as are all the computer models employed by finance and strategy. It also represents Greater Taylorism's finally grinding its way down to plain old Taylorism, but with computer algorithms to complement the stopwatch.

What the systems don't capture is Keynes's famous "animal spirits," entrepreneurial energies and imaginings that bring a business to life. They also miss out on the aspirations employees may harbor to think a bit on their own, experiment with new ways of doing the same old drill, and perhaps even be recognized by the company for what they create. For most of strategy's history, those are precisely the factors that the paradigm hasn't found a way to work into its calculations. If the discipline is to continue to be of service, it will have to find that way.

In seeking models of an organization that succeeds in weaving together corporate purpose, first-rate analytics, and individual aspiration, the quest might start with the very consulting firms that gave intellectual structure to the rise of strategy. At their best, BCG, Bain, and McKinsey apply the same empiricism and rigor to the management of themselves as they do to client work. The firms devote as much attention to hiring as Bruce Henderson did, but they're far more systematic about it. Consultants are evaluated after every project, and junior members of the team appraise the performance of their managers. Aspirants who are not going to make it to partner are given lots of warning and often helped to find a new position elsewhere. (Among the firms' most valuable assets, assiduously cultivated, are their networks of alumni proud to have been part of the endeavor.) Partners evaluate one another on a variety of dimensions, not just the ability to land clients (again, when the consultancies are at their best). They also elect the leadership of the firm, this for fixed terms and without politicking so overt as to leave lasting wounds.

The result is to create many of the features that one would hope for in a twenty-first-century enterprise: organizational due process that leaves most people feeling that they have been treated fairly. Democratic meritocracy open to talent from around the world. (Who among business outfits does globalization better?) A system of self-management that works even for people who adamantly don't want to be managed, never wanted a boss.

Most of all, it seems a form that encourages members to venture down the paths where curiosity, imagination, and entrepreneurial energy lead them. In conversations with these new-style intellectuals, I repeatedly heard, "The firm is good about letting you do that"— whether "that" meant chasing down a new idea, trying a novel approach to working with a client, or opening an office in Stockholm or Seoul.

Bruce Henderson would have been pleased with his legacy in this respect. Its possibilities are exactly what he wanted for himself.

Notes

Chapter 1

1. The actual percentage may be considerably higher but is known only to the mind of God, the sole entity whose omniscience extends to the client lists of all three firms. I tried to get them to submit those lists to a neutral observer to be crosshatched against lists of the largest companies but one balked, apparently after much deliberation. Nevertheless I'm confident in the three-quarters figure, which derives from conversations with senior partners at the firms and other sources. Indeed, nowadays big corporations that *don't* use the strategy consulting firms stand out, exceptions that are much talked about among denizens of the industry. Often they attribute the failure to the prejudices of a willful CEO, as at Oracle under Larry Ellison, Citigroup under Sandy Weill, and Ford Motor Company after then CEO Bill Ford "kicked all the consultants out."

Chapter 12

1. The tale of Bain and Guinness is told in riveting if occasionally flawed detail by James O'Shea and Charles Madigan, *Dangerous Company* (New York: Times Business, 1997). The title sums up what the authors think of consultants. The purpose here isn't to replow that well-turned ground, though I'll obviously tread in some of their footsteps, but rather to point up the elements of the story that recall and reinforce Bain's role in the strategy revolution.

Chapter 13

1. Some of the less-well-known founders were women: The 1950s work on corporate growth by Edith Penrose, an American-born British economist, was cited by many resource-based-view scholars as feeding their thinking. Cynthia Montgomery, at Michigan with Wernerfelt—and, reader, she married him—makes continuing distinguished contributions to the field, including coauthoring one of the best textbooks

on the resource-based view. Porter would hire her away from Northwestern's Kellogg School to HBS in 1989; she currently heads the school's strategy unit. Wernerfelt isn't far away, across the river at MIT's Sloan School.

2. And what form is the plural to take, by the way, *competences* or *competencies*? The 1989 piece used the former; the 1990, the latter, subsequently leading some confused souls—including me, on occasion—to use a back formation, *core competency*, for the singular.

Chapter 14

1. All this makes for jokes like the slightly bitter taxonomy-as-jest proposed by a Bain & Company partner: Bain consultants are, of course, "Bainies"; BCG consultants, still celebrated for their conceptual bent, "brainies"; and the sleek, self-satisfied denizens of McKinsey, "vainies."

2. The revenue numbers are provided by Kennedy Information, Inc., publisher of *Consultants News*. Kennedy has been described as "the Dun & Bradstreet of the consulting industry." Since the strategy consultancies are not publicly owned, they are not obliged to publish their financials figures. Kennedy's are informed estimates based on its research, typically with "guidance" from the firms themselves.

3. Indeed, in his polemic *Managers Not MBAs*, Henry Mintzberg briefly summarizes, in "How Management Became Strategy," the changes Porter wrought.

4. A recent United Nations report observed that worldwide, illiteracy rates have declined by half since 1970, to the lowest global rate in history, around 18 percent. Whatever else the 10,265 programs tallied up by the Association to Advance Collegiate Schools of Business around the world may be doing, they're providing their students some familiarity with numbers and with quantitative techniques as applied to enterprise, together with at least a bit of insight into the energies that propel commerce.

5. Not that client companies aren't paying a lot for the consulting they receive. Many veterans of the early days of strategy consulting, now corporate directors on the other side of the commissioning process, register amazement at the prices their old firms command. "It will cost you $150,000 *a week* to get in a team from BCG or McKinsey," one incredulous pioneer told me. "Four or five million dollars for a six-month project!" another marveled.

6. A partial list would include from Bain: Ken Chenault at American Express; Kevin Rollins, formerly CEO of Dell; and Meg Whitman, until recently CEO of eBay. (When she stepped down, the company named John Donahoe, who a year earlier was managing director of Bain, as her successor.) From BCG: George David, a partner who went on to a long, successful run as CEO of United Technologies; Neil Fiske, head successively of Bath and Body Works, then Eddie Bauer; and Indra Nooyi, CEO of PepsiCo, Inc. From McKinsey: John Malone, head of Liberty Media; James McNerney, CEO of Boeing; Phil Purcell, who used to be at the top of Morgan Stanley Dean Witter & Co.; Jeffrey Skilling of Enron fame or infamy; and Jonathan Schwartz, CEO of Sun Microsystems and formerly its chief strategy officer.

Apologies and Thanks

Every day, in offices and plants across the face of the earth, thousands labor to forge strategy for their companies and, even more difficult, to implement their designs. Over the course of thirty years I've had the benefit of talking with many of these people, of having them explain what they're about, and of learning from them. I admire them and what they do. If, per the suggestion of one witty observer, business occupies as dominant a place in world civilization today as the Roman Catholic Church did in fifteenth century Europe, they are the vital clergy in a worldwide movement making for the betterment of mankind.

But this book isn't about them, or at least not as much as it perhaps ought to be. For all the articles and books written about particular companies, the story of how corporate strategy was conceived and enacted at most of them remains largely untold. Whatever its failures on that front, I hope that *The Lords of Strategy* will perhaps encourage intellectual history on that more granular scale, where in so many ways the real story of strategy is to be found.

In *The Player*, his satirical novel about Hollywood and the movie industry, Michael Tolkin commits a thoroughly sneaky act of authorial legerdemain: from this world of actors, directors, producers, and extras, he totally excises agents; they're nowhere in the narrative. I fear I may have committed a comparable sin with respect to corporate planners. While their ranks have waxed and waned over the course of the strategy revolution, many of them are among the most thoughtful students of the discipline. They frequently stand at the intersection of ideas and action, and have often served to make the traffic flow more smoothly. Their history probably deserves a book of its own.

When the study of American civilization was at its height under F. O. Matthiessen, the joke ran that the Harvard faculty taught everything about the subject that its members could see from the roof of Widener Library. Some may accuse this book of a similar not-straying-far-from-the-banks-of-the-Charles insularity in its treatment of the academic study of strategy. My reporting benefited from interviews with the likes of Dan Schendel of Purdue, the founding president of the Strategic Management Society. As those conversations reminded me, important work in the area is being done at scores of institutions (though you can get into debates with specialists in the field as to whether the number of full-time faculty exclusively devoted to strategy is still on the increase). I regret that I wasn't able to include more of their thinking within the scope of my narrative.

Any inquiry into the history of strategy should begin with Pankaj Ghemawat's monograph "Competition and Business Strategy in Historical Perspective" and his textbook on the discipline. The tracks he cut through the brush, particularly through the early, linear stage of the story, have made the going vastly easier for the rest of the writing of this book. My thanks to him to that, and for taking time to discuss the subject at length, both at Harvard Business School and at his current billet at IESE in Barcelona.

Almost all the lords of strategy and of anti-strategy were extremely generous with their time and with access to their recollected histories, as is reflected in the pages of this book. My thanks as well to the many partners and consultants at the strategy firms who submitted to interviews; to list all their names would add require almost another chapter. These "action intellectuals" are constantly on the move from bases around the globe—I recall one day when the three I was scheduled to talk with were, respectively, in London, Vietnam, and Poznan, Poland.

Arranging for me to speak with such a mobile cadre required choreographic skills worthy of a Balanchine. Kay Mosher of BCG, who once worked directly with Bruce Henderson, supplied just that kind of invaluable help over the course of months, indeed years; I hope she finds the resultant portrait of Henderson accurate, fitting, and suggestive of the excitement of being in his presence. Jim Dresser, a veteran BCG partner and a presiding administrative genius there for many years, shared insights critical to my understanding of its operations. Wendy Miller and Heidi Merlini performed scheduling and logistic magic at Bain; Michael Stewart and Diane Wilson, at McKinsey.

My agent Kathy Robbins provided imagination, discipline, and support to the original proposal, to successive drafts, and to the author all the way through the process. Hollis Heimbouch, my favorite fellow Nebraskan, served as this book's first editor and champion at Harvard Business Press. After she left to become publisher at Collins Business, Jeff Kehoe ably took up the cudgels. His thoughtfulness, care, and constant injunction—"Try to make it more like Hemingway and less like bad Henry James"—have spared the reader much. Jennifer Waring and her colleagues at the Press helped the prose become crisper and more telling while Stephani Finks provided an elegant design to house it.

My long-time HBP colleague Angelia Herrin applied her acute editorial and journalistic insights to the project from the outset. Bill Matassoni, the only person I know to have had distinguished careers at both McKinsey and BCG, helped calm his colleagues' fear at the prospect of my reporting. Joel Price sat through hours of talk about the book that understandably may have left him a bit weary but constantly served to reinvigorate its author. Janice Pikey, a world-class photo editor and no slouch as a reader, served up generous research on the images available of the lords and good counsel on how they could best be used (i.e., on the Web site, not in the bound volume). Conversations with my daughter Julia have made this a more informed and even-handed enterprise; with my son Nathaniel, a more tough-minded one.

The book is dedicated to its true begetter.

Index

About the Author

In the course of a thirty-year career as a journalist, Walter Kiechel III has served as the editor of *Fortune* and as editorial director of Harvard Business Publishing. He is also the author of *Office Hours: A Guide to the Managerial Life*.